D0531383

Language, Culture
and Identity in the
Early Years

Also available from Bloomsbury

Anti-Discriminatory Practice (3rd edition), Rosalind Millam
Communication, Language and Literacy, Nichola Callander and
   Lindy Nahmad-Williams

Language, Culture and Identity in the Early Years

Tözün Issa and Alison Hatt

B L O O M S B U R Y

LONDON • NEW DELHI • NEW YORK • SYDNEY

Bloomsbury Academic
An imprint of Bloomsbury Publishing Plc

50 Bedford Square	175 Fifth Avenue
London	New York
WC1B 3DP	NY 10010
UK	USA

www.bloomsbury.com

First published 2013

British Library Cataloguing-in-Publication Data
A catalogue record for this book is available from the British Library.

ISBN: HB: 978-1-4411-4581-9
PB: 978-1-4411-4614-4

Library of Congress Cataloging-in-Publication Data
Issa, Tözün.
  Language, culture and identity in the early years / Tözün Issa and Alison Hatt.
    p. cm.
  Includes bibliographical references and index.
  ISBN 978-1-4411-4581-9 (hardcover) – ISBN 978-1-4411-4614-4 (pbk.) –
ISBN 978-1-4411-8658-4 (ebook) – ISBN 978-1-4411-4701-1 (pdf)
1. Multicultural education–Great Britain. 2. Education, Bilingual–England.
3. Education and state–Great Britain. I. Hatt, Alison. II. Title.
LC1099.5.G7L36 2013
370.1170941–dc23
2012036079

Typeset by Newgen Imaging Systems Pvt Ltd, Chennai, India
Printed and bound in Great Britain

We dedicate this book to the memory of our colleague
and friend Hilary Claire

Contents

Acknowledgements

We are grateful to all the staff at the settings we have visited for their support and co-operation. We are particularly indebted to the Early Years Centre for facilitating our meetings with parents and our contacts with the two primary schools. We acknowledge the interest in our research shown by the parents and their willingness to contribute to discussions by inviting us into their homes. Most especially we would like to thank all the children we met throughout our research who made it extremely enjoyable and enriching.

Abbreviations

ATEPO	Association of Teachers of Pupils from Overseas
BIS	Department for Business Innovation and Skills
BMRB	British Market Research Bureau
BUF	Bilingual Under Fives
CEC	Commission of the European Communities
CGFS	Curriculum Guidance for the Foundation Stage
CLL	Communication, Language and Literacy
CRE	Commission for Racial Equality
DCSF	Department for Children, Schools and Families
DES	Department of Education and Science
DfE	Department for Education
DfEE	Department for Education and Employment
DfES	Department for Education and Skills
ECC	European Community Commission
EEC	European Economic Community
EMAG	Ethnic Minority Achievement Grant
EMTAG	Ethnic Minority and Traveller Achievement Grant
EYC	Early Years Centre
EYFS	Early Years Foundation Stage
ILEA	Inner London Education Authority
LEA	Local Education Authorities
NCB	National Children's Bureau
NCCI	National Committee for Commonwealth Immigrants
OFSTED	Office for Standards in Education

PEAL	Parents, Early Years and Learning
PGCE	Post Graduate Certificate in Education
PSE	personal, social and emotional
PSED	Personal, Social and Emotional Development
PSRN	Problem Solving, Reasoning and Number
QCA	Qualifications and Curriculum Authority
RE	Religious Education
SACRE	Standing Advisory Council for Religious Education
SAT	Standard Assessment Task

Introduction

In an interview given to the *Guardian* newspaper on 30 September 2011, the Education Secretary Michael Gove proposed that 'every child aged five or over should be learning a foreign language'. He highlighted the fact that fluency in another language reinforces the understanding of the linguistic systems such as grammar, syntax and sentence structure; however, it is interesting to note that one of the main reasons he put forward for learning another language was that it helped 'the understanding of English better' [*sic*]. To hear this narrow view of language learning is hardly surprising as we seem to have developed a tradition in this country where language *learning* is synonymous with learning of *English*. We appear to view the tendency to perceive children's languages, cultures and identities as somehow invisible in this process. Did Mr Gove miss the wider point on bilingualism?

We realized, on reading this statement from the Secretary of State, that he and his advisers had no or very little knowledge of bilingualism or language acquisition and learning. It was also clear that the body of research and knowledge that has accumulated over the past 40 or 50 years was being (wilfully?) ignored in government thinking and policies. We wish we could detect a new emphasis on children and childhood in all its wonderful variety rather than a relentless emphasis on children as 'learning machines'. Our view seems to be confirmed by the content of the proposed new Teachers Standards (due to come into effect in September 2012) and the new OFSTED (Office for Standards in Education) inspection framework. In the Standards there is neither a positive commitment to bilingualism nor an understanding of languages and language acquisition. Instead, we see only a reference to children with EAL (English as an Additional Language), who are placed alongside, yet again, children with special educational needs and disabilities.

In the OFSTED framework, there is also constant reference to achievement and standards but with no associated understanding of all the factors that affect these. In addition, while the importance of parents is recognized, this appears to be largely as working with the school as agents in children's learning. What parents might contribute beyond this does not appear to be acknowledged.

Therefore, our anxiety about this situation has affected the content and direction of this book. While we are keen to share the outcomes of our research visits, we also want to give our readers, who may not be familiar with the background, an insight into some of the research, documents and initiatives that formed such a vital part of education in the 1970s and 1980s until the arrival of the Education Reform Act of 1988. Earlier, there was considerable excitement and activity in schools and certain local education authorities (LEAs) about children's languages and cultures and how best these could be integrated into the curriculum and school ethos. The reader who is less familiar with this history might be surprised to learn how much material and how many resources were being devised and published to support bilingual children and their teachers.

To deal with this, we have provided in Chapters 1 and 2 two historical overviews: the first looks at general historical developments in early years education and the second presents an overview of political policies, legislation and documentation especially connected with language and bilingualism.

Britain is a multicultural country in its truest sense. There are over 300 languages spoken in London alone. Statistical information – some of which is provided by the government's own sources – support our claim that the number of children who have access to a language in addition to English is actually increasing in our schools. These children have varying degrees of bilingualism. Mostly they are born into families that use a home language which is not English and experience the added benefits of bilingualism. The linguistic systems (e.g. vocabulary and grammar) the government is referring to exist – and often used – in the home language with these children. Learning of the second language – in this case English – develops in relation to the existing linguistic systems which are in the home language. It is therefore important to highlight the benefits of bilingualism particularly the difference between language acquisition and language learning.

Some of the concerns that guided our thinking in writing this book relate to a narrow perception of multicultural education which is historically ingrained in our society. where multiculturalism was merely viewed as 'valuing' the culture and languages of the children that made up a significant portion of our schools. Organizing international days, children performing traditional dance, music from different parts of the world were all included under the practice of multiculturalism. Often these practices were 'tacked on' to the school curriculum and it could be claimed that one result was to present some children's cultures as other or 'exotic' rather than an integral part of school and society.

Therefore, we feel that the practice of multiculturalism cannot really be viewed as separate from the practice of multilingualism. If we are really to show that the children's social and cultural practices are to be celebrated in their truest sense, we need to include their languages as well. For instance, celebrating different festivals needs to be perceived in the context of presentations of songs, stories, poems in that particular language. This is the only way to capture the magical sense of that particular festival, as we would do with the beautiful carols that are sung in English during Christmas. However, we do think it would be a fantastic experience for all children if some of the carols in other languages were sung as well.

The celebration of festivals is one of the many approaches that contribute to an inclusive school ethos. Including children's community experiences in the home language as part of the teaching and learning in the classroom is positively multicultural. Jim Cummins, in his numerous research work, points out the benefits of utilizing children's home experiences embedded in their home languages can contribute to their self-esteem as well as their literacy development. We will refer to Cummins' work throughout this book.

In this book, we also explore the importance of maintaining the home languages of young learners. We show that valuing and encouraging the use of the home languages by adults in early years settings help young children with learning of English and develop their bilingualism. The problem was that once the child became linguistically competent in English – at least in conversational settings – it was deemed as fine, 'mission accomplished'. There was no need to continue home language development. The main problem with this traditional model of multilingualism was that it viewed the languages, cultures and identities of different minority groups as inherently separate and distinct entities from each other. We refer to these programmes and approaches to multilingualism when we discuss some of the government sponsored 'mother tongue' initiatives in the United Kingdom during the 1970s and 1980s.

In this book, we take a critical look at this point, arguing that notions of language, culture and identity are dynamic processes constantly evolving out of complex interrelated relationships between different linguistic and cultural groups. These dynamic processes, we believe, provide a healthy relational development of such groups towards much more holistic and inclusive practices.

When we set out on our first project visit to find out more about a 'highly innovative' (a quote from its OFSTED report) Early Years Centre (EYC), we were not very sure what we were going to see in the name of inclusive practice. People often assume that when one talks about supporting language, culture and identity of children it only refers to children from minority ethnic backgrounds. Our main concern in embarking on this project was to challenge this in some way; to show that inclusive practice means inclusion of all children regardless of their social and cultural backgrounds, including monolingual English speaking children from all strands of life with different variations of English used by staff and children alike. In our innovative EYC, we found that inclusion was happening at an amazingly natural pace. Hearing greetings and phrases in different languages used by adults and children was the norm in the Centre. Parents were fully involved with the life of the EYC, some taking the children for short language sessions as others were reading to them. We saw a parent walking in with her guitar settling in for a singing session. Everybody was included. Every single child attending the EYC had something to relate to which was an extension of what they brought from home. Cultural pluralism was at work permeating from the senior managers to teachers, other adults and parents to the children and back to the top again.

About the book

The ideas and discussions presented in this book are the result of 24 months of data collected from an EYC and two receiving schools in South London. We had a number of concerns and interests about inclusive education that guided our investigation and subsequently make up the overriding themes explored in this book. First we would like to clarify the use of some of the key vocabulary and our understanding of the meanings attached to them.

Bilingual/bilingualism

We use the term bilingual to refer to children who use or are exposed to a language or languages other than English at home and/or in community settings. Our focus however is not so much about the level of competence children have in the home language but rather to explore how the concepts and vocabulary used in that language are shaped by children's individual, social and cultural experiences. This is one of the central themes of the book as we discuss its significance in linking this to children's learning of English. A particular model we put forward relates to the development of both languages as equally enriching components of children's home and school experiences. Here it is also useful to develop our argument on home and school experiences further to underline the importance of developing home and school experiences of all our children. So, by referring to culture we are no longer using it to imply merely to the experiences of children from linguistic minority communities but to all children who reflect distinct aspects of their home and community experiences. One of the questions we sought answers to is:

> As active learners what experiences, skills and knowledge are these children bringing into the learning environment and to what extent are these utilized in early years settings?

Culture and identity

On the whole, we use these terms interchangeably. We aim to challenge the traditional view that describes them as static and insular concepts with clearly defined boundaries. We argue that they are dynamic and fluid, constantly evolving around an individual's own perception of self at personal and social levels. If we were to apply these concepts to the context of our study, we could say that having arrived at early years settings, young children extend and develop their cultural identities through interaction with peers and adults in their environment. Newly arrived young learners are not expected to be overtly evaluating their 'new' experiences in relation to their existing conceptual attributes. However, we know that these inquisitive young learners make sense of their new surroundings silently through their inner mechanisms as they interact with their environment. We are not going to devote the rest of this introductory chapter to explain the intricate details of this process but simply to say that the end results of these mechanisms of internalization facilitate the formation of new knowledge in the context of that already acquired. This, as we argue, is the process through which such new dimensions form the basis of children's thinking from something which is particular and monolithic to that of general and pluralistic. Here we would like to inform the reader that our intention in using of the word 'particular' is *not* in a negative but more of a Piagetian sense, that is, from egocentric to becoming more abstract and formal in the child's developmental stage to maturity.

If we were then, to merge the two concepts to sum up what we mean by *cultural identity* we could talk about a dynamic process which facilitates the transformation of particular social and cultural experiences of the child's home and community from a particular to a more pluralistic set of values.

Language

Language with its richness and diversity – certainly in a London context – is another topic which preoccupies our thinking in this book. The Education Secretary's statement, referred to above, about learning a foreign language cannot hide the dim reality of language uptake at Key Stage 3. Again a compartmentalized view of languages and successive governments' failure to convince learners of the benefits of language learning, are some of the issues associated with language learning. However, it is the hierarchical notion of languages and language learning that concerns us as educators in this field. It is the lack of policies and practice relating to the utilization of learners' home languages as points of reference in language learning which we think is absent from government languages agenda. We feel this is an important issue as it posits language learning perspectives firmly within the multicultural/inclusive agenda. It signals a positive message to those learners that as bilinguals they already have the most necessary skills in additional language learning. It gives the message that everyone's linguistic and cultural experiences are firm basis for additional language learning. It is inclusive, democratic and humanist in essence.

In Chapter 1, we provide a historical overview of policy and practice in early years settings and evaluate these in relation to major government reports and legislation. We then develop these ideas further by providing an account of the current Foundation Stage requirements and wider developments in the United Kingdom and Europe.

In Chapter 2, we discuss the education of the minorities from a historical perspective, exploring successive government legislation in the context of wider social and political developments.

We continue our exploration of developing perspectives on young children's Personal, Social and Emotional Development (PSED) by relating it to the Early Years Foundation Stage (EYFS) in Chapter 3. We explore the relationship between Communication, Language and Literacy (CLL) and PSED and argue that this is an important prerequisite for young learners' reading and writing development. We support these with examples from early years practice.

In Chapter 4, we explore aspects of children's PSED, placing it in historical, political and contemporary contexts. In this chapter we also identify and disseminate good practice relating to children's own constructions of their multiple identities in multilingual and multicultural settings.

In Chapter 5, we explore some key issues and debates about multilingualism. We start by discussing some of the misconceptions of multilingualism and the use of first languages in schools and research that supports the nurturing of children's languages, linking these to their conceptual development. We investigate how children from a variety of linguistic and cultural backgrounds can be supported through a range of supportive practices which are based on knowledge and understanding of emotional/social development of young children. In this respect, we highlight the important processes related to first and subsequent language acquisition.

We begin Chapter 6 by first providing an overview of research which supports positive correlations between second language acquisition and related themes explored in previous chapters, namely young learners' individual, social, emotional and cultural development. We link these to the present national picture as well as the developments in Europe.

In Chapter 7, we reflect on our observations in an EYC of activities, data and practice collected from children, staff and parents. In doing this, we identify examples of good practice which recognize the key role of the first language in the nurturing and support of children's identities via their social, emotional, linguistic and cultural development.

In Chapter 8, we present parents' views on the ways in which good early years practice can foster children's personal, social, emotional, linguistic and cultural development. We draw attention to parents' views that home languages should be recognized and supported in early years settings and we consider the professional relationships that can be promoted between all adults concerned in young children's overall development.

In Chapter 9, we revisit the EYFS curriculum in the light of our preceding discussion of young learner's language development and consider how it could be extended further in relation to children's language and identities. We draw on research that highlights the importance of communicative competences and speaking and listening as forerunners to becoming literate. In the final part of this chapter, we return to the CLL area of learning and development and, drawing from current practice, suggest ways in which this might be made more responsive to children's languages.

We devote Chapter 10 to a discussion of the transition to Reception classes. We look closely at the ways in which early years settings and Reception classes could work together to support children's identities, languages and cultures in order to bring about successful transition from the early years setting to primary school. In this chapter, we revisit the EYFS Curriculum in the light of our findings to examine how effectively it is working as a mechanism for supporting young learners' multiple identities and languages.

In our final chapter (Chapter 11) we summarize our findings and make recommendations for future policy development and practice.

We end each chapter with 'Reflective activity' containing key questions to help all staff who work with multilingual children to reflect on their own practice. Practical suggestions and strategies are threaded throughout the book. We also include data on conversations with staff, parents and children. Finally, we are aware that some of the data from our interactions and observations with staff, children and parents presented in this book may appear in other chapters. Our justification for reusing them is their suitability to meet the purpose of each chapter.

The Early Years Foundation Stage: Historical Context and Recent Developments

1

Chapter Outline

This chapter briefly summarizes some of the main historical and educational developments in the growth of state provision in this country for young children's education. It also considers changes in the UK population which derive from its own history of empire and colonization and how these have affected education.

We start by stating that in our (and not just our) view, the history of what is now called the United Kingdom is one that illustrates that its growing populations are, and always have been, linguistically and culturally diverse. Our history encompasses more than the arrival of the Norman French in the eleventh century or the installation of a German Hanoverian monarchy (and its entourage) in the eighteenth century and the post-Second World War émigrés. If we read widely enough we will find that there is evidence going back to around 7,000 BCE (Before Common Era), when this country was separated from Europe by the rising sea level, that there were settlers in the south of 'England' and that some one thousand years before the Romans invaded (54–5 BCE) there were other settlers from Central Europe (Winder, 2004, p. 18). Our country has constantly absorbed new arrivals, modified its language to reflect their various influences and, of course, been responsible for our own various arrivals on other shores. In addition, the reader should also bear in mind (if s/he does not know this already) that the majority of the world is bi- or multilingual and that the monolingualism of Britain (and America) is the exception rather than the norm.

This book is mindful of how these facts link to our contemporary situation and this chapter is therefore written in the belief that this knowledge is fundamental for all who work with young children, whatever be their ethnic, cultural or linguistic background.

Where should we start?

We have to find a suitable starting point for our consideration of the historical background that precedes the discussion of children's linguistic and cultural identities. For us, this starting point is in the nineteenth century with the Elementary Education Act of 1870 which led eventually to the provision of free elementary education funded by the state. We will find, though, that it is many years later that the interests and needs of young children begin to take centre stage and even later that their linguistic and cultural heritages start to receive due attention. In fact, it is in the Bullock Report of 1975, that these heritages begin to receive their due.

The title of the Bullock Report was 'A Language for Life'; it was a report that took a very generous view of language development and promoted an inclusive vision of the meeting of the cultures of home and school between which children necessarily travelled every day.

> No child should be expected to cast off the language and culture of the home as soon as he [*sic*] crosses the school threshold, nor to live and act as though school and home represent two totally separate and different cultures which have to be kept firmly apart. (Bullock Report, 1975, para 20.5)

This sentiment is, or ought to be, one with which those who work with or care for young children should be familiar and one which such workers strive to realize in their different settings. The title of the report – 'A Language for Life' – seemed radical at the time since it did not pin the language down as 'English' but appeared to be acknowledging broader dimensions to the linguistic experiences of children and pupils. Nevertheless, chapter 20, 'Children from Families of Overseas Origin' (the chapter the quotation comes from), even though it includes a (brief) discussion of children in infant and nursery classes, is a long way from chapter 5, 'Language in the Early Years' suggesting that the authors did not see any connection or overlap between the two headings. Chapter 5, indeed, presents a fairly neutral account of early language development, drawing on what was then recent research and considering the effects of social class on young children's language proficiency but surprisingly, considering the nature of the report, making little reference to their linguistic, cultural and ethnic heritages. The Report, however, did make a strong pronouncement in favour of bilingual children:

> When bilingualism in Britain is discussed it is seldom if ever with reference to the inner city immigrant populations, yet over half the immigrant pupils in our schools have a mother-tongue which is not English and in some schools this means over 75 per cent of the total number on roll. The language of the home and of a great deal of the central experience of their life is one of the Indian languages, or Greek, Turkish, Italian or Spanish. These children are genuine bilinguals, but this fact is often ignored or unrecognised by the schools. Their bilingualism is of great importance to the children and their families, and also to society as a whole. In a linguistically conscious nation in the modern world we should see it as an asset, as something to be nurtured and one of the agencies which should nurture it is the school. Certainly the school should adopt a positive attitude to its pupils' bilingualism and wherever possible should help maintain and deepen their knowledge of their mother tongues. (Ch. 20.17)

In fact we find that very little attention has been paid to this aspect of young children's lives in most government documents and legislation. Worse still, the broad and wide-ranging needs and the education of young children have received patchy and spasmodic attention since the school starting age was arbitrarily set at 5 years via the 1870 Elementary Education Act. Nevertheless, the under fives have had their champions, although it is not, as we have said, until we reach the end of the twentieth century that we see attention being paid, in this country, to their languages, cultures and identities. The history, then, is a twofold picture of political neglect – that of young children generally and their languages and cultures specifically.

Katherine Bathurst – An early 'champion' of young children

Concerning young children, it might be useful to consider some of their previous 'champions'. One such figure was Katherine Bathurst (1905), an Infant School Inspector, who drew attention to the plight of 4- and 5-year-olds who, were 'entitled' by the 1870 Act to go to school but were receiving a totally inappropriate curriculum. Her report graphically describes the discomfort and distress experienced by very young children assailed by a curriculum, surroundings and teaching which were all completely unsuitable.

> Let us now follow the baby of three years through part of one day of school life. He is placed on a hard wooden seat . . . with a desk in front of him and a window behind him. . . . He often cannot reach the floor with his feet, and in many cases he has no back to lean against. He is told to fold his arms and sit quiet. He is surrounded by a large number of other babies all under similar alarming and incomprehensible conditions, and the effort to fold his arms is by no means conducive to comfort or well-being. . . . If he cries quietly, he becomes aware of the following proceedings. A blackboard has been produced and hieroglyphics are drawn upon it by the teacher. At a given signal every child in the class begins calling out mysterious sounds: 'Letter A, letter A' in a sing-song voice, or 'Letter A says Ah, letter A says Ah', as the case may be. (Bathurst (1905) cited in Woodhead and McGrath, 1988)

There is much more in this bleak account of life in an elementary school and Bathurst also has some pithy remarks to make on the unhelpful 'contributions' made by male Inspectors. She quotes one such person who in a Manchester school logbook wrote that 'the babies should learn to sit still and attend'. Amazingly, this statement was echoed in the proposed Early Learning Goals of the late twentieth-century early years curriculum.

By the time that Bathurst wrote her report, schools were no longer run by the School Boards which had been established by the 1870 Elementary Education Act to run non-denominational schools. An

Education Act of 1902 handed this responsibility to the recently established local authorities, extending this to London in 1903. In 1918, towards the end of the First World War, an Education Act enabled the local authorities to provide nursery education. Women were already at this stage forming a large part of the work force so that nursery provision served an economic and national cause, not just an educational one. As we will see, economic arguments have been a main factor in the provision of early years education. In addition, the South African wars in the late nineteenth and early twentieth century and, of course the First World War itself, fought between 1914–18, revealed the appalling physical condition of many of the army and navy recruits from the impoverished working class. Much of the ensuing health and welfare legislation stemmed from the discovery that fighting men were undersized and malnourished.

It should also be noted that many people, probably over 1 million, from the British empire and its colonies fought in the First World War. This has a bearing on the arrivals, later in the century, of the grandparents and great grandparents of the young bilingual and multilingual children that our book will be describing in the following chapters.

Other important women educators

Around the time that Katherine Bathurst was arguing on behalf of young children, the McMillan sisters, Rachel (1859–1917) and Margaret (1860–1931), both with training in Health, Hygiene and Sanitation, were also concerned about young children's (and young women's) health, diet and physical development and, rather less attractively, with the racial health of the nation. They established health clinics in Bradford and, later, in South-East London, and Margaret eventually established the Rachel McMillan Nursery, an open-air nursery school, where outdoor physical activity formed a central part of children's education.

In the 1920s Susan Isaacs (1885–1948), later to become the first Professor of Child Development at the University of London, worked in a progressive school in Cambridge, ratifying observation and conversation as one of the key methods for extending children's learning and thirst for exploration and investigation. Her major interest was in children's intellectual development and she was much influenced by the work of Jean Piaget (1896–1980).

Two of the Hadow Reports

Susan Isaacs contributed evidence to two important reports, whose committees were chaired by Sir W. H. Hadow, on primary education (1931), that is, schools which included Infant classes, and Infant and Nursery Schools (1933). These two reports set the tone for primary education as can be seen by this brief quote:

> Hitherto the general tendency has been to take for granted the existence of certain traditional 'subjects' and to present them to the pupils as lessons to be mastered. There is, as we have said, a place for that method, but it is neither the only method, nor the method likely to be fruitful between the ages of seven and eleven. What is required, at least, so far as much of the curriculum is concerned, is to substitute for it methods which take as the starting-point of the work of the primary school the experience, the curiosity, and the awakening powers and interest of the children themselves. (Hadow Report, 1931, Introduction quoted in Maclure, 1986, pp. 190–1)

The Infant and Nursery Schools report provides an extensive chapter on the history of Infant education and other chapters include aspects of child development, school organization, teacher training, premises and equipment. Much that was recommended in this report was not implemented, as the Plowden Report of 1967 made clear. Susan Isaacs, with Sir Cyril Burt, provided an appendix discussing the emotional development of children up to the age of 7. They were both psychologists; not surprisingly, the appendix reflects this. Ideas about and knowledge of child development have increased since this report but one striking observation they make is one that perhaps contemporary practitioners might think it worth their while to consider in their work with young bilingual children.

> Observers who have approached the study of the young child from many different angles are all agreed upon one outstanding point: namely, that the emotional intensity of the young child's life reaches its zenith about the end of the third year. At this age, every emotion the child undergoes

is felt with a vividness and a strength that is never again experienced either in later childhood or in adult life; from this stage onwards experience and the integration of impulses tend more and more to control and moderate the child's emotional excitement. This early vividness and intensity are seen with every type of feeling. (The Hadow Report, 1933, Appendix 3 para 3, pp. 246–7)

These two reports exerted considerable influence over the nature of a curriculum for Primary aged (or Junior) children particularly in relation to physical health and diet; certainly there was an expansion of provision for open-air activity and recreation (many local outdoor swimming pools were built in the 1920s) and of the schools' medical services, schools meals, and so on. They set the tone for the expansion of education for the under 11s and for gradual changes in educational philosophy and pedagogy until the Plowden Report of 1967, although they do not directly address our concerns of language as it relates to identity and culture.

After the Hadow Reports

It is perhaps not until the Education Act of 1944 that we begin to see some governmental recognition of diversity in the population. In this Act, religious education was the only named compulsory subject and while this was embodied in Christianity, the national faith, it was also recognized that within this there were many denominations (Anglican, Catholic, non-conformist Churches, Quakers, etc.). There were also, of course, those who practised no religion. To begin to reflect this diversity, the Act established SACREs (Standing Advisory Council for Religious Education) which would address the beliefs and practices of the religious groups in each local authority. The Act also upheld the rights, via a conscience clause, of parents and teachers to withdraw children or themselves from any aspect of Religious Education (RE) with which they could not agree.

It should be remembered that this legislation, and indeed all preceding legislation, was enacted in a country which was still an imperial and colonizing force in the world. It is this complex and troubled history which led to the arrival of people from the countries that formed the empire, and, later, the commonwealth which will lead to the ideas that stem from the title of this book.

Empire, colonization and their after-effects

As stated in the introduction to this chapter, it is fair to say that the population of this country has always been mixed. Invasions and settlements by Romans, Scandinavians and Norman French, among many others, left their mark in many ways, not least by the intermarrying of the new populations with the established ones. There have been black people (i.e. people from African, Caribbean and Asian countries) living in this country certainly since the time of Henry Viii and probably even earlier (Merriman, 1993; Visram, 2002). The development of the slave trade in the seventeenth and eighteenth centuries, one of the most repellent features of this country's history, also led eventually to greater movement, settlement and intermarrying of people from a wide range of ethnic backgrounds. However, one of the many negative outcomes of empire and colonization was the racism that became an institutionalized part of every day life and thinking and which encouraged white Britons to consider themselves superior in every way to black non-Britons. This is a legacy still to be worked through as the Parekh Report (2000) suggests:

> expunging the traces of an imperial mentality from the national culture, particularly those that involved seeing the white British as a superior race, is a much more difficult task (than shedding the empire). This mentality penetrated everyday life, popular culture and consciousness. It remains active in projected fantasies and fears about difference, and in racialised stereotypes of otherness. (Parekh, ch. 2, pp. 24–5)

Nevertheless, during the Second World War, Britain found itself obliged again to call on its empire and colonies to join in the war effort – and thousands of their people did. After the War, as the country began to rebuild itself, it called again on its colonial members for help in the reconstruction of the 'Mother Country'.

Thus in 1948, the *Empire Windrush*, a troop ship, docked in Southampton with its 500 passengers (mostly young men) largely from the Caribbean, all seeking careers and employment in England. This was the first of many ships that brought migrants from the Caribbean over the next 12 or 13 years (Phillips and Phillips, 1998; Dabydeen et al., 2007).

In the ensuing years, further groups from European, Asian and South American countries arrived and settled in various parts of the United Kingdom (see Merriman, 1993; Visram, 2002 and Winder, 2004 for detailed information).

New arrivals: Language issues and initiatives and legislation

While this is not the place to rehearse the different responses to these arrivals, for the purposes of this book it should be noted that support for the children of new migrants gradually began to emerge in the 1960s when, for example, organizations such as ATEPO (the Association of Teachers of Pupils from Overseas), the British Caribbean Society and the National Committee for Commonwealth Immigrants were formed with a view to assisting children whose first language was not English and to provide information and training for the children's teachers (Plowden, 1967, para 186).

The Plowden Report of 1967, 'Children and Their Primary Schools', included a chapter headed 'Children of Immigrants' that drew attention to various factors that were affecting the progress of these children, not the least of which were their languages and their teachers' lack of knowledge and training in how best to support them. We also have to consider the social and political contexts into which the children and their families arrived. To say that the 'host' country was endemically and institutionally racist is not an extreme statement since the negative reactions to people from overseas who were visibly 'different' have been well documented (see, for example, Phillips and Phillips, 1998).

Government responses veered in two opposing directions: legislation that began to reduce or eliminate opportunities for people from the former empire to settle here and legislation that began to tackle the discrimination that families already here were experiencing. The first Race Relations Act of 1976 outlawed both direct and indirect discrimination on 'racial' grounds (which includes anti-white discrimination) and established the Commission for Racial Equality (CRE) which oversaw the workings of the Act.

There can be no doubt that the arrival of families from overseas brought about considerable social upheaval and put pressure on various agencies – employment, housing, schooling, for example – to accommodate and provide support. But, because of the legacy of empire, attitudes, both personal and institutional, towards new arrivals and settlers leaned towards locating the difficulties within the new groups themselves, rather than towards structural rigidities. Thus 'problematizing' of so-called immigrant groups and ambivalent attitudes towards the use and teaching of children's 'mother tongues' led to varied outcomes. On the one hand, the 'problematizing' of African-Caribbean boys in particular, resulted in many being wrongly assigned to special schools (see Coard, 1971) and the question of their language and dialects largely passed over. On the other hand, children from South Asia who so obviously spoke languages other than English, required support of a different kind. There is more here than can be covered in this chapter but suffice it to say that the Home Office established in 1966 what was known as 'Section 11' funding which has its own interesting history and is accompanied by various developments in Europe via the European Union. We will discuss migration patterns and successive government initiatives in more detail in Chapter 5.

Provision for bilingual children: United Kingdom and Europe

As stated above, Section 11 refers to a specific section of the Local Government Act of 1966 which provided for the payment of a grant to local authorities and to some education institutions. The purpose of the grant was to

> address disadvantage – brought about by differences of language or culture – that is experienced by members of ethnic minorities in accessing education, training, employment and a wide range of other opportunities, services and facilities that are available to other people. (Home Office, 1986, www.nationalarchives.gov.uk/ letter concerning the future of Section 11)

The grant also paid part of the costs of employing additional staff for projects which were designed to help minority group members to cover such disadvantages. Note that it was the Home Office dealing with this, not the Education Department.

In Europe, too, there was debate about the education of the children of migrant workers (e.g. Turkish 'gastarbeiters' in Germany). The Council of Europe that was established to promote European unity also became concerned about the children's education and in 1970 passed a resolution (701/35) that made such recommendations as:

- Children of migrant workers should be supported in national school systems
- Provision should be made for the maintenance of the migrant children's linguistic and cultural links to their countries of origin
- Smooth reintegration of children to their countries of origin should they return
- Recognition of the child's qualifications whether obtained in their home of host country. (Skutnabb-Kangas, 1981, quoted in Issa, 1987)

The European Community Commission (ECC) Directive (1977) recognized the importance of mother tongue provision but was itself a problematic document and one which was not whole-heartedly supported by member countries. We refer to this Directive again in other parts of our book.

In spite of this apparent positive approach to children's bilingualism, schemes to support their first language in this country were localized and spasmodic. The work of the Linguistic Minorities Project 'The Other Languages of England' (Stubbs, 1985) and the Schools Council Mother Tongue Project set up in 1981, provide useful information of the different language communities of the time, as did the Inner London Education Authority's (ILEA) biannual language censuses which revealed in fascinating details the range of languages spoken at home by its school population. The 1987 census, for example, estimated that 64,987 pupils, representing 23 per cent of the ILEA school population, spoke a language other than or in addition to English at home, with a total of 172 languages identified as being used by pupils (ILEA, 1987).

Eventually, Section 11 funding was taken over by the then Department for Education and Employment (DfEE) and became named as EMTAG (Ethnic Minority and Traveller Achievement Grant). Commitment to EMTAG or EMAG work on the part of government and local authorities continued to be patchy and the intricacies of questions around languages, language for learning, mother tongue teaching, generalist and specialist teaching (not to mention training) never fully addressed. The Parekh Report (2000) makes this stringent criticism:

> There has been a decline in resources for many schools; considerable inse-
> curity among staff; a continuing loss of experienced and expert teachers;
> even less provision of specialist training; lack of informed leadership by
> head teachers and scarcely more attention to the plight of African-
> Caribbean pupils than in the past. (Ch. 11, p. 150)

Following the General Election of 2010, it appears that EMAG funding is to be drastically reduced, leaving schools and local authorities in a problematic situation.

Two significant reports of the 1980s

It should also be borne in mind that there was also a ground swell, in the 1980s, in response to racist stereotyping and inadequate institutional provision towards first, multicultural education or a recognition of the culturally plural nature of Britain and, more radically, towards anti-racist education and a realization that the impact of racism and poor policy making had to be contested and children, parents and teachers empowered to make such contests. Two seminal reports in this area were the Swann Report of 1985 ('Education for All') and the Report of the Macdonald Inquiry of 1989 (Macdonald et al., 1989).

The Swann Report of 1985

It is impossible to do justice here to the Swann Report but its scale and scope merit further study. Suffice to say in the context of this chapter that part of its remit was to:

> review in relation to schools the educational needs and attainments of
> children from ethnic minority groups taking account, as necessary, of fac-
> tors outside the formal education system relevant to school performance,
> including influences in early childhood and prospects for school leavers.
> (Swann Report, 1985, p. vii)

The Committee recognized the importance of preschool provision for all children and

> for the child from a home where English is not the first language, it is clear that nursery provision can be a particularly valuable stage of the overall educational experience and can we believe serve to ease the sometimes traumatic transition between home and school. (Ch. 7, p. 393, para 2.11)

and in its discussion of language and language education endorsed in much of the Bullock Report (1975), Swann makes positive comments on the nature of a multilingual society:

> in order to lay the foundations for a genuinely pluralist society the education system must we believe both cater for the linguistic needs of ethnic minority pupils and also take full advantage of the opportunities offered for the education of all pupils by the linguistic diversity of our society today. (Ch. 7, p. 385, para 1.1)

Nevertheless, after an intriguing discussion, the committee pulled away from endorsing 'mother tongue teaching' or bilingual education programmes in state schools (apart from such national programmes as in Welsh schools), preferring to recommend:

> mother tongue maintenance as best achieved within the ethnic minority communities themselves rather than within mainstream schools, but with considerable support from and liaison with the latter. (Ch. 7, p. 406, para 3.15)

Britishness

Another important aspect of the Swann Report was its discussion of 'Britishness'. The Swann committee followed on from the earlier Rampton committee of inquiry which was established to investigate the causes of social unrest in areas with large African-Caribbean populations, in the early 1980s. The Swann Report made it clear that despite legislation (e.g. the 1976 Race Relations Act) against discrimination, it was still very much in evidence and that racism was an endemic part of society. Chapter 2 of the report should be read for its discussion of racism, its effects and the role of education in combating it.

What the Swann committee urged was an understanding and acceptance that being British now includes those from ethnic minority groups. Indeed the report quotes the then Home Secretary:

> it is no longer appropriate to speak of ethnic minorities in this country as immigrants. Already almost half of Britain's population whose origins lie in the New Commonwealth or Pakistan were born here. Many more were brought up in this country and, for practical purposes, know no other. Britain is their home. They belong here: they are here to stay and to play their part of the life of their country. (Ch. 1, p. 7, para 6)

The Swann Report also had many recommendations to make in relation to teacher education, some of which began to be implemented in the later 1980s but these were overtaken by the determination of the then Conservative government to introduce a national curriculum, which it did via the Education Reform Act of 1988.

Report of the Macdonald Inquiry (1989)

The Macdonald Report, which investigated the circumstances that led to the murder of a teenager in a Manchester school, highlighted the weaknesses inherent in anti-racist policies and practice which were imposed by the school's poor senior management, which failed to support minority ethnic staff and which failed to recognize that anti-racist practice had to apply to *all* pupils, not just those from minority backgrounds. There is much to think about in this report and its profound and moving investigation into the events surrounding the murder and the subsequent comments and recommendations all merit further study.

Where is this leading us?

By this point, the reader may well be asking if all has this anything to do with early years education and the languages and identities of young children? The answer to this must be 'yes'.

The preceding background has been intended to help the reader arrive at some understanding of where we are now if their own background is not that of a minority ethnic group. Indeed, even if the reader is from a minority group, it is possible that they may not know some of this history. And teachers, perhaps especially of young children, should be as fully informed as possible of events that still resonate today and which will have a bearing on the policies and decisions of the current government.

So questions of language and identity have long been a part of education even while early years education remained on the margins and the political implications of these aspects of early development not fully explored.

Research into young children's language development

There has been very little overt promotion or understanding of the role and emotional significance of children's first language/s in both their intellectual and cultural identities until relatively recently. That is not to say there was not considerable research and interest in the role of language and talk in young children's development; significant and still relevant work was carried out and published in the 1980s by Tizard and Hughes (1984) and Wells (1987) which revealed the depths of the conversations between children at home and their carer (at that time usually the mother) and the contrasting frequent paucity of the interactions between children at school and their teachers. Their work explicitly challenged the notion, held by some educators, that children's communicative experiences at home were necessarily inferior to those of school or nursery and that children from working-class homes also necessarily experienced limited linguistic input – a notion that replicates the 'problematizing' referred to earlier and one that is still remarkably prevalent but not, so far as we are aware, founded on any reliable body of evidence.

At this time (1980s) there was a very wide range of early years provision, from childminders, playgroups, social services day nurseries, nursery classes in primary schools to nursery schools, all examples of state or private provision led by staff with very different training and experiences but with no overarching regulatory body.

On the plus side, early years education has and continues to have, a very impressive history of philosophy and pedagogy that follows on from the work of the nineteenth- and early twentieth-century educators. In the late twentieth- and early twenty-first-century writers such as Bruce (2005) set out ten principles (variously modified in ensuing editions) from the 'pioneers' that underpinned work with young children. While these tend to concentrate on children's personal and emotional well-being as experienced in relationships and stimulating environments, they do not explicitly address the fundamental roles of language and culture in nurturing individual and group identities nor attend in much detail to children whose first learning has taken place in the home language.

The beginning of legislation relating to equality

One of the first pieces of legislation that began to address these factors was the Children Act of 1989. In this the situation of children under 8 was specifically considered and the duties of local authorities concerning the day care of young children made explicit. The Act also made specific reference to race equality by requiring local authorities and voluntary organizations to give: 'due consideration to the child's religious persuasion, racial origin and cultural and linguistic background' (Section 22(5)(c)).

The Guidance to the Act 'reflects the changes that have come about as a result of a wider acceptance of the importance of the early years for developing positive cultural identity and a recognition that, even in these early years, children learn racial attitudes and place values on them'. It continues: 'children from a very young age learn about different races and cultures including religion and languages and will be capable of assigning different values to them. . . . It is important that people working with young children are aware of this, so that their practice enables children to develop positive attitudes to differences of race, culture and language' (Lane, undated paper).

The Rumbold Report

In 1990, the report 'Starting with Quality' (Rumbold Report) was published. Its committee was established to:

> consider the quality of the educational experience which should be
> offered to 3 and 4 year olds, with particular reference to content,

continuity and progression in learning, having regard to the requirements
of the National Curriculum and taking account of the government's
expenditure plans. (p. 1, para 1)

The committee addressed the unequal range of provision for young
children and also set out some of the principles of early education that
should underpin good provision (play, role of parents). But here we
have, at last, a report dedicated to the under fives and, optimistically
perhaps, one which showed considerable insight into early learning and
what might constitute a 'curriculum' for young children. We return to
this report in Chapter 3.

The Education Reform Act (1988) and afterwards

As mentioned earlier, one of the most far-reaching pieces of Conservative government legislation was the Education Reform Act of 1988
which included, among many other changes, the introduction of the
National Curriculum with its subject centred content. Although the legislation required it to be 'broad and balanced' its structure has militated
against this expectation (the Core subjects taking priority over the
Foundation). There have been various tinkerings with the curriculum in
the intervening years which appear to have temporarily ended with the
version of 1999. Following the election of the 'New' Labour government
in 1997, the Literacy and Numeracy Strategies were introduced for primary schools. While these were not statutory, many schools, under
pressure from the government, OFSTED (the mechanism for inspecting
schools which was established via the Education Reform Act) and the
media allowed these programmes to dominate the teaching so that English and Mathematics (reduced to being called Literacy and Numeracy)
were allocated 50 per cent of the week with all other subjects (8, plus RE)
allocated the other 50 per cent.

This is not the place to go over the arguments about the National
Curriculum, the role of Standard Assessment Tasks (SATs), OFSTED
inspections and grading of schools, measurable outcomes and
the country's economic performance but they are all interrelated and
the insidious impact of these on early years teaching should not be
ignored.

The National Curriculum

In schools, the imposition of a subject centred curriculum was particularly inappropriate for young children. The National Curriculum legally only applied to children of statutory school age (5 years), which left those teaching in the Reception class in a difficult position.

The under sevens, once considered to be 'Infants' were renamed via the Education Reform Act as Key Stage 1, with children in Reception classes, many still only 4 years of age, beginning to be subjected to a curriculum that had something in common with that observed nearly a hundred years earlier by Katherine Bathurst, with whom this chapter started.

The subject curriculum was swiftly embarked upon; the realization that a curriculum encompassed more than a number of subjects came later with various cross-curricular dimensions and themes. Attention to children with Special Educational Needs or children with EAL also came as something of an afterthought. It should be reiterated here that children's language needs are not the same as learning needs – bilingual children are all too often seen as having a learning deficit and grouped or labelled as such rather than having their specific linguistic needs and talents acknowledged and catered for.

The Foundation Stage

By the time the National Curriculum was revised in 1999, the government was beginning to address the variation in provision for the under fives and a new Key Stage – the Foundation Stage – for the 3–5-year-olds was introduced. Accompanying this was a new advisory (not statutory) document: 'Curriculum Guidance for the Foundation Stage' (CGFS) (2000). In contrast to the National Curriculum, this Guidance was based, not on single subjects, but on one of the underlying principles of early years learning that: 'Areas of learning involving the humanities, arts and sciences cannot be separated; young children learn in an integrated way and not in neat, tidy compartments' (Bruce, 2005, p. 17).

Thus the curriculum was one of six areas of learning and experience:

PSED, CLL, Mathematical Development, KUW (Knowledge and Understanding of the World), Creative Development and Physical Development. All these were and are deemed to be equally important.

The accompanying guidance notes for early years practitioners repeated many of the principles on which well-informed early years provision were already based. PSED, in particular, highlighted the central role of relationships in young children's lives and their need to be part of a caring relationship between home and school/nursery. CLL, too, emphasized the role of language and culture in forming children's identities. Chapter 3 looks more closely at these two areas of learning and development.

A controlled curriculum?

Unfortunately, the record of the previous government in relation to education is a mixed one. While there is no doubt that schools' funding and staffing improved dramatically over the past 13 years or so, the government's tendency to meddle in pedagogy and practice has had less admirable outcomes. Centralized control of the curriculum, for instance, and an obsession with measurable results has led to a curriculum which is dominated by formal assessments (SATs) and questionably 'broad and balanced' (which is the legal requirement).

This apparent need for control has spread steadily towards the early years, resulting in England (the Framework is not statutory in Wales, Scotland or Northern Ireland) in the Statutory Framework for the EYFS (DfES, 2007b) which replaced the CGFS, the Birth to Three Matters Framework and the National Standards for Under 8s Daycare and Childminding.

Accompanying this Framework is the Foundation Stage profile through which practitioners are required to record *and give points for* (our italics) children's progress as charted in chronological stages in the document. At the time of writing, these amount to a 117-point scale per child.

The Framework posits four guiding themes that should underpin provision:

- A Unique Child,
- Positive Relationships,
- Enabling Environments and
- Learning and Development. (DfES, 2007, p. 9, 1.11)

However, it does not actively recognize and promote the fact that many young children can operate in more than one language and should be encouraged to do so, although it does make frequent references to parents' bilingualism in its discussion of 'Positive Relationships'. The Early Learning Goals for CLL make no specific reference to children's home languages but merely state that children should 'know that print carries meaning and, in English, is read from left to right and top to bottom' (DfES, 2007b, p. 13, 2.10). It could, perhaps, be argued that because there is no specific reference to home languages, CLL could be seen as incorporating them but unless this expectation is spelled out, language variety is in danger of being ignored and children's personal linguistic experiences undervalued or not valued at all.

We would have expected a government document to take into account the huge amount of scholarly and research work carried out over the past 40 years or so and to use this to enhance its ideas about a curriculum. Under each of these four guiding principles, there were clear opportunities to draw attention to all children's linguistic and cultural backgrounds – aren't these part of what makes each child 'unique'? The role of the family and family networks could have been highlighted under 'Positive Relationships'. 'Enabling Environments' could have required all settings and staff to examine carefully their own provision and how well it acknowledged the children's homes and cultures and enlarged all children's experiences of cultural differences. 'Learning and Development' could have incorporated the body of knowledge referred to above and ensured that early years provision was based on secure philosophical and intellectual understanding of bilingualism, first and second language acquisition and language variety. We would also have expected there to be a bolder requirement for all staff working with young children to understand and be able to contest the workings of racism and discrimination.

Contrasts with other parts of the United Kingdom

Interestingly, there is, in Northern Ireland, Scotland and Wales, a marked and increasing concern about the use respectively of Irish Gaelic, Scots Gaelic and Welsh. We do not have the space to go into the histories here but for all three the indigenous languages were explicitly (and cruelly) repressed when each nation was brought, or coerced, into union with England and English imposed as the main language of communication. Moves during the later twentieth century towards greater independence from England, particularly on the part of Scotland and Wales, have led to state intervention in establishing programmes for the teaching and use of Gaelic and Welsh and in Wales in the prominent use of Welsh and English in government and public documents.

In Northern Ireland, too, there have been clear moves to increase the teaching and learning of the Irish language.

Europe

We referred to the EC Directive of 1977 earlier in this chapter. Stubbs (1985) suggests that while it was positive in its recognition of the importance of mother tongue provision and

> the actual right of an individual child to receive such provision was taken out of the original draft proposal at the insistence of Britain and West Germany' (as it was then); in addition, arguments surrounding mother tongue maintenance were also strongly linked to other social, economic and political questions including the residential status of migrant workers. (p. 297)

The Directive did, however, place a responsibility on the British government, among others, to 'take appropriate measures to promote, in coordination with normal education, teaching of the mother tongue, and culture of the country of origin' (Stubbs, 1985 pp. 315–16).

It could be argued that this was in reality to help children readjust when they and their families returned to their country of origin rather than settle in a new country (Alladina and Edwards, 1991) but, for all its limitations, the Directive certainly drew attention to multilingualism and obliged member countries to start to devise language programmes for bilingual children (see Skutnabb-Kangas and Cummins (1988) for a detailed discussion).

Baetens Beardsmore (1993) outlines what were, nearly 20 years ago, some of the models of bilingual education then operating in parts of Western Europe, but also notes that these were programmes that generally catered for children of civil servants and aimed to develop proficiency in other European languages as well as an appreciation of other cultures and a sense of European identity. In such possibly elitist programmes, the language needs of the children of migrant workers were not addressed.

Revisiting the EC Directive almost 34 years later it is quite clear that the Commission had got it wrong: The so-called migrant workers did not all return to their country of origin. Many of them settled in the new country where their children and their children's children were born. These children now see their country of birth as their own and have no particular desire to return to their parents' and grandparents' country of origin. In a more recent publication by the Commission of the European Communities (CEC, 2008) of a Green Paper on migration and mobility, there is a discussion of the challenges of providing adequate educational provision to students from the 'migrant communities'.

It also attempts to remedy the educational disadvantage facing them in mainstream European schools.

Note that the Commission is, in 2008, still using the terminology of 1974 to describe the students, particularly those from low socio-economic backgrounds.

A recurring question here is how much longer are subsequent generations of families endure being labelled as 'immigrants' or 'migrants'?

Looking beyond Europe, the reader might like to investigate New Zealand's 'Te Whariki' early years curriculum which is part of a ten-year plan that 'seeks to acknowledge diversity in provision, within and across cultures' (David et al., 2010, p. 40), with the Maori and Polynesian cultures particularly being addressed. As far as we know, neither the present nor the previous government has expressed much interest in this kind of programme for the United Kingdom.

Summary

This chapter has provided an overview of developments in education in this country, encompassing the historical changes and movements in its populations. The long-standing diversity of cultures and languages has been highlighted as well as the impact of empire and colonization and their influence on the arrival of 'new' populations particularly after the Second World War.

The neglect of young children and specifically young bilingual children in government education policy until the late twentieth century has been noted and the impact on schools of the 1988 Education Reform Act's National Curriculum considered.

The establishment of the EYFS and its now statutory curriculum will be explored in more detail in the Chapter 4. Having looked at the EYFS in this chapter we now explore the history of minority education in some detail in Chapter 2.

Reflective activity

1. How much of the information in Chapter 1 was familiar to you?
2. How much was new?
3. What do you know about the language backgrounds of the children you work with?
4. Do you know how many children speak a language other than or as well as, English at home?
5. What do you think you now need to find out?

2 Minority Education: Developments in Britain

We have already mentioned some of government legislation and migration patterns to the United Kingdom in Chapter 1. In this chapter, we develop these in more detail by exploring some of the policy initiatives by successive governments to argue that overall these were not supportive of children's bilingualism in UK schools. As we will discuss in Chapter 5, debates and research around negative aspects of bilingualism play a considerable part in shaping general public view about language acquisition in general and help create negative assumptions about second language acquisition in particular. What appeared to be particularly damaging about these studies was the wrong association of bilingualism with lower levels of intelligence and cognitive functioning.

In this chapter, we set a historical context of the education of minority ethnic children in Britain. This in our view will help to explain the present provision for minority groups. We argue that successive government policy initiatives on minority education should be seen in the context of wider political developments. We present the development of such initiatives within specific periods. Although the periods outlined are specific, in time they do overlap and are in no way discrete. They are an aid for analyses and discussion rather than commentary on changes in education affecting bilingual children. We begin by identifying the factors that have contributed to the adoption of new policies and discuss the eventual change in some practices in the classrooms. We analyse the educational provision for children of migrants who, for a variety of reasons came to settle in Britain, and began to appear in the British schools since the early 1950s. We look at these key issues in some detail.

These factors affecting some changes in the practices were multidimensional, and at times formed the ingredients for powerful initiatives. Such changes, however, found themselves within the embrace of greater political forces. Despite claims that the decisions taken could be justified on educational grounds, many decisions were in the end the product of power relationships (Rogers, 1997). Political parties had their own views on education, and successive governments made it quite clear as to how they thought best to educate the so-called immigrant child (Tomlinson, 1983). There was also strong public opinion on education and successive governments had to take account of this. It was not so much the case of having a sound policy and from this position trying to change public opinion on the education of migrants, as of 'making-up-policy-as-you-go-along' in line with the pressures presented by public opinion on education. For each successive government policy was based on how best to win public opinion on education – that meant winning votes for power – while maintaining the party line on education of migrants. Change came only gradually and was supported by a rather patchy picture of LEA initiatives (Townsend, 1971; DES, 1971; Craft, 1981).

What were the factors influencing change? First, there were social factors, particularly the views of the minority ethnic communities themselves. For the West Indian community there were increasing concerns about a disproportionate number of West Indian children who were finding themselves in schools for the educationally subnormal (Coard, 1971). For the Asian and other minority communities this related to their desire to preserve their cultural traditions and practices, namely teaching of their religion as well as their mother tongue (Taylor and Hegarty, 1985). There were also growing concerns about racism in schools. The parents from the minority ethnic communities became powerful social agents, demanding change.

Secondly, there were psychological factors. There was a growing awareness among some educators that the way that minority children perceived themselves within an 'alien' education system was important and needed attention (Mehmet Ali, 1984).

Thirdly, there were environmental factors. These were supported by studies in Britain and abroad which advocated the importance of educationally enriched environments in promoting the quality of life and learning for those who were disadvantaged (Issa, 1987). There were also demographic factors. Migration was of a scale, never been previously experienced, which changed the demographic characteristics of whole areas (Rose et al., 1969). Many of the original migrants had relied on kinship ties both to sponsor their migration and find jobs and housing when they first arrived here. For example, according to the 1971 census data, 70–75 per cent of Cypriots were living in the Greater London area. This focus on London came from the pre-war concentration of Cypriots in the restaurant and clothing trade, particularly in Soho. These patterns led to the concentration of migrant families living within close proximity to one another. Local authorities felt the need to respond to such changes in their catchment areas. There were further complications: while there were broad similarities between central and local government attitudes to minority education, as reflected for example, in the funding arrangements of central government directly conditioning local government practice, there were also occasions when local authority practices varied considerably from central government policy. Government policy on dispersal is an example of this (DES, 1965).

Setting the debate

Children from a range of different minority ethnic backgrounds have long been present in this country, but it is only since the early 1950s, when there was sharp rise in immigration from Commonwealth countries that this was seen as affecting the nature of British society, that educators and politicians began discussing the particular implications such children had for educational provision.

There is a clearly defined chronological pattern of attitudes towards the educational needs of minority ethnic groups moving from the initial policy of assimilation. This was followed by integration, in which attempts were made in schools to recognize the backgrounds of minority ethnic children. More recently, moves were made towards creating a more coherent and practical approach to what became multicultural education. We will contextualize each of these in turn within the period of discussion.

The 1950s signal the beginnings of a change in the perception of so-called minority education in Britain. For the first time, the children of the migrant workers became visible within the system, and there was a realization that the education of immigrant children might require a somewhat different approach than that of their monolingual peers (Hawkes, 1966; Khan, 1980). What were the reasons contributing to this realization? Why did the government change its practice on assimilation? We argue that the evolution of policy initiatives and practices reflect periods of development in educational thinking. Dominant policy and practice remained within central government's power so the apparent autonomy of the LEAs were undermined by the practical (funding) and theoretical (political) activities of successive governments.

It is important to discuss central government's role within the context of changes in educational thinking (Rogers, 1997). The educational arguments about bilingualism, like those about other educational philosophies, evolved over a period of time. Thinking about the education of bilingual pupils has developed rapidly, but only become dynamic, challenging the actual practice of the advocates of monolingualism in classrooms, from the early 1980s onwards.

The role of successive governments will be a central theme. The constant preoccupation of each government with teaching of English has prevented a comprehensive approach to be adopted towards the education of minorities. This can be traced through publications and reports that have appeared through the decades. One of the published surveys by the Department of Education and Science (DES) is an example of this: the teaching of English was seen as: 'the most urgent single challenge facing the schools' (DES, 1971).

At certain periods the attitude of government to the education of minorities has been sympathetic and genuine. The real point of concern is government's preoccupation with preserving existing systems, that is, how to accommodate and support bilingual children within the boundaries of existing systems. It was never the government's intention to change the system to meet the more complex needs of bilingual pupils. The local initiatives and practices were important, and contributed positively towards the education of bilingual children. But, without national endorsement of approaches to bilingual children these practices remained local and confined within community boundaries.

Despite LEAs apparent autonomy to adopt and implement policies for bilingual pupils, they were often dominated by the central government, which had a degree of leverage over the decision-making mechanisms of the LEAs. With few exceptions government influence on the LEA's was formidable. In a way, this was no surprise as government agents, LEAs had always been expected to carry out central government initiatives.

This was not an open, calculated intervention but a subtle 'reading between the lines' approach. There was no clear direction by the government on the education of the minorities. This is shown in the practice of most of the LEAs, which while well intentioned was without a coherent strategy and tokenistic. There was, of course, more to the LEA/central government dimension. Although having the power to initiate change, most LEAs lacked leadership and knowledge to innovate programmes. Some of those who did value and support bilingual approaches were nervous about implementing a system that would require a complete change in the organization of teaching and learning in their schools. The very few LEAs who bravely pursued their aims encountered financial difficulties because local authority funding was determined by central government. In the case of the Conservatives, who dominated the British political scene for nearly two decades, from 1979–97, this control was displayed quite blatantly, not only in the form of intolerance towards bilingualism, but also through active opposition to any change favouring bilingual education. The real purpose of such attacks was often disguised under other justifications against the so-called subversive left-wing LEAs (Rogers, 1997). The result left these LEAs with significant reductions in their budgets.

The 1950s: The first arrivals

The 1950s were not the first time that Britain had seen large-scale immigration. During the latter part of the nineteenth century, there were Italians, Jews, Blacks, Huguenots, Maltese already settled here. In 1861 there were 6,504 Italians living in the United Kingdom (King, 1979) and in the early part of the twentieth century, Chinese settled in the Docklands area of East London and Liverpool (Watson, 1975). During the Second World War around 100,000 Polish settlers came to Britain as political refugees. 30,000 Ukrainians settled in Britain after the War (Proudfoot, 1956). These peoples were soon assimilated into the British society. One of the main reasons for this was their physical appearance. With the exception of the Chinese and the black people they looked relatively similar to the indigenous British people, which meant they were white. For some of these migrants, the attempts to maintain their own cultural values in closely knit communities was the direct result of hostilities and racism experienced in other countries.

Britain in the 1950s was different from that of the 1930s. The expanding British economy needed more workers to meet the growing demand for unskilled and semi-skilled work, in, for example, London Transport, British Rail and Underground as well as mass production lines. These were also jobs that the indigenous working force was no longer prepared to do. Recruitment started in British colonies and former colonies where relatively cheap labour was available. These countries had high unemployment with substantial agricultural subsistence economies. The Caribbean, the Indian subcontinent and the Mediterranean supplied the first wave of workers. Recruitment was started with young males in mid-twenties and thirties. This was often done through official advertising in these countries with the involvement of Colonial administrations. In other cases, interested companies set up recruitment centres in those countries: London Transport recruited in the West Indies through such initiatives in 1955. As the new work force arrived, the job vacuum that had existed in the transport, hotel and catering services slowly started to be filled.

Some negative feelings emerged from some sections of the society towards the arriving work force and against what began to be known as 'coloured immigration' (Rose et al., 1969, p. 43). The feelings were soon used by some Conservative politicians, who began to articulate them as political material to attract more votes. They were also used by some extreme political groups to fuel anti-immigration feeling among the population, perpetrating the myth that the country was being swamped with immigrants. In reality, numbers were relatively small and falling as the decade came to an end. The trend seemed to have had some link with levels of unemployment. As unemployment went up in the United Kingdom, immigration appeared to be going down (Patterson, 1969).

The intention of some of these predominantly male settlers was either to make enough money to go back home to marry or to earn enough money to provide a more comfortable life for their families back home. As many of these male workers decided, for a variety of reasons not to return to their countries, more and more families started to join their next of kin in the United Kingdom (Anwar, 1979).

With the arrival of those other family members the demography of some inner city areas, for example, in London, Manchester, Birmingham, Coventry and regions of South Yorkshire started to change. It was during this period that Britain's position as a colonial power was beginning to decline, and Britain was involved in colonial conflicts around the world.

These events did not help the host society's perception of the newcomers: they already held a 'colonial' view of their countries and their peoples. As early as 1958 Britain witnessed its first riots between black and white people in the Notting Hill district of London. About 2,000 young people and adults attacked black people's houses, breaking windows and causing extensive damage. A black man was murdered. Police

Table 2.1 Estimated net inflow of immigrant workers and total number of unemployed persons between 1957–9

Year	Total West Indian, Indian and Pakistani net inflow	Mid-year total unemployment in United Kingdom
1957	34,800	276,000
1958	25,900	406,000
1959	20,200	420,000

Source: S. Patterson (1969), *Immigration and Race Relations in Britain, 1960–1967*

investigation revealed the involvement of extreme political groups (Briggs, 1992). After the riots there were calls for legislation to stop immigration: the Conservatives supported this and began to make administrative arrangements to deal with growing concern on immigration (Dickinson, 1982). The Home Office became responsible for the Commonwealth immigrants' affairs in 1956 as the whole 'immigration issue' was conceptualized in two broad categories: control over entry and laws against racial discrimination. The Commonwealth Immigrants' Advisory Council was set up to review discrimination. Apart from this, very little was actually done by the government to legislate against racial discrimination during the period.

The local authority response

The initial problem that confronted local authorities was finding suitable accommodation for the newcomers. Initially, families were temporarily housed in bachelor homes, often rented privately. For families who arrived with children, finding suitable accommodation became a council priority. Assessing the needs of each household required a degree of organization. Recruiting interpreters for different language groups and arranging training for them was one difficulty. Analysing the information collected and putting people in them in order of priority required time and extra staff resources. These were all cost related issues.

Discussion of services for minorities was influenced by negative attitudes of some councillors towards minorities. Provision for minorities was often influenced by the local party power relationships within councils. Some Conservative councils were influenced by right-wing groups, who influenced policy and practice on local provision for minorities.

Action of this sort was quite widespread among some councils within large urban centres such as London, Manchester and Birmingham. The prejudice displayed by some of the councillors was a reaction to the wider political debate outside the council chamber. Some of the white majority population were beginning to draw parallels between the growing numbers of the unemployed and what they saw as increasing number of immigrants. The resentment of seeing what was 'rightfully theirs' 'taken' by those from other countries produced the early seeds of racism. Extreme right-wing political activists had a political agenda that functioned independently of the major parties, and they played on these negative feelings.

The 'race' issue was to become a powerful and dangerous influence on public opinion and policy decisions at local and national level for many years to come. It became ingrained in public thinking and was seen as a potential vote winner by the political parties. Public demands changed and it influenced policy decisions, particularly in the educational provision for immigrant children (Power, 1967; Tomlinson, 1983). The initial response of the system was to absorbing them into the majority pupil population as rapidly as possible.

The second period: 1960–5

This period was characterized by the implementation of the Commonwealth Immigrants Act (1962). There were growing pressures from sections of the public and politicians who were alarmed at the numbers entering Britain as Colonial and Commonwealth citizens. Immigration from the ex-colonies slightly increased by the rush to beat the ban caused by the Act. The numbers were not significant. A new Labour government was elected in 1964 with a very small majority and issued a White Paper in August 1965 which suggested further restrictions on entry into the United Kingdom. The sudden rise in the immigration just before the 1962 Act was sufficient for extremists to spread the myth that the country was swamped with foreigners.

During the 1960s, some parts of the urban centres became areas of high concentration of immigrant groups from particular countries, such as Cypriots in Camden and Islington, Punjabi-speaking Muslims and Sikhs in Bradford, Italians working in Bedford (King, 1979). The employment opportunities in the service sector (Cypriots), the textile industries in the North (Punjabis and Sikhs) and the brick industry (Italians) were attractive for the newcomers.

Immigration continued as more of the families of these groups arrived, as well as those from different countries, for example, from Portugal and Gujarati speakers from the Indian subcontinent. As newcomers settled with fellow country folk or with relations in the area, earlier settlers began to move out or stayed to buy their own homes. For example, it is estimated that more than two-thirds of Cypriot immigrants became homeowners during the 1960s (Stubbs, 1985). Concentrations of newer groups were beginning to emerge in other parts of large cities.

The first wave of ethnic minority children in English schools: Some changes in policy and practice

English is used here to refer specifically to England, as opposed to the term British, which may include other parts of the United Kingdom, which is Wales, Scotland or Northern Ireland. Immigration during this first period was very much an urban English experience. The patterns of immigration described earlier meant that children started to appear in schools from the early 1960s onwards. The initial practice was to immediately place children in centres to teach them English. Other practices were the result of pressure groups concerned about the concentration of a significant number of minority children in their schools. These groups were to influence policy decisions on minority pupils. There were also economic reasons for change as the service sector and other industries expanded. Growing economic prosperity made it possible for the Labour government to provide funding for English language support for minorities, implemented under the Section 11 of the Local Government Act (1966). Such initiatives were seen as a step towards repairing fragile race relations in Britain that had been strained by the implementation of the 1962 Commonwealth Immigrants Act and by the White Paper on Immigration (1965).

There was growing pressure on the government to further restrict entry into the United Kingdom. Some extreme political groups, sensing discontent among the majority population, were actively using the issue as political propaganda to attract attention and to provoke. The government yielded to this because the delay in implementing change could cost them the next general election. Both the Commonwealth Immigrants Act (1962) and the White Paper on Immigration (1965) were attempts by respective Conservative and Labour governments to address fears about the coming elections in 1964 and 1966. While justifying the need to control entry, the Labour government also set out to convince the electorate that the minorities already settled here would be part of society, integrated into the British way of life. The Labour party declared that only those migrants who wished to integrate into the system should be allowed to stay (Power, 1967). In reality, the government was facing difficulties in justifying their policy decisions: As Power (1967) indicated: 'Ministers and civil servants alike were under pressure from one quarter (of the community) or another. Anything they did was likely to be called wrong (p. 5).

This period saw an increase in the concentration of immigrant children in English schools. The policy and practice in most LEAs was the same as that of central government: to assimilate bilingual children into mainstream classes as quickly as possible, without causing too much disruption to the existing school system (Rose et al., 1969). Learning English was key to this. Speaking another language was strongly discouraged in schools and English language instruction was seen as the only way to achieve the aim: 'from the beginning, the major educational task is the teaching of English' (DES, 1965).

Special units for receiving pupils were set up, in the school buildings or at separate locations near the schools. There was separate language teaching in some schools through the practice of withdrawal for certain hours each day. The methods used were based on teaching English to foreign students and were carried out by teachers who were foreign language teachers. LEAs also followed the lead of central government in language provision. Policy documents were produced to support their position on teaching immigrant pupils. *English for Immigrants* was produced to help teachers about methods of teaching immigrant pupils English (Ministry of Education, 1963). The work of the Commonwealth Immigrants Advisory Council – set up as a result of proposals made during the passage of the Commonwealth Immigrants Bill in 1962–, was to endorse the government's position on the importance of assimilation and to help create a national system that perpetuated one value system, and a particular way of life. The following example, taken from their second report, expresses concern about the possible effects of large numbers of immigrant pupils in English schools:

> The presence of a high proportion of immigrant children in one class
> slows down the general routine of working and hampers the progress of
> the whole class, especially where the immigrants do not speak or write
> English fluently. . . . Immigrant pupils in such a school will not get as good
> an introduction to the British way of life as they would get in a normal
> school. (Commonwealth Immigrants Advisory Council, 1964)

During this period, anti-immigration hostilities were continuing to manifest themselves. For example, angry parents might protest against the concentration of large numbers of immigrant children in their local schools. This concern was based on the assumption that there would be a drop in standards as schools would spend time teaching these children English, neglecting the needs of other children (Tomlinson, 1983). In one school in Southall, parents claimed that the high numbers of Punjabi-speaking children presented a problem and demanded that something be done about it. The Conservative Minister of Education, Edward Boyle, made a personal visit to the school in 1963 to defuse the tension. He later reported in the Commons that something needed to be done about schools that were 'irretrievably immigrant' and suggested that a limit of 30 per cent immigrant pupils be allowed in a school. The minister was signalling the beginning of the practice known as *bussing*. Children who exceeded the 30 per cent limit in a school were bussed to other schools and centres for English language instruction. In 1965, the DES incorporated this in *Circular 7/65*, and this was later incorporated into the White Paper later that year (1965). All LEAs, with the exception of two, accepted the proposals and *bussed* their children when the limit was exceeded.

Issues facing West Indian children were equally as serious as those facing bilingual children. There were growing concerns among the community that West Indian children's language needs were not understood sufficiently or catered for. Some teachers had a negative perception of the particular variety of English used by these pupils. It was assumed by some teachers, that the different dialect of English spoken indicated a deficiency in English language skills. This was one of the reasons why West Indian pupils were placed in schools for the educationally subnormal (Coard, 1971). These issues will be discussed in more detail below.

It took the government some time to realize the ineffectiveness of its bussing strategy. Children were taught in an environment away from their own classrooms, through a language that was in many ways alien to them and there was no direct connection between what was learned in the withdrawal classroom and what was going on in the child's mainstream classroom. Teaching approaches were also criticized by many educators as inappropriate: these children were being taught English through the same methods for teaching English as were used with adult students. Another highly debated point among the educators was the use of children's cultural values as starting points for learning. Increasing numbers of educators believed that teaching should refer to aspects of children's cultural experiences, for example, geographical and historical information on the Caribbean, Asia, lives of famous black people.

By the end of the second period (1960–5) these distinct educational groups were beginning to influence the views of the public. The public was also influenced by political activities in the United States: race riots, bussing, mass boycotts of services by black people were generating wide interest in Britain. The Labour government appeared to be sensitive but remained indecisive. The apparent dilemma for the Labour party seemed to be linked to the contradiction that existed between policy decisions that was to be egalitarian and progressive on one hand and the practical decisions that ensured keeping in line with tradition on the other. The Labour party agenda was also about how to stay in power after the next general election.

Third period: 1966–72

The third period was marked by an escalation of political activity that engulfed educational debate. Migration to Britain decreased considerably with the 1962 Commonwealth Immigrants Act and the fall in availability of unskilled jobs. Immigration fell further, cut with the 1971 Immigration Act, which replaced the 1962 Commonwealth Immigrants Act. The new Act got rid of the voucher scheme and the right to be partial. Those who had no right to settle or no relations in Britain were only allowed to come through using the work permits.

Racism continued to manifest itself through anti-immigration hostilities. It seemed to carry more weight as it came from those holding official positions. The situation was more serious than what appeared on the surface. The real intentions of these people were hidden under the 'anti-immigration' banner. These ideas seemed to have greater influence on the general public than any government policy. Their actions were preventing public debate to be centred on the real issue, *racism* rather than immigration. Enoch Powell and Peter Griffiths, both Conservative MPs, were instrumental in provoking racist tendencies through their speeches. Powell was an opposition front bench MP for Wolverhampton South-West. In his series of speeches around the country in 1968, he displayed his views clearly on immigration and citizenship: 'like the Roman, I seem to see the River Tiber foaming with much blood' (*Immigration and Race in British Politics*, 20 April 1968 (quoted in Foot, 1969)). What similarities Powell drew between rivers Tiber and Thames is unclear but the tone of his speech was sufficient to escalate racial tensions within the communities. 'The West Indian or Asian does not, by being born in England, become an Englishman. In law, he becomes a UK citizen by birth, in fact he is a West Indian or Asian still (Birmingham, 20 April 1968).

The Labour government continued to introduce further legislation in response to such calls. It also continued to initiate new programmes to support the deprived areas with immigrant settlers in them. In 1968, two new laws were enacted: The Commonwealth Immigrants Act (1968) removed the right of entry from the British Asians in East Africa, and the Race Relations Act (1968) generally widened the scope of race relations to include housing, employment and many services, but with many limited powers for the board.

This Act also established a new statutory body, the Community Relations Commission to replace the National Committee for Commonwealth Immigrants (NCCI). From around 1970, by which time the entry of Commonwealth immigrants for work had ceased under the increasingly strict requirements which the Department of Employment had established under work voucher schemes, ethnic minority affairs became the responsibility of the Home Office. The emphasis of central government policy, and the bulk of expenditure, was on immigration control rather than upon community relations work and anti-discrimination initiatives (Swann Report, 1985). It was a widely shared view among the minority communities that the positive achievement of the relevant bodies set up by the government was very small when compared to the impact of successive Immigration Acts on their lives (Berk, 1972).

The Urban Aid programme, originally set up in 1968 as a response to Enoch Powell's anti-immigration speeches by the then Labour party, was to fund projects among immigrant communities. It rapidly became a general source of funding for urban projects, and was not noticeably used to finance educational provision (Tomlinson, 1983). There was also a diversity of provision between LEAs. This was documented by Townsend, who surveyed the practices and policies of 146 LEAs. Some placed a much higher priority on arrangements for schools with immigrant pupils than others while others deliberately played down arrangements as they were unwilling to be seen to divert resources to immigrant communities (Townsend, 1971, p. 69).

These programmes, as well as their modified versions, were mainly designed to cater for the *areas* rather the groups in them. In fact, it has been argued that Labour's expenditure in areas of high immigration was directed more towards diffusing tension within the communities than any planned effort to help ethnic minorities within them to achieve success. The Labour government's Section 11 Grant was introduced in 1966 to help children of the Commonwealth in the British education system 'whose language and customs differ from those of the community'. Section 11 of the Local Government Act 1966 shares a common origin with the government's Urban Programme. LEAs with a schools population of 2 per cent and more of immigrant population were eligible for government grants under the Act. The Act was primarily designed for areas with large numbers of immigrants 'whose custom and language may throw an additional burden on the resources of the authorities'. Implicit in this was a concern that the number of immigrant children in school may have a detrimental effect on the 'standards' of the school. The Act was significant for two main reasons: first, for the first time in the history of education in Britain, a central government was directly paying for the education of immigrant children. Secondly, the funding necessitated the collection of statistical data about the children to be supported. This information on numbers determined the need, and thus the funding to be allocated to each area.

Educational provision during this phase was moving from assimilation to an integrationist model. There was a growing realization – at the local level by the teachers and professionals working in this field – that assimilation practices had not succeeded. The argument for including children's cultural experiences in their learning was shared by some educators and a small minority of teachers (see Bernstein, 1971; Trudgill, 1975; Rosen, 1973). The use of children's cultural experiences, it was argued, would prevent alienating the child and help integration. The government line on the education of the immigrants still appeared to be advocating the mastery of English as the only possible means through which the minority children would gain access to mainstream society. According to the government, this process needed to take place in a much more planned way, and funding was needed for this purpose. Studies were funded that would highlight the language learning of minority children (see Townsend (1971) based on the survey of the LEAs and schools undertaken by HM Inspectorate 1972).

Practices in schools concerning the education of the minorities were varied during this period. The education of these children emerged on an ad hoc basis, with few teachers trained to cater for the language needs of immigrant children (Tomlinson, 1983). School responses split between those with significant numbers of minority children and those who were all white and hence felt they had no problems (Townsend and Britten, 1973). Practice across the country varied, with some boroughs still practising bussing. Some schools linked poor achievement to poor self-image, and made changes to their curriculum to give some minority cultures greater recognition (McNeal and Rogers, 1971). But neither the Conservative government nor most LEAs responded to the issue of achievement. It was felt that producing appropriate policies would alleviate the problem. Any research on underachievement stressed causation, rather than policies to overcome the problem (Bernstein, 1972). The position of the DES summarized the government's view 'Practical help and advice to teachers faced with the challenge of teaching immigrant children (1971, p. 15).

Although funding continued for the education of minorities, the policy and practices of first the Labour and then the Conservative government remained assimilationist in character. This, with few exceptions, was also the case in the LEAs. One reason for this reluctance for change was the pressure on the government from the general public, instigated chiefly by pressure groups within both parties and considerably dramatized by the mass media. Power (1967) wrote that the educational policies of this period had to take account of the public feeling against coloured immigration.

As the debate on education intensified, the Labour government's programmes and initiatives for the migrant communities lacked cohesion and real planning. Callaghan's 1968 Urban Programme demonstrated how civil servants were often left to deal with hurried policy decisions that were unplanned by the politicians. The result was policies that lacked clarity and objectives.

The statistics debate that emerged as a major policy issue in the late 1960s was an indication of this pressure. In order to provide the statistical basis for the dispersal policy and also to quantify the degree of language need, the DES initiated the collection of statistics on immigrant children through Form 7(i) returns from the LEAs from 1966 onwards. The information was to establish the length of stay of immigrant children or children of immigrants' parents within the education system. It was asserted that if a child had been in Britain for more than ten years, he or she would no longer suffer from any education difficulties. This was bitterly opposed by the minorities, who argued that this would be used to gather statistics on them that would provide information for right-wing propaganda.

The government maintained that this data was needed to determine the most needy areas. This position reflected the general feeling of the period and was further strengthened by studies in Britain and abroad, which advocated progressive child centred approaches to learning that explicitly supported the child's cultural/home environment as important experiences in their learning. Some children, it was argued, 'are most handicapped by home conditions' (Plowden Report, 1967, p. 426; also Bernstein, 1972; Rosen, 1973 in Britain; Labov, 1966; Breiter and Engelmann, 1966) in the United States. Paradoxically, these studies while pointing out the 'deficiencies' in minority children's home environments were also paving the way for studies on minority children's home backgrounds. As we will see, the emphasis was to shift from the 'deficiency' models of the home environment to one of 'enrichment' where the cultural experiences of the child were to be regarded as important ingredients for teaching.

As the debate on the standards in education was intensified under Mrs Thatcher's Conservative government (1979 onwards), new initiatives from Europe put the education of the minority children back on the policy agenda. Governments were needed to do something for the minorities for two reasons. First, as a member of the European Union, Britain's actions were watched closely in Europe from 1973 onwards. Secondly, governments were needed to promote equal opportunities, as they believed this was a potential vote winner.

Fourth period: 1972–82

While the 1960s had been dominated by the student unrest, the beginning of the 1970s was marked by an escalation in racial tensions, exacerbated by the economic recession of the 1970s that characterized decline and economic unrest in the Western economies. The OPEC oil price rises sent shock waves into the industrial world. In Britain, Labour and Conservative governments alike were unable to prevent drift towards economic chaos, of which a three-day working week (1973–4) and the winter of discontent (1978–9) became potent symbols. It was a period of rising inflation and of waves of strikes that paralysed Britain, and that too many of her European neighbours became known as the 'British disease'. It affected the race relations negatively, as rising unemployment was blamed on the minorities. The period was also characterized by the upsurge of extreme right tendencies such as the National Front, who staged demonstrations against 'foreigners' 'who came and took their jobs'. Countering these tendencies were demonstrations organized by the Anti-Nazi League.

Government attitudes to minorities during much of the 1970s were dominated by the perception of them as 'disadvantaged'. While the assimilationist view regarded immigrant children's needs as requiring short-term, ad hoc measures, it was now becoming clear that the educational needs of ethnic minority children were not so easily met. The government's thinking was towards a new stereotype in which minorities suffered what was traditionally termed the 'cycle of cumulative disadvantage'. This move towards categorizing ethnic minority groups as disadvantaged was resisted by the ethnic minority communities themselves as an Open University (1982) course book expressed it: 'To them (the Government) it implied that "immigrants" could be lumped together in a crude, undifferentiated way with the most unfortunate members of the indigenous community' (Open University, 1982, E354-Block 4, Units 13 and 14).

The assumption made by the government was that, since the education system had not succeeded in devising a programme appropriate to the needs of the indigenous communities, by implication the needs of ethnic minority pupils must be another aspect of a wider problem. The stereotype of ethnic minorities as disadvantaged was furthered by the correlation drawn between their situation and the plight of the inner cities. This point was the subject of increasing public concern during the 1970s. As the 1975 White Paper on 'Racial Discrimination' put it:

> the problems of racial disadvantage can be seen to occur typically in the context of an urban problem whose nature is only imperfectly understood. There is no modern industrial society, which has not experienced a similar difficulty. None has so far succeeded in resolving it.

Meanwhile, the minority communities continued to be uneasy about forms of discrimination, particularly those who suffered in the workplace and in housing applications. The policy recommendations put forward by the 1976 Race Relations Act were primarily to help local authorities to eliminate racial discrimination and disadvantage.

It is debatable how useful the Act was in countering racial discrimination at the work place. The Act was thought to have 'illuminated' (Young, 1983, p. 294) the deficiencies of the Section 11 Act of 1966 in countering such discrimination and put certain moves into motion for its replacement. In April 1977, a Green Paper was published proposing changes to the British Nationality Law. This suggested that the existing immigration control structure remain unchanged but the possibility of transmitting British Nationality from male citizens of the colonies and from the remaining British Asians in East Africa to wives and children be removed. In 1981, the British Nationality Act was passed amid considerable controversy and there was some confusion about whether it was really a nationality measure or rather an immigration law in disguise: 'Logically however it marked a further step on the same road that immigration laws had followed since 1962 (Swann Report, 1985, p. 210).

During this period, there was a lack of clear and coherent guidance from central government on the education of minorities. Discrepancies in practice between central and local authorities continued amidst increasingly politicized notions of what constituted the right kind of education. The concern of Conservative politicians on what they saw as falling standards found support among some educators. The mass media were also often critical of progressive education, and there seemed to be considerable support around the country for such views. The teaching profession did not always help itself, and the William Tyndale affair in 1975 provided evidence for those seeking to discredit progressive teaching methods.

Such messages were instrumental in giving the traditionalists a boost in their argument for traditional methods in teaching. Similarly, the methods of teaching for minority children continued to be nothing more than an extension of the previous programmes, aimed at improving the 'deficiency' of the home environment of ethnic minorities. It did not bring about a national consensus in approach nor achieve any results in addressing the issue from a bilingual perspective; hence, the role of the first language – with the exception of a few isolated cases – remained outside central and local government initiatives. Meanwhile the debate continued.

Fifth period: 1981–8

This period was characterized by tensions within government about the kind of curriculum that should be delivered in schools. The outcome of this debate was to influence the provision for minority children in later years. Debate between the DES and the HMI began a few years earlier with the publication of the DES document titled *A Framework for the School Curriculum* (DES, 1980a). The document appeared to advocate a much more centralist approach to learning (Lawton, 1989), and prescribing how subjects were to be taught nationally (Ross, 2000, p. 38). The HMI publication *A View of the Curriculum* (DES, 1980b) appeared to have a broader perception of the curriculum: '(It) presented a variety of views of the curriculum acknowledging the 'necessary tension' between the broad and common aims of education and individual abilities and characteristics (Ross, 2000, p. 41).

One of the more positive outcomes of this debate between the DES and the HMI was the considerable revision of the framework by the DES (1981) to take account of the individual needs of the pupils. More vocational and economic dimensions to the curriculum were emphasized. There was also a support for multiculturalism:

> The stress on multiculturalism, as an essential element for all pupils is noteworthy. Many teachers and LEAs – particularly, but by no means exclusively those in the inner city areas where most of the ethnic minority population were living – had been advocating (and implementing) curricula that recognised and used such cultural diversity. These approaches had been generally ignored and derided by the Conservatives. (Cited in Ross, 2000, p. 44)

The 1979 Conservative Party election victory lead by Margaret Thatcher produced a series of Education Acts. Local authorities were made to introduce Comprehensive schemes (Rogers, 1997). An Act in 1980 introduced an Assisted Places Scheme to give financial assistance to some children from working-class families, so that gifted children of lower income families would get government help for private education. Despite these innovations for education, the appointment of Keith Joseph as the Education Secretary in 1981 led to a slight reduction in spending on education. Joseph argued that 'the basis of all good education is high quality teaching' (Knight, 1990, p. 146) and implied that methods of teaching were more important than the resources to support teaching. It was hardly surprising to see a more traditional approach to teaching being supported by the Conservatives.

Some ideas of the 'new right' were soon to be taken into Conservative policy. Policy was now focusing on a return to more formal methods, where teaching is teacher directed, within more structured lessons. Although multiculturalism was accepted as a reflection of modern British society, the education of the minorities was seen very much in the context of learning English. The main thrust of Conservative policy on education was to establish standards within a centrally controlled education system in which teachers were to be accountable for the content of their teaching. This was an ideology that had no time for diversity and saw education in the context of raising standards.

Educational initiatives at local and national levels were described in reports that seemed to endorse the government's provision for minority education. The first major study on the education of minorities was undertaken by the Committee chaired by Lord Swann (DES, 1985). This provided an in-depth study of minorities and their language use in the United Kingdom, and put the educational developments in policy and practical levels into context. The report provided a climate for healthy debate on the education of the minority communities. However, its position on the role of English was viewed with scepticism by some members of the minority communities. The report's overall emphasis was on raising achievement levels of minority pupils under the 'unifying' (Swann Report, 1985, p. 385) function of the English language. The report had a carefully drawn agenda within which bilingualism was not acceptable. The report conveyed the government's position on the issue of bilingualism: 'We find we cannot support arguments put forward for the introduction of programmes of bilingual education in maintained schools in this country' (Swann Report, 1985, p. 400).

The final phase: 1988 to present

The 1988 Education Reform Act introduced the National Curriculum, with core subjects of English, Mathematics and Science and seven additional foundation subjects. Programmes of Study and Attainment Targets for each subject were to be drawn up by the National Curriculum Council, with the School Examination and Assessment Council detailing arrangements for testing in the core and foundation subjects. The Secretary of State had the final say over matters of the Curriculum. The Act strengthened the rights of parents to choose schools and abolished the LEAs right to set the number of children who could enter a school, instead establishing the 1979 entry as a base line. Schools were made responsible for the management of their own budgets (Local Management of Schools). The power of school governors was enhanced, and they became responsible for the appointment of staff, the management of school finances and the overall conduct of schools. New categories of school were also established, such as Grant Maintained schools and City Technical Colleges (CTC). Other schools were able to opt out of LEA control after a ballot of parents and there was a possibility of schools changing their character.

The Act made teachers more accountable to the Secretary of State by increasing reporting, by testing and by the evaluation of tasks on an annual basis. It also established the OFSTED to monitor progress of schools. For minority children, the Act signalled again the importance given to Standard English as the only measure of achievement within the system. The administrative burden of these served as the catalyst for the test boycott activities in 1992. Sir Ron Dearing's final report (1993) also supported these claims and resulted in the slimming of the curriculum into its present form.

Despite such criticisms, the government was not totally insensitive to the needs of ethnic minorities. In 1988, Kenneth Baker, the Secretary of State for Education wrote a letter to the National Curriculum Council asking it to take account of: 'Ethnic and cultural diversity and the importance of the curriculum in promoting equal opportunity for all pupils regardless of ethnic origin or gender' (DES, 1988).

In response, the NCC set up a task group consisting of educators and representatives of minority groups (six of the group members were of Afro Caribbean or Asian origin). The main task of the group was to: 'Consider the ways in that the National Curriculum could broaden the horizons of all pupils in a multicultural society and address the curriculum needs of ethnic minority pupils, especially bilingual pupils' (Tomlinson, 1993, p. 22).

The task group met regularly and prepared guidelines which they assumed would be published along the lines of the eight National Curriculum Guidance booklets that dealt with 'aspects of the curriculum not subject to statutory orders' (NCC, 1990). It was also assumed that the guidelines were to be published by autumn 1990. However, the Guidelines were never published. The members of the group wrote about this to the NCC: a letter written by one of the officers of the group stressed that the NCC 'Recognized multicultural education as a controversial area and subject of considerable debate that should be central to the thinking of all those throughout the country with a responsibility for curriculum planning' (Tomlinson, 1993, p. 22).

It was clear that ideological conflict was still influencing national policy initiatives. The use of the words 'all', 'multi' and 'anti' in the task group aims was enough to encourage nervous traditionalists to lobby government (Lewis, 1988). Multicultural policies and practices were a potent weapon in attacks on Labour controlled education authorities from right-wing groups such the Salisbury Group, the Centre for Policy Studies, the Hillgate Group and a number of smaller organizations claiming parental support.

These groups attacked any form of multicultural education, their influence on central government received wide press coverage. Their main focus point was to discredit multicultural education on the grounds that any national initiative would be counter to the previous local policy. This was the main point of support for the groups. One of the other concerns of the Hillgate Group was the content of the curriculum, and they had a particular desire for the curriculum to reflect Britain's cultural heritage, and this led to considerable debates over the English and History orders (Knight, 1990).

The education of minorities was never seen as a national issue. Even when the most dramatic changes were taking place at the local level, some predominantly white areas were successful in staying outside it. This demonstrated the government's perception of the education of minorities, as did the decision not to publish the Task Group's guidelines. The only references after the revised curriculum in 1992 were to the 'translation' difficulties that some minority children might face, thus totally ignoring the linguistic needs of the second- or third-generation minority children in this country. Attempts by some institutions to look into the levels of achievement of minority ethnic children provided very little guidance. A Report by Leeds University of SAT results of Key Stage 1 ethnic minority children in 17 LEAs, openly stated that the use of mother tongue was one of the reasons for educational underachievement. The mother tongue issue was clearly seen as a problem: 'The major factor in some of these differences (different levels of underachievement) was the fact that the home languages of many of the children from different ethnic origins were not English' (Shorrocks et al., 1992, p. 101).

A clear implication of such a narrow definition of underachievement was that the children who were underachieving within the National Curriculum were doing so because they were speaking another language at home. Double standards were clearly evident in the government's position on the education of Welsh/English bilingual children in Wales.

The Welsh language was recognized as the regional language and endorsed within the 1992 (revised) National Curriculum. The success of bilingual programmes in Wales was the result of the policies of the LEAs rather than due to the support of successive governments. During a visit to an education authority, Gwynedd in North Wales in 1997, one of the authors of this book observed that the Council adapted a bilingual policy which required every Council employee to be bilingual in order to work in the authority. This was supported by teacher training institutions that produced graduates who were bilingual Welsh/English speakers. Teachers in the classroom admitted that it was more demanding to teach a bilingual class, but they added that it was also more rewarding as children became more diverse thinkers. There were indications of a correlation between the rising levels of achievement and the introduction of bilingual policies in Gwynedd (Williams et al., 1996). Statistical information also supported the view that bilingualism has contributed positively to all aspects of life in Wales. Some research supports the view that the number of Welsh speakers is increasing in Gwynedd because of its promotion in schools rather than its use at home (Baker, 1996).

The post-1997 Labour government's policy did not appear to be different from that of the previous government. The slimmed down National Curriculum has a heavy emphasis on the National Literacy and Numeracy Strategies, and appears to promote achievement through the development of English. In a jointly published handbook for teachers *The National Curriculum: Handbook for primary teachers in England* (1999) the position of the QCA (Qualifications and Curriculum Authority) and DfEE on the provision for EAL learners is put forward. In a 150-pages document their views are given on a single page:

> Pupils for whom English is an additional language have diverse needs in terms of support necessary in English language learning. Planning should take account of such factors as the pupil's age, length of time in this country, previous educational experience and skills in other languages. (1999, p. 37)

The responsibility for the education of minorities under the Section 11 Grant was transferred to the DfEE from the Home Office as a new Ethnic Minority Achievement Grant (EMAG). The EMAG's emphasis is on achievement of all ethnic minorities.

The emphasis is therefore placed on the provision within schools. While Department for Education (DfE) (then DfEE) guidelines on partnership teaching have helped clarify roles for class teachers and EMAG teachers, they have fallen short of its aim to provide appropriate training for relevant staff. The training programme has had to give way to more urgent priorities such as training for the National Literacy and Numeracy initiatives, which have left very little release time for EMAG and class teachers to receive appropriate training. The greater autonomy for headteachers in relation to the use of the EMAG, and a lack of clarity from the DfEE in relation to some problematic issues has brought into question their effectiveness within schools.

Summary

In this chapter, we have provided a historical account of policy initiatives that has shaped successive government legislation on minority education. We argued that there has never been a commitment to bilingual education in this country, and that the notions of bilingual education and education for bilingualism have not been on the agenda of successive governments. Successive governments have held the view that the education of bilingual pupils mainly related to their ability to learn English. Successive governments have always controlled such decisions and the few LEAs who had other ideas for their bilingual pupils often found themselves at odds with the central governments' policies and had difficulties. We also argued that compensatory initiatives have mainly been taken on an ad hoc basis and were politically motivated. Even when positive ideas were generated in some LEAs, policy and practices were not sufficiently implemented to produce lasting outcomes.

Reflective activity

1. Can you recall some the key policy decisions for each of the phases discussed in the chapter?
2. In your view, what were the main factors affecting those decisions on ethnic minority education?
3. Which is the key learning point for you in this chapter?

Setting the Context: Historical Perspectives on Personal, Social and Emotional Development and the Early Years Foundation Stage

3

Why would anyone want to create a curriculum for very young children? What could such a curriculum possibly consist of? Could there be a National Curriculum for the under fives?

This chapter does not intend to examine curriculum theory but it intends to start by considering the contributions made by various early years 'pioneers' and learning theorists to some of the broadly accepted understandings in the Western world of young children's developmental needs. It will then examine the emergence of the Foundation Stage, the Curriculum Guidance and the Statutory Framework and their approach to PSED. We also refer to CLL linking it and PSED to what we know about young bilingual children's emotional needs and personal/cultural identities.

As stated in Chapter 1, much of the writing about young children tends to be culturally and linguistically neutral, with bilingual experiences generally limited to individual case studies, themselves usually very interesting accounts, of children of academics growing up bilingually but with the emphasis placed on the child's simultaneous acquisition of grammar and vocabulary. This is still of use to us in our work with young children but we hope to go further by adding a socio-cultural dimension to the children's own metalinguistic knowledge.

What preceded the EYFS?

The Curriculum Guidance and the later statutory EYFS Curriculum have only been in existence for just over ten years and yet young children of nursery age have been educated in this country in state and private settings for closer to 100 years. How have early years teachers managed for so long without a government prescribed curriculum for them to follow? How could they possibly know what to provide for young children?

Surprising as it may seem to some in government departments, there has been a body of knowledge about young children and their development and learning that goes back several centuries in Western European countries. This knowledge has accumulated over time, from individuals and groups in different countries and in this country, at least, contributed eventually to the formulation of ten common principles for early years education. These have been succinctly outlined by Tina Bruce (2005).

Ten principles for early years education

1. Childhood is seen as valid in itself, as part of life and not simply as preparation for adulthood. Thus, education is seen similarly as something of the present and not just preparation and training for later.
2. The whole child is considered to be important. Health – physical and mental – is emphasized, as well as the importance of feelings and thinking and spiritual aspects.
3. Learning is not compartmentalized for everything links.
4. Intrinsic motivation, resulting in child-initiated, self-directed activity, is valued.
5. Self-discipline is emphasized.
6. There are specially receptive periods of learning at different stages of development.
7. What children can do (rather than what they cannot do) is the starting point in the child's education.
8. There is an inner life in the child which emerges especially under favourable conditions.
9. The people (both adults and children) with whom the child interacts are of central importance.
10. The child's education is seen as an interaction between the child and the environment in which the child finds itself – including, in particular, other people and knowledge itself. (Bruce, 1987 cited in Bruce, 2005)

So who were the writers, thinkers and practitioners whose work eventually inspired principles such as the ones above? We now look briefly at some of their key ideas to try to identify their influence on the formation of the ten principles and current thinking about young children's education. As with all our historical figures, there is much that has been learned since they wrote; nevertheless, we can be grateful to them for their original contributions to our knowledge of young children's developmental needs.

The contribution of previous writers/practitioners

Jean-Jacques Rousseau

Jean-Jacques Rousseau (1712–78) is often credited by many writers as being one of the first key thinkers about infancy, childhood and later stages of development. He was also a writer, philosopher and a political radical, but not a teacher in the currently accepted sense of the word. However, he broke new ground by his original (for the time) thoughts on childhood and its characteristics, the stages of development towards adulthood and the ways in which he thought adults should educate children (or, at least, boys).

Certainly, he writes persuasively in *Emile* (published in 1762) and argues convincingly for giving children physical freedom and the types of learning or activity that they will find congenial and fitting to their current mental development.

> Work and play are all one to him, his games are his work; he knows no difference. He brings to everything the cheerfulness of interest, the charm of freedom, and he shows the bent of his own mind and the extent of his knowledge. Is there anything better worth seeing, anything more touching or more delightful, than a pretty child, with merry, cheerful glance, easy contented manner, open smiling countenance, playing at the most important things, or working at the lightest amusements? (Book II, p. 126)

Books I–IV of 'Emile' are devoted to the education of Emile, and by extension all boys. In Book V, he introduces Emile's 'promised helpmeet', Sophy. Here Rousseau is much more closely tied to the mores of his time and rigid notions of male and female: 'The man should be strong and active; the woman should be weak and passive; the one must have both the power and the will; it is enough that the other should offer little resistance' (Book V, p. 322).

Although he does allow that Sophy should have some freedom as a girl and is clearly uneasy about the narrow, restricted upbringing that many (well-born) girls of the time endured; in the end his conclusion seems to be that girls should be shaped to suit their future roles as wives and mothers, to be subordinate to their husbands. This echoes through the next two centuries.

Setting aside misgivings about his thinking for girls, we still owe a debt to Rousseau for his role as a catalyst in Western thinking about children and childhood and to his ideas about giving children an upbringing of relative freedom and play. Note how his ideas underlie Principles 1 and 2.

Johann Heinrich Pestalozzi (1746–1827)

We may find richer pickings in Johann Heinrich Pestalozzi who was greatly influenced by Rousseau but was also one of the first teachers to try to describe the methods which he used when working with children as well as the philosophy that supported them. He did not find this an easy task but the following are some of the key principles underlying his work that clearly link to the ten principles listed above.

Like Rousseau, Pestalozzi saw the unity of all aspects of childhood – a key point for twentieth-century early years principles. He believed that children's learning is integrated and holistic and that the starting point for their education should be the children themselves.

He also outlined, possibly following on from Rousseau, children's psychological development based on what he saw as the crucial relationship between child and mother:

> (1) the development of his [sic] feelings (love and confidence) through the physical satisfaction provided by his mother, and the naming of the things which give him pleasure (infancy); (2) the development of his consciousness, the recognition of persons and things in his environment, still under the protection of his mother (childhood); (3) his growing independence of her through his increasing powers and knowledge; his joining the community of persons and making use of the objects of his world (boyhood); (4) the widening of his range of action, his urge 'to know, master, and possess the world' without the help of his mother, the knowledge of evil. (Silber, 1960, pp. 202–3)

He believed that children's first education was in the home and that the educational institution should try to replicate home conditions.

Pestalozzi's one experimental school (in Stans, Unterwalden, in 1798–9) for orphans of a civil religious uprising lasted only five months but during this time he was able to transform traumatized, aggressive and unhappy children into settled, confident beings who were able to learn. One of the ways in which he succeeded was to place the children at the centre of his work:

> he was trying to create an atmosphere of home life in which the children could develop naturally. . . . He was of the opinion that the characteristics of a home had to be emulated in institutional upbringing, that the 'spirit of the living room' was the basis of a good education, and that parental love was the first demand on a good educator. (Silber, 1960, p. 113)

In all his ensuing school experiments, Pestalozzi worked on the principle that love, not fear, should be the basis of teaching, that teachers should commit themselves whole-heartedly to the children and that the children themselves should be constantly active both in mind and body.

As we have seen, he also had some interesting ideas about the relationship between home and school. In his own schools, Pestalozzi made sure that there was contact between parents, teachers and children, arranging meeting times and drawing on parents' expertise too. Principles 2, 3, 6, 7 and 9 link to Pestalozzi's work.

There were many visitors to Pestalozzi's most famous residential school – that at Yverdon in Switzerland – which he established early in the nineteenth century and where boys and girls were given a very similar education.

Friedrich Froebel (1782–1852)

One such visitor to Yverdon was Friedrich Froebel who, although impressed by much of what he saw at Yverdon, was not convinced by Pestalozzi's methods. However, like Pestalozzi, he was much influenced by the European Romantic movement and evolved his own mystic, religious approach to god and the natural world, seeing, as Pestalozzi did, unity in all things and unity of development in children. He also saw a sequence in children's development, from infancy, to childhood where language emerges, to boyhood [*sic*] when the age for schooling is reached.

In addition, Froebel took Pestalozzi's (and Rousseau's) conviction of the importance of activity even further and placed children's own play at the centre of their learning, both physical and spiritual, and their personal growth.

> for at first, play is the child's natural life. Play, then, is the highest expression of human development in childhood, for it alone is the free expression of what is in the child's soul . . . it induces joy, freedom, contentment, inner and outer repose, peace with all the world. . . . Childhood's play is not mere sport; it is full of meaning and of serious import. (Fletcher and Welton, 1912)

Froebel's work exerted a massive influence on attitudes to early years provision and is represented mostly in Principles 1, 2, 3 and 8.

Maria Montessori (1870–1952)

Another significant figure we should consider is Maria Montessori whose name and reputation continue to be recognized in the many Montessori nurseries that still exist and are based on her methods. Montessori also deserves recognition for her own courageous determination to succeed in education and work in fields where women in nineteenth-century Italy had previously been debarred. Against all odds she became a doctor of medicine in 1896 and later began her work in Rome with what were then labelled as 'defective' children. Whatever the children she worked with, Montessori observed them closely (as Pestalozzi did) and she came to realize that there were hidden depths in children's minds that adults constantly underestimated. She saw how children could choose and work with materials spontaneously and concentrate on these for considerable lengths of time, that autonomous repetition had meaning for them, that if children were engrossed in work (an important distinction from play for Montessori) there was no need for rewards or punishments.

Montessori (cited in Oswald and Schulz-Benesch, 1997) also believed that children had an 'important mental life' (p. 53) which had been formed in embryo and which helped prepare the child to live in its society. Thus, far we can see her influence in Principles 4, 5 and 8.

But she was also one of the first early years educators to consider how language is a crucial element in children's development on personal as well as cultural levels.

> In the period of unconscious activity language is indelibly stamped upon the mind and becomes a *characteristic* which man [*sic*] finds established in himself. No language that one may wish to add can become a characteristic and none will be so sure a possession as the first. . . . One's mother tongue is not entrusted to the conscious memory. (Cited in Oswald and Schulz-Benesch, 1997, pp. 59–60)

Furthermore, Montessori understood how young children absorb their particular culture or 'race' and how integral this is, with language, to their identity:

> [i]t is easy to acknowledge that in a similar way (to the unconscious acquisition of language) the other characteristics which differentiate one race from another must be fixed in the child. These are habits and customs, prejudices and feelings and generally all those characteristics which we feel to be incarnate in ourselves – features that are part of us independently, and even in spite of changes which our intelligence, logic and reason might be desirous of bringing about. . . . The child really builds up something. He reproduces in himself, as by a form of psychic mimesis, the characteristics of the people in his environment. Thus while growing up, he does nor merely become a *man*, he becomes *a man of his race.* (p. 62)

Montessori also put forward the notion, which she drew from De Vries' work with animals and insects, that in children's development there might also be 'sensitive periods' (or the 'receptive periods of learning' of Principle 6). These are times of specific, short-lived inner impulses which promote a specific form of growth. In human beings, Montessori claims:

> We are dealing on the one hand with an inner impulse that gives rise to the most admirable results, and on the other with a periodic indifference that leads to blindness and unproductiveness. The adult is unable to exert any type of external influence on these fundamental stages of development. But if the child has not had the chance to act in accordance with his inner directives during the periods of sensitivity then he has missed the opportunity to acquire a particular ability naturally and this opportunity

has gone for ever . . . should the child encounter an obstacle to his efforts during a period of sensitivity, then a type of breakdown, a deformation occurs in his soul. The result is a spiritual ordeal about which we understand next to nothing though almost everyone bears its scars without knowing it. (p. 64)

It is the unconscious acquisition of language and the unconscious absorption of the child's culture which ultimately form its identity. It is important for us to remember that this is why they are so emotionally powerful. They are rooted in our early, largely unremembered experiences of parental and family care and practices. But while they may be unremembered, these experiences remain incredibly strong and exert deep emotional reactions. We cannot help being who we are and this is why perceived attacks, from whatever quarter, on our own language and culture are an attack on our personal identity.

If we accept a notion of sensitive or receptive times in young children's development and link these to the experiences of young bilingual children entering a nursery armed with their own language and culture only to find that the nursery silently (or actively) ignores and excludes both of these assets, we should surely not be surprised that young children's emotional well-being could be severely damaged by such behaviour.

No doubt we could argue with some of Montessori's theories, but, bearing in mind when these were written (the late 1940s), they seem to us to show a far-reaching insight into these two crucial factors in all children's personal and social development and a sensitivity towards the innate power of language and cultural identity.

Susan Isaacs (1885–1948)

Not so far removed from Montessori's ideas about periods of sensitivity might be the time of emotional intensity outlined by Susan Isaacs and Sir Cyril Burt in the 1933 Hadow Report that was referred to in Chapter 1. Susan Isaacs may not have much to offer us concerning language and bilingualism since her interest lay more with intellectual growth, social behaviour and sexual development. Nevertheless, in her role as a teacher at the experimental Malting House School in the 1920s and later as the first Professor of Child Development at the London

Institute of Education, as well as her contributions to the Hadow Reports, she merits our attention.

She reminds us of the importance of providing space for children to pursue their own interests and learning without unnecessary interference from adults: that is, she reminds us too that we should trust children to make their own decisions. Central also to her work was observing, recording and interpreting the children's behaviour and investigations (remember that Pestalozzi was doing this some 200 years earlier). Adults were there to respond to activities and questions and nurture the children's natural curiosity.

Her work at the Malting House School then, relates to Principles 2, 4, 7, 9 and 10 and her contribution to the serious study of young children's intellectual and social growth should not be underestimated. Isaacs' book *The Nursery Years* (1932), for example, may not discuss language and culture in the ways that we now see them, but it does reiterate her firm belief in the role and power of action in young children's growth and the importance of adults who encourage rather than deter them.

> Walking and running, jumping and climbing, throwing and balancing, threading beads and drawing – each is tried and attained in its turn. We don't have to teach children to do these things. They do them with passion and delight, if we leave them room and opportunity. We can hinder them by saying 'don't' and 'sit still'; by asking the wrong things of them, and giving them the wrong things to play with – to 'sew a fine seam', for example, or to do fine writing at a time when their muscles need large things to hold and large sweeping movement. On the other hand, by studying the ways of their growth, we can give them things to do and to play with which will feed their skill and power. (p. 69)

Her constant advice to adults is to trust children to make their own decisions about their own play and activity and to respond constructively and honestly, especially with regard to their questions about and investigations of the world.

Mia Kellmer Pringle (1921–83)

Pringle's contribution develops from Isaacs' work on emotional growth and that of Maslow on primary needs. She was another key figure in early years development and the integration of children's services and provision. She herself had experienced flight from Nazi occupied Vienna as a young woman and arrived in the United Kingdom in 1939 with virtually no possessions or money. From this background and her professional work she was able to construct a theory of children's emotional needs linked to a set of principles which also relate to children's rights.

In 1963, Pringle became the first director of what was to become the National Children's Bureau (NCB). With Dr Neville Butler she worked on a long-term study (the National Child Development Study) of all the children born in Britain in one week in March 1958. The NCB was founded on the principle of putting children first and on two others, which have since become generally accepted:

1. that there should be co-operation between all key service providers in education, social care and health and between voluntary and statutory sectors
2. that research should influence policy and practice and vice versa
   (www.nurseryworld.co.uk/news/716362/Putting-children-first/?DCMP=ILC-SE)

Pringle's major research, based on the long-term project, was published in 1975 as *The Needs of Children*. In this she highlighted the importance of:

- the early years of life to later development
- the environment in which children grow
- children's social and emotional needs as well as their physical needs

She added another tier of secondary needs that included love, security, praise and recognition (see Bruce, 2005, p. 37) which we know are fundamental to children's PSED.

She also was committed to the following statements of principle:

- children need love and security, new experiences, praise and recognition and responsibility
- failure to meet children's needs in the early years leads to long-term difficulties
- parenting is too demanding and complex a task to think it can be performed well merely because we have all been children
- the school curriculum should include human psychology, child development and preparation for parenthood. (Pugh, 2006)

Principles 1, 2 and 10 would appear best to relate to Pringle's thinking.

Implications for practitioners

Pringle makes strong claims for the early years – claims which are at last being recognized (in the previous government's Sure Start Centres, for example).

And her identification of the importance of meeting children's emotional needs is crucial for those who work with young bilingual children.

The work of Pringle and all the other educationalists mentioned should remind us of the importance of providing young children, as far as we can, with secure and happy relationships. All being well, these will have been formed at home and with this foundation children can successfully venture out into new worlds and experiences, developing, perhaps, the 'resilience' (we will discuss this in Chapter 10) that enables them to begin to cope with difficulties and problems. In their homes, children will have gained all their early learning – emotional, social and intellectual – and this will have been learned through whatever language or languages the family use. Through the medium of language and through customs and conventions, children will have absorbed the life of the family and the ways in which it relates to family cultural history. As must be obvious, these are the building blocks of identity on which children rely. It should be equally obvious that early years settings must consider how they provide continuity in supporting and nurturing children's different identities. We cannot state too often how seriously practitioners should consider how well they provide for all children and how seriously they tackle differences of language, culture and identity.

Freud's contribution

There is, however, another major area of interest and research which we have not yet explored and that is psychology and its later offshoot – neurology, or neuroscience. Both of these disciplines enable us to make further discoveries about young children's inner or psychic development and its connection to their well-being.

Sigmund Freud (1856–1939)

Freud is a major figure in psychology and, later, psychiatry. He was an influence on the thinking and work of Susan Isaacs, among others, and he is still regarded as a significant pioneer who in many ways broke new ground in the analysis of human behaviours. His interest in the unconscious workings of the mind was extremely radical at the time (he practised in Vienna towards the end of the nineteenth century). His work has given rise to many branches of psychology but he probably should be credited with being: 'the discoverer of the first instrument for the scientific examination of the human mind . . . no systematic method of investigation existed before Freud' (Strachey, 1977, p. 17).

His work with patients with various neuroses and his discoveries made via his own self-analysis led to: 'a hypothesis of the mind as something dynamic, as consisting in a number of mental forces, some conscious and some unconscious, operating now in harmony now in opposition with one another' (Strachey, 1977, p. 18).

In his long life, Freud wrote a prodigious number of books illustrating his practices in psychoanalysis and his ideas about human behaviours and endeavours. Freud's investigations into and revelations about the workings of the unconscious mind brought to the surface unpalatable details; many found these hard to swallow. Nevertheless, his work was becoming widely translated and the practice of psychoanalysis spread across Europe and in America.

What can we learn from Freud?

The range and amount of writing that Freud produced is prodigious but what might be most illuminating for us now in the early twenty-first century? Psychoanalysis is way beyond our scope as early years practitioners but we should remember that his practice's primary purpose was healing. Freud was convinced that most of the neuroses he dealt with had their roots in very early childhood, in experiences that had become buried in the unconscious. It was the unconscious mind that exercised such inexplicable power over behaviour.

Freud was working in a largely monocultural, white society and one in which knowledge and ideas about cultural differences were very much at the starting point (although it should be remembered that he was Jewish and that anti-Semitism was prevalent in Europe. His books were destroyed in Nazi occupied Austria).

So for those who work with young children in multicultural settings, it might be helpful to hang on to the idea that while early experiences may not be articulated, they may nevertheless be extremely powerful and may exert an equally powerful influence on outward, observed behaviours.

Summary of the selected theorists

This has necessarily been a brief outline of some of the major ideas of a selected group of Western European educators, theorists and psychologists, spanning about 200 years. Whatever we may make of some of their ideas now, it is, we hope, abundantly obvious that all of the educators placed children at the heart of their thinking and doing. Not only that, they also saw that young children are worthy of the respect of adults who should trust children's ability to lead their own learning. Play, exploration and investigation, both indoors and out, are all seen to be essential to children's successful emotional and mental well-being.

Freud differs, of course, since he was not, in the strict sense of the word, an educator, but at the heart of his practice was a desire to return his patients to a state of mental well-being. As we all now know, for him it was the experiences of childhood that lay at the root of psychological disturbance.

Therefore, what is required of adults is to attend closely to the ways in which children develop and to seek to nurture and support the processes, rather than place unnecessary obstacles in their path.

Government guidelines

As formally instituted educational systems evolved in the nineteenth and twentieth centuries, these absorbed in various ways and to various extents the ideas of the educators. These found expression in legislation, reports such as those chaired by Hadow, which we discussed in Chapter 1, and in handbooks and guidelines.

We outline one of these below.

- Codes of practice for teachers – the beginnings of formalizing the curriculum

The Board of Education (forerunner of the current Department for Education) had been set up in 1899. The Local Boards that ran the state elementary schools were abolished by the 1902 Education Act and their function was handed over to the newly established local authorities (Aldrich, 1982). It is from the Board of Education that a Code for teaching was written and in place from 1904–26. It was then variously revised, taking account of the ideas of the Hadow Reports. The 1944 edition, preceding the imminent Education Act, shows the underlying philosophy and principles that it was hoped that all teachers and schools (as abstract entities) would adhere to.

The 'handbook of suggestions for the consideration of teachers and others concerned in the work of public elementary schools'

It is interesting to note that this 1944 edition repeats the introduction to the 1904–26 code where we find, among some very lofty ideals (and perhaps the Code is none the worse for these), this paragraph:

> In all these endeavours the School should enlist, as far as possible, the interest and co-operation of the parents and the home in an [*sic*] united effort to enable the children not merely to reach their full development as individuals, but also to become upright and useful members of the community in which they live, and worthy sons and daughters of the country to which they belong. (p. 11)

This concern that schools and parents should work together in the interests of the children is a constant thread in much of the legislation, starting with the 1870 Act and continuing through to the present day.

Preceding the 1944 Code's section on the Nursery School is a paragraph that reminded teachers then, and reminds us now, of the significance of the home for children's development:

> It would be a mistake to imagine that the child, though untaught, has learnt nothing before he [*sic*] comes to school . . . by the age of five a child has amassed a considerable though unsystematic knowledge of his own small world. (p. 72, para 7)

The Nursery School section emphasizes the nursery's role in nurturing children's physical health and also expects that 'the small child will find in the Nursery School *an atmosphere of natural affection*, a feeling of space and security, an ordered and regular way of life' (p. 74, para 11).

In addition, the 'daily programme' should be 'elastic enough for him to exercise initiative and learn to adapt himself to changing experiences' (p. 74, para 12) and there should be what the Code describes as 'Free activities' (i.e. child initiated) in which the teacher acts as observer helper and 'Directed activities' (teacher led) which are the specifically organized events, outings, group times, and so on.

The summary of what the child learns in the nursery school suggests that the school will be successful if the children, among various listed attributes, also are: 'able to look after themselves, companionable and willing to respect the rights of others' (p. 77, para 15).

It seems obvious from this that the work of the key figures we have highlighted had penetrated the thinking of the personnel of the Board of Education so that a body of accepted knowledge came to form the practice of those working in nurseries with the under fives and continued relatively untouched through to the end of the twentieth century. As has been said, this knowledge may have been formed for an apparently monocultural society but its precepts, although they need extending, are applicable to one that has become more obviously multicultural. At the least, the Code recognized how strongly the family influenced early development and how it was in the best interests of children that home and school should work together. It also made clear that children needed security and affection to help them thrive.

The impact of the Second World War (1939–45)

The cataclysmic events of this event also provided the impetus which prompted international concern about the emotional well-being, security, healthy growth and, eventually, rights of children.

We have only to remember just a few of the effects of adult actions on children during the Second World War to realize how traumatic many of these must have been. In Germany, there was at first the 'Kinder transport'– the removal of Jewish children to safe homes in other parts of Europe before the war started. In the cities of England and especially London, there were the various schemes of evacuation of children from their homes. At the end of the war, there were thousands of orphans in all the participating countries, displaced children, children in refugee camps, child survivors of the occupied countries as well as the different concentration camps and child survivors of at least six years of disruption, anxiety, fear and uncertainty in unoccupied countries.

The Declaration of the Rights of the Child

From the appalling situations which arose from the Second World War came, eventually, a widespread understanding of the term 'human rights'. As Parekh (2000) says:

> The term 'human rights' has come to be widely used only since the second world war, when experiences of state terror and ethnic cleansing strengthened determination to develop a body of international law to prevent their recurrence. (p. 92, para 7.5)

In 1948, the United Nations (UN) adopted the Universal Declaration of Human Rights. There have been subsequent additional conventions and agreements including the UN Declaration on the Rights of the Child (1959) which, according to Parekh, is the most widely ratified of all the conventions and which followed on the principles of the Declaration of Human Rights.

The United Nations called upon:

> parents, upon men and women as individuals, and upon voluntary organisations, local authorities and national Governments to recognise these rights and strive for their observance by legislative and other measures progressively taken in accordance with the following principles:

The first makes clear that ALL children are entitled to the rights of the Declaration.

> Every child without any exception whatsoever, shall be entitled to these rights, without distinction or discrimination on account of race, colour, sex, language, religion, political or other opinion, national or social origin, property, birth or other status, whether of himself [*sic*] or of his family.

Principles 6, 7 and 10 are perhaps the ones that most concern us in our work with young children:

> (6) The child, for the full harmonious development of his personality, needs love and understanding. He shall, wherever possible, grow up in the care and under the responsibility of his parents, and, in any case, in an atmosphere of affection and of moral and material security; a child of tender years shall not, save in exceptional circumstances, be separated from his mother.

> (7) The child is entitled to receive education, which shall be free and compulsory, at least in the elementary stages. He shall be given an education which will promote his general culture and enable him, on a basis of equal opportunity, to develop his abilities, his individual judgement, and his sense of moral and social responsibility, and to become a useful member of society.

The best interests of the child shall be the guiding principle of those responsible for his education and guidance; that responsibility lies in the first place with his parents.

> The child shall have full opportunity for play and recreation, which should be directed to the same purposes as education; society and the public authorities shall endeavour to promote the enjoyment of this right.

> (10) The child shall be protected from practices which may foster racial, religious and any other form of discrimination. He shall be brought up in

a spirit of understanding, tolerance, friendship among peoples, peace and universal brotherhood, and in full consciousness that his energy and talents should be devoted to the service of his fellow men. (www.un.org/cyberschoolbus/humanrights/resources/child.asp)

When we look at subsequent educational documents and legislation it is clear that the Declaration underlies much of their ideas and proposals.

After the 1944 Act: Two major reports – Plowden and Rumbold

The Plowden Report – children and their primary schools (1967)

As we noted earlier, there is interplay between teaching, research and government policy. The Plowden Report (chaired by Lady Bridget Plowden) reflects the influence of then current ideas about children and their development. It devotes a section to 'The Emotional Development of the Child' (paras 65–74) which merits attention. Obviously, our knowledge of child development has increased and deepened since the Report but there is much that is relevant still. The writers of the Report state:

Emotional, social and intellectual aspects are closely intertwined in mental growth: the child is a total personality. Emotional life provides the spur and in many ways gives meaning to experience.(para 65)

The child is vulnerable to his [*sic*] emotions, not so much experiencing them as being swept by them. Even the five year old, despite his apparent balance and control, remains subject to overpowering impulses and fears and is still dependent on those close to him for guidance and control. . . . The emotional life of the child of two to five is intimately bound up with his relationships with those who care for and are close to him (para 66)

One of the most important aspects of the child's early learning is his dependence on the adults around him. . . . Consistency of handling, too, is an important factor in helping the child to pick his way through the confusion of acceptable and forbidden types of behaviour which, at the time of learning, he cannot fully understand. The quality of the care and security provided by a child's home during the early years of his life are of extreme importance for his later emotional development. The emotional climate of the home, parental attitudes, values and expectations, whether personal or derives from their social and cultural background appear more important than specific techniques of child rearing. (para 69)

Moral development is closely associated with emotional and social development. The child forms his sense of personal worth and his moral sense from early experiences of acceptance, approval, and disapproval. (para 72)

The committee was clear about the nature of early learning and the central role of play and creativity. Thus, perhaps, lay behind their decision that 5 was, in this country, still a suitable age to start school since:

It was with this age group that informal ways of learning, and teaching geared to individual needs, were first extensively developed in this country. . . . In this country, learning through play and creative work continues throughout most infant schools; elsewhere this approach seemed to us on our visits often to be lacking. We think that it is probably sacrificed to the formal work which a later date of entry may easily seem to demand. We should not want this to happen in England. (para 357)

We wonder how the committee would react to the statutory curriculum now in place?

There is much in the Plowden Report that repays reading. We recommend our readers to dip into it, if they can.

The Rumbold Report (1990)

Following the 1944 Education Act, provision for young children was largely divided between the government departments for education and health. State funded nursery schools were part of education, day nurseries part of health and their functions and philosophy often dissimilar. This division between education and care continued for the next few decades with other fee-paying provision for young children occurring via private nurseries, the PPA (formerly the Pre-School Play Association now the PLA – Pre-School Learning Alliance) and home-based care such as childminding. Gradually, it became evident that this variety of provision required some investigation and attention, particularly as the government of the time was creating a society where it was becoming more imperative for both parents to work. Thus, it was that the Rumbold

Report (its committee chaired by Angela Rumbold MP) was published following research into early years provision.

It consisted of a survey of the provision then current for the under fives, with a remit to ensure that whatever its nature, the provision was of good quality. Here we find again the role of the parents being recognized as crucial: after estimating that about 10 per cent of children have no experience of preschool provision, the committee states that:

> we believe it is important to recognise that the remaining 90 per cent spend more of their waking hours with their parents than they do in nursery provision; the role of parents as the first educators of their children must not be underestimated. (p. 4, para 37)

In Section 3, the report summarizes the 'characteristics of young children', placing emphasis on their differences and different experiences as well as the shared attributes such as activity, enquiry and curiosity as modes of learning, of the undisputable role of play in learning: 'Play is a powerful motivator, encouraging children to be creative and to develop their ideas, understanding and language' (p. 7, para 56).

In addition, the interaction between children, adults and other children is also noted as a positive element and that 'establishing a partnership with the home at this stage provides a firm foundation on which subsequent educators can build' (p. 7, para 58).

Even more important as evidence of demographic population changes are the paragraphs that consider the children's different home and cultural experiences. It is worthwhile quoting here most of paragraphs 59–61 complete.

> 59: Educators should also recognise and respond to the diversity of society, and the need to avoid stereotyping on the basis of race, sex or special needs. How this may best be done will vary according to local circumstances; but the aims will be to enable all children to respect and value ethnic and cultural diversity, to encourage positive self-images among ethnic minority children, and to ensure that high expectations attach to all groups alike.

60: A good relationship between preschool setting and home also fosters the establishment of *a loving atmosphere of approval and acceptance which young children need.* A child's emerging self-awareness and self-confidence depend upon the quality of these early encounters with other people.

61: Finally, it is easy for adults to forget that young children growing up in the 1990s have been born into a different world from that in which their own childhood was spent . . . such differences may be the more marked where the parents were born overseas and the children in the UK. Young children will, in consequence, have a very different view of the world from their parents' generation; and those adults who encounter the under fives must always keep this in mind.

Note how both Plowden and Rumbold emphasize the importance of emotional and personal relationships as the base from which children's successful growth emerges. Rumbold goes further into addressing the realities of late twentieth-century Britain's multicultural populations and responsibility of educators to accord recognition and respect to children's various heritages.

The beginnings of an early years curriculum

Rumbold also considers what a curriculum for the under fives might consist of. Sections 14 and 15 of part two of the report are well worth investigating. In these a possible early years curriculum is outlined based on eight areas of learning and experience. These are described as: aesthetic and creative, human and social, language and literacy, mathematics, physical, science, spiritual and moral and technology.

These are obviously the precursors of the current statutory early years curriculum.

The committee at that time saw no place for a formal National Curriculum for young children but it did draw on the work carried out by HMI (under the title 'Curriculum Matters') in the 1980s. HMI stands for 'Her Majesty's Inspectorate' – a body of education inspectors who were independent of the government, unlike the current inspection system of OFSTED.

HMI curriculum matters (1985)

This document outlined the 'areas of learning and experience' that could constitute an appropriate curriculum even though the framework HMI presented was for children aged from 5–16. The areas of learning and experiences they suggested were:

> aesthetic and creative, human and social, linguistic and literary, mathematical, moral, physical, scientific, spiritual, technological.

HMI (1985) also stated that:

> these are not suggested as discrete elements to be taught separately and in isolation from one another. They constitute a planning and analytical tool. Nor are they equated with particular subjects (for example, pupils may gain scientific or mathematical experience from art, and aesthetic experience from mathematics), although inevitably individual subjects contribute more to some areas than to others. (p. 16, para 33)

Interestingly, in this proposed curriculum which was for England and Wales, the following is said about Welsh language and culture:

> it is natural that, given its unique heritage, the Welsh language and culture should occupy a distinctive place in the curriculum of schools in Wales. In some, because the Welsh language is in daily use at home and in the community alongside English, it will be accorded a priority in curricular terms similar to that of English. But all children in Welsh schools should have access to the means of extending their familiarity with it and extending it as a means of communication. (p. 1)

There is disappointingly very little about children speaking languages other than English or Welsh other than the point that: 'many children from ethnic minority groups speak two languages, English at school and another language at home, (which) can help to create a context of reality for work in foreign languages' (p. 23, para 52).

In spite, then, of all the work and research into language and culture that had been carried out, or was being carried out, at the time that HMI were deliberating about the curriculum, they managed to avoid paying it any serious attention. All credit to the Rumbold committee for going much further.

The arrival and impact of the National Curriculum

This Curriculum was born of the Education Reform Act of 1988. Suffice it to say that far from attending to 'areas of learning and experience', it was formulated as a subject curriculum and deemed suitable for children of statutory school age (i.e. from 5–16), as we saw in Chapter 1. It has undergone various modifications over the years, as teachers have battled to cope with the demands of its heavy content. As the reader will probably know, the legislation expected the Curriculum to be 'broad and balanced' but with the creation of Core and Foundation subjects this has in reality in most schools ceased to be the case so that the Core subjects dominate, particularly English and Maths, while the others are relegated to subsidiary status.

In addition, in the 1990s, schools also had to contend with the National Literacy and Numeracy Strategies and their descendant, the Primary Strategy. Although the Literacy and Numeracy strategies were non-statutory, they were presented to schools as though they were a legal requirement, backed up with a plethora of training programmes, advisers and teaching materials.

Both these strategies, unfortunately, in our view, included sections for children in Reception classes (children who reached the statutory school starting age of 5 during the reception year). This has led to young children being given, much as they were in 1905, an inappropriate curriculum where aspects of more formal, whole class, teacher led learning were introduced and the role of play, home languages and culture minimized.

Champions of young children did not take this lying down. Individuals and groups such as the Early Years Curriculum Group worked to publicize young children's requirement for a 'developmentally appropriate' curriculum based on the principles outlined by Bruce (1987) and on research (see, for example, Curtis et al., 1992).

The development of an early years curriculum

Notwithstanding all the evidence to the contrary, the previous government pressed ahead with introducing the first state early years curriculum when it produced the CGFS in 2000 (just after the 1999 revision of the National Curriculum). This guidance was, at least, non-statutory but it was greeted with some alarm by early years practitioners. Its 'stepping stones' of development outlining progression from 3 to the end of the Foundation Stage (Reception class) was for some too mechanistic a description. However, it did confirm the integrated, holistic nature of young children's learning and drew upon the 'areas of learning and experience' described by HMI in 1985 to illustrate this. The areas were reduced to six: PSED, CLL, Mathematical Development, Knowledge and Understanding of the World, Creative Development, Physical Development.

After the CGFS: The Statutory Framework for the EYFS (2008)

It would appear to be the case that government (of whatever political persuasion) encroachments into education have led inexorably towards greater concern with measurable outcomes linked directly to the statutory requirements of the National Curriculum. The early years sector thus became as vulnerable to this thinking as all the other education sectors. Thus, it was that in 2007 three documents: the CGFS, the Birth to Three Matters Framework and the National Standards for Under 8s Daycare and Childminding were all conflated or consumed into the Statutory Framework for the EYFS which became a legal requirement from September 2008.

This Framework was to be used in all provision for children from 0 to 5 and was to be inspected by OFSTED. It differed from the CGFS in its hierarchical and chronological description of children's development which was accompanied by an extensive assessment profile, on which a child 'scored' points. For many involved in early years work, this comes very close to the thinking and structure of the National Curriculum itself.

Summary

In this chapter, we have considered some of the contributions made by historical and more recent figures to our thinking on the development and education of young children. We have looked at a range of government documents and reports particularly in relation to under fives and started to query the early years curriculum as it currently stands. We have also started to ask questions and raise concerns about the omissions in documents and initiatives around the areas of language, culture and identity.

Reflective activity

1. Did you find the historical information (and there was a lot of it!) informative? Is there any part of it you would like to research further?
2. If you have the CGFS (2000) in your place of work, are there any parts of it that you think would be helpful to you in your thinking about young children's development and your own practice?
3. How would you describe your own linguistic and cultural identity? Can you remember what attention was paid to it in your own early years and/or primary education?
4. How well do you think your workplace provides opportunities for the children to explore and share different linguistic and cultural experiences? Is there anything more you could do? How would you go about it?

Personal, Social and Emotional Development: Exploring Language, Culture and Identity

4

Chapter Outline

In Chapter 1 and 3, we made a brief survey of some of the ideas of leading writers and theorists and of government documents and reports in relation to the development of young children culminating with the Statutory Framework. We touched on the importance of personal, social and emotional (PSE) factors in the lives and education of young children and intend now in this chapter to look more closely at PSED and the ways in which it meshes with matters of linguistic and cultural identity. We also consider how CLL approaches them too.

Where does PSED come from?

Certainly in the West, the writers we have alluded to, starting with Rousseau, formed a strong foundation through their demonstration of interest in children's 'natural' growth and how their education might take place alongside this. As we have also seen, many of these individuals and subsequent government departments and agencies have drawn and built on each others' work and ideas, so adding to the general reservoir of knowledge.

We know that, all being well, by about 2 years of age, children have acquired a huge amount of their first language or languages. For children who are yet to acquire English and who will do so largely in an early years setting, it is not only important that they are disposed to learn the new language but that the adults there facilitate its learning. We have pointed out already that young bilingual children come to the early years setting armed with their first language and all that it has represented to them for their first 2 or 3 years of life. They have already achieved an impressive linguistic competence that for them is nothing out of the ordinary. If the adults who will be working with them do not understand this, the children may then undergo the experience of feeling that their language and by extension their home life and culture, are not welcomed. Worse still it may even be seen as a hindrance rather than an asset to their acquisition of English. Young children may not be able to express verbally how this affects them but it will be something that they *feel*.

In this respect, the actions of the adults who work with young children will have a remarkably strong impact. A child's environment has an equally strong effect on emotional and social growth. Young children may have to balance the expectations and nurturing of the home environment and those offered by the nursery, centre, childminder or grandparents or whoever may be caring for the child if the parents are at work. If these are markedly different, the child may face some extraordinary challenges in coping with different principles and practices, however well intentioned they are.

In Chapter 3, we mentioned the Plowden Report of 1967 and its comments on emotional development. The Rumbold Report (1990), mentioned in Chapter 3, also emphasized this aspect of early years provision in its discussion of children's personal and social growth. One of the eight areas of learning and experience was 'human and social'.

The committee described 'human and social' learning as being:

> 'concerned with people, both now and in the past, and how and where they live' (para 25). That is, it addresses historical and geographical ideas. It continued:

'Young children are naturally interested in people, in their families and homes and the community in which they live. From an early age they are aware of the work that members of their families do and often reflect this in their role-play.' (para 26)

'Many young children are curious about the past. They are interested in . . . what things were like when their parents, teachers and helpers were children; and in what they were like as babies. (para 27)

Adults can help satisfy this curiosity, and in so doing help children to develop a sense of time and change . . . *and by talking about events in their own lives and those of the children and their families.*' (para 28; our italics)

Interestingly, it is in the 'spiritual and moral' area of learning that the committee makes most reference to personal and emotional development and links these explicitly to children's cultural/religious experiences. This is a selection:

Most children have the support of caring families through which they are helped to develop self confidence and a understanding of right and wrong.

By the age of three or four, most children will have taken part in celebrations and ceremonies such as birthdays and marriages. Some will have joined in religious celebrations such as Christmas, Diwali, Eid-ul-Fitr or Hannukkah and be aware of the rituals or special foods associated with them. Some may come from homes where prayers and readings from religious literature are everyday events. Festivals often provide valuable opportunities for under fives to share celebrations with parents and other members of the community.

Children's experiences in their immediate and extended families provide a basis from which adults working with under fives can help them explore ideas, for example, of fairness, forgiveness, sharing, dependence and independence.

Developing respect for others, themselves and for their surroundings are important basic elements in this area of the curriculum which good social relationships in pre-school provision can do much to establish.

Children's self-esteem is profoundly influenced by the regard in which they are held by others and the way they are treated in day to day activities. (paras 57–62)

Evidently, the members of this committee took emotional and social development very seriously and understood how fundamental it is to children's well-being and ability to grow intellectually as well as socially.

We found this understanding reflected in the EYC we visited.

Our research in the EYC

We saw many examples of supportive practice in the EYC. Both indoors and out, the staff had set up a 'reflective' space, rather like a miniature tent with mirrors where the children could sit alone or with a friend and literally 'reflect' on themselves and life. It was from the indoor 'tent' that Jeremiah rushed out, telling us 'I speak my language'.

The importance of families was demonstrated by the display of photos in the entrance where the children were shown with family members and their home languages identified in the accompanying captions.

As we prepared to leave (on a local visit), Preeta showed Alison Hatt (AH) the picture of herself and her family in the nursery entrance (where photos of families and a caption referring to their family language are displayed) with the caption that Preeta's family spoke Yoruba. When asked if she herself spoke Yoruba, Preeta nodded.

Because many of the children's family roots were outside the United Kingdom, travel figured frequently in play and provision. In one visit, Malcine was playing on the 'train' (wooden blocks) observed by Alison Hatt (AH).

AH:	Where are you going?
Malcine:	We're going to Barbados.
AH:	What will you do there?
Malcine:	Play with the sand (pointing to sand pits) and the water.
AH:	Where will you stay?
Malcine:	In the restaurant, in the hotel have to go on the aeroplane, train to the airport, mum and dad lived in Barbados when I was born.
	(Malcine was actually of Eritrean background but was going to Barbados for a family wedding. 'Journeys' had been one of the topics of the nursery and one worker had been looking at the world map with children for family origins, etc.)

On another visit, there was a new display about journeys and visits to tie in with Katisha's return from Japan. AH had a discussion with Katisha's mother and learned that they had been to Japan for an extended visit to maternal grandparents. After being there for one month, Katisha was speaking Japanese. The family tried to visit once a year; so far Katisha's grandparents had not visited England since her grandmother was anxious about flying such a long way.

AH:	Do you speak Japanese to her (Katisha) at home?
MO:	Yes, all the time.
AH:	And her dad?
MO:	No.
AH:	So he speaks English and you speak Japanese to her so she's got the two languages together . . . brilliant!
AH:	What about the writing?
MO:	Not Japanese writing yet.
AH:	So do you think she'll learn to write English first, at school?
MO:	Yes, Japanese writing is difficult.
	(all the above taken from field notes)

One observation we made was of Sadia 'teaching' the Deputy Head, Claire, about her family's country of origin, her religion (Islam) and describing via an information book her own knowledge of some of the practices she and her family performed.

CL and SA are looking at a book about Islam, with SA 'teaching' CL about it.

CL:	. . . big place but on this map it's very small but this is a map of the whole world so Eritrea is a very big place, isn't it?
SA:	This is not Eritrea (indistinct), Eritrea's very far from this place (?)
CL:	Let's have a look . . . teach me about Ramadan.
SA:	Well, they pray (CA: yeah) and Ramadan we celebrate, Muslims all celebrate, my dad at Ramadan he pray.
CL:	Every day?
SA:	Sometimes he pray at home.

CL:	(Looking at a photo in the book) What are they doing on this page? Why so they have to do that?
SA:	Muslims always do that (she then went on to recite one of the Arabic prayers). All the time at pray time you do that . . . all Muslims do that (shows position of hands).
CL:	Who can speak then?
SA:	Then when you're finished . . . quiet when you . . . Discussion of language – CL: It's English?
SA:	When they pray on the carpet . . . my mum always did that . . . on the pray carpet – so we mustn't put . . . on it.
CL:	So you do fasting in Ramadan? (transcribed from recording)

And of course, sometimes the researcher missed the point entirely:

Jeremiah:	I was born in England.
AH:	In a hospital?
J:	No in England.
AH:	Do you have any brother or sisters?
J:	No, just my mum (not actually true!) (taken from field notes)

The EYC and language

The EYC staff demonstrated a very strong understanding of the relationships between language, culture and identity and was very committed to nurturing all three. As we have said, the entrance to the Centre, during the year of our visits, had photos of the children and their families with captions informing the reader of the language/s used at home. There was an electronic screen in the entrance with greetings in different languages and information concerning centre activities for children and adults.

Parents were seen as partners in the Centre. In conversations with some of the parents it was clear that this approach to working with the whole family on an equal footing was embedded and very much appreciated. The parents commented on the positive attitudes towards the children's home languages, on the staff's willingness to learn greetings and phrases from family languages, on the open way languages were discussed or featured as 'language of the week' and how the children were becoming adept at attributing greetings to parents (*ola* to a Spanish speaking parent, for example) and learning songs or counting in different languages.

Language awareness appeared to be embedded in the ethos and everyday practice of the nursery. This was most visible in children's knowledge of their own and other languages as clearly demonstrated in Tözün Issa's (TI) conversation with Ernesto in the following extract:

TI: Ernesto, what language do you speak?

ER: Portuguese

TI: *obligado*

  Ernesto looked at TI and smiled.

  On another occasion Selma was sharing photos with TI

TI: (Looking at the photo) Ah, I love cheesecake.

SE: Yes, I like it too.

TI: (Looking at Italian version) How do you say cake in Italian then?

SE: *torta*

SE: (Looking at her name written in Arabic) Here is Selma in Arabic, these are Arabic, my dad speaks Arabic.

TI: Do you know Arabic?

SE: I speak Arabic, Italian and English.

TI: How do you say daddy in Arabic? Is it *baba*?

  (transcribed from recording)

In another example a photograph of Ayse, who came from a Turkish and English speaking home (Turkish mother, English father) appeared in the album of another child in the nursery with the caption: 'This is my friend Ayse, she speaks Turkish and English at home.'

Under another child's picture was the caption 'Jayden can say hello in Spanish' the writing *ola* clearly visible under his picture.

Our conversations with parents (discussed in Chapter 8) showed how deeply they were committed to maintaining children's first language/s and how positively they felt towards their children becoming bilinguals as well. Many of the children came from very linguistically rich homes and some were being exposed to three languages simultaneously.

We would argue that the close relationships between parents and the centre staff and the shared agreement over the importance of home languages to the children combined to provide part of the Framework that enabled the children to continue to grow not only as individuals but as members of the community of the centre. Explicitly embracing languages and cultures gave all the children opportunities to learn about each other and to respond positively, as far as we could see, to their differences.

We now move to a discussion of PSED and CLL in the CGFS and the Statutory Framework – the documents that should provide support for the work of early years practitioners.

Ten years after Rumbold, the CGFS was introduced in 2000. It was guidance, not a legal requirement.

The CGFS was, though, intended to:

> underpin all future learning by supporting, fostering, promoting and developing children's personal, social and emotional wellbeing: in particular by supporting the transition to and between settings, promoting an inclusive ethos and providing opportunities for each child to become a valued member of that group and community so that a strong self-image and self-esteem are promoted. (p. 8)

CGFS and PSED (pp. 28–43)

While this section applies to all children in its emphasis on the importance of constructive relationships between children, children and adults (practitioners and parents), of establishing a climate of trust, respect and of valuing children, there are nevertheless certain statements that are particularly applicable to young bilingual children. We select these as ones we feel are especially useful for practitioners to remember:

respecting children's culture so that they develop a positive self-image

This statement is expanded in the accompanying paragraph which says:

> gaining a knowledge and understanding of their own culture and community helps children develop a sense of belonging and strong self-image. *Each child has a culture defined by their community and more uniquely by their family.* (Our italics)

The section on PSED emphasizes its 'critical' role in all aspects of children's lives. Statements that are particularly relevant to our book include:

- establishing constructive relationships with children, with other practitioners, between practitioners and children, with parents and with workers from other agencies, that take account of differences and different needs and expectations
- planning activities that promote emotional, moral, spiritual and social development alongside intellectual development
- providing positive images in, for example, books and displays that challenge children's thinking and help them to embrace differences in gender, ethnicity, religion, special educational needs and disabilities
- providing opportunities for play and learning that acknowledge children's particular religious beliefs and cultural backgrounds
- providing support and a structured approach to achieve the successful social and emotional development of vulnerable children and those with particular behavioural or communication difficulties. (p. 28)

As the above examples showed, the Centre we visited had such principles firmly embedded in its own practice.

CGFS and CLL (pp. 44–67)

The CGFS has a section (p. 19) on 'Children with English as an additional language' which clearly states:

> Many children in early years settings will have a home language other than English. Practitioners should value this linguistic diversity and *provide opportunities for children to develop and use their home language in their play and learning.* (Our italics)

It follows this with examples given of the support that bilingual children should receive:

> Building on children's experiences of language at home and in the wider community by providing a range of opportunities to use their home language(s), so that their developing use of English and other languages support one another;

> Providing a range of opportunities for children to engage in speaking and listening activities in English with peers and adults;
>
> Ensuring all children have opportunities to recognise and show respect for each child's home language;
>
> Providing bilingual support, in particular to extend vocabulary and support children's developing understanding;
>
> Providing a variety of writing in children's home languages as well as in English, including books, notices and labels;
>
> Providing opportunities for children to hear their home languages as well as English, for example through the use of audio and visual materials. (p. 19)

Work and contact with parents and carers is emphasized particularly with a view to gathering information about their children which: 'may include children's competence in their language at home, whether or not it is English' (p. 24).

The section on CLL, in our view, is rather disappointing in its approach to this area of learning and development. It is a shame that it is not more closely linked to the section on children with EAL and to PSED. This was also our opinion about the comparable section in the Rumbold Report. The CGFS section on CLL provides overarching guidance but, we feel, could have gone further into the relations between different forms of communication. Literacy (knowledge of and expertise in written forms of language) is rooted in spoken language and depends on the child acquiring competency in its spoken repertoire before it begins to understand the purposes of written language. Young bilingual children have, or potentially have, a rich repertoire of language which receives little recognition in this section.

The CLL section recommends that practitioners should 'give particular attention to':

> Providing time and opportunities to develop spoken language through conversations between children and adults, both one-to-one and in small groups, with particular awareness of, and sensitivity to, the needs of children for whom English is an additional language, using their home language when appropriate; (p. 44)

And as part of another recommendation a rather grudging:

> Children's experience of different scripts at home should be acknowledged and built on when learning about English. (p. 45)

No-one is likely to deny that learning English is a central function of early years provision but it is disappointing to see children's languages, in which so much of personal, family and cultural feeling is invested, given such perfunctory treatment. We can see no reason why different scripts should not have gone beyond 'acknowledgement' to overt utilization in early reading and writing activities and to be given equal but separate status with English.

It is regrettable that in this section there are neither any explicitly positive statements about bilingualism nor any acknowledgement of how identity is formed through the meshing together of language and culture.

Assessment of children: The CGFS and the 'stepping stones'

The approach taken in the CGFS towards identifying children's development across the six areas of learning and experience was one of 'progression' from 3 years of age to 5, that is, the Reception year which is the end of Foundation Stage. The 'Early Learning Goals' are the developmental milestones which children were expected to reach at this stage. While none of this is without attendant problems, the CGFS appeared to take the view that children invariably do progress this progression was set out through its notion of 'stepping stones'. In the document, each of these has a different colour background (four in all) on which each 'stepping stone' is described. These clearly imply that children, supported by the adults who work with them, will move towards ever-increasing sophistication in their ideas and understanding across all six areas of learning and development. The CGFS largely avoids a judgemental approach; that is, it does not suggest that if a child does not reach a stepping stone or an Early Learning Goal, that child has somehow 'failed'.

There is much that is praiseworthy in this government document and we would recommend our readers, if they can, to take some time to look at it in order to compare it with the current Statutory Framework which we now go on to discuss.

The Statutory Framework for the EYFS (2008)

Its subheading is: 'Setting the Standards for Learning, Development and Care for children from birth to five'. It is worth noting the order in which the capitalized nouns are presented, particularly when we consider that this Framework is for children from birth to 5 years of age.

As we have already said, this EYFS legislation became mandatory in 2008 for all schools and those in registered settings providing for young children aged 0–5 years. It still extends to the Reception year. The Framework is therefore applicable to a much wider range of early years provision and a wider age range than was the CGFS. Apart from the Statutory Guidance there is also a plethora of additional, non-statutory materials which may or may not enhance the workload of those involved professionally with young children.

The Framework's structure

The Framework bases itself on the four 'themes' which we outlined earlier in Chapter 1:

- A Unique Child
- Positive Relationships
- Enabling Environments
- Learning and Development

It retains the six areas of learning and experience but renames them as areas of learning and development; it also renames Mathematical Development as 'Problem Solving, Reasoning and Number' (PSRN). The Early Learning Goals of the CGFS, which children at the end of their Reception year should achieve, are also retained. PSED remains the first on the list.

The four themes

We are disappointed that the apparent commitment to equality indicated by the Framework is not overtly present in each of the four themes.

Instead, we have a marked insistence on children as 'learners' and little here that emphasizes personal and emotional development.

- A Unique Child – every child is a competent learner from birth who can be resilient, capable, confident and self-assured.
- Positive Relationships – children learn to be strong and independent from a base of loving and secure relationships with parents and/or a key person.
- Enabling Environments – the environment plays a key role in supporting and extending children's development and learning.
- Learning and Development – children develop and learn in different ways and at different rates and all areas of Learning and Development are equally important and interconnected. (DfES, 2007b, p. 5)

Each 'theme' is followed by a 'commitment' which is 'focused around' the implementation of each theme:

- (unique child) – development, inclusion, and health and well-being
- (positive relationships) – respect, partnership with parents, supporting learning and the role of the key person
- (enabling environments) – observation, assessment and planning, support for every child, the learning environment and the wider context-transitions, continuity and multi-agency working
- no specific 'commitment' is added to the fourth theme (Learning and Development).

At the time of the introduction of the Framework, the government was requiring all providers to attend to the outcomes of 'Every Child Matters'; this partly accounts for the bureaucratic nature of the themes and commitments. In addition, the Framework was to be adhered to by all early years settings/provision which included childminders, workplace nurseries, day care centres, EYCs, nursery schools and nursery classes in primary schools.

The themes come across as assertions rather than principles and are written, as is the rest of the document, in the strange, dehumanized language we have come to expect from government publications with their curious separation from reality. We seem to have moved a long way from the ten principles outlined by Bruce (2005) and even further away from the principles that underpinned the CGFS. Somehow, children seem to be as distanced from the heart of their own education as they were a century ago.

Our thoughts on the themes

We focus here briefly on the 'themes' to show some of the ideas that we would include under these headings in relation to young children's languages, cultures and identities.

A unique child

We certainly agree that all children, to different degrees, are born with the ability to learn. Piaget's, Vygotsky's and Bruner's ideas about active minds we whole-heartedly endorse. But as Pringle (see Chapter 3) pointed out, as humans we have needs that go beyond intellectual capacities. These needs are things that we all share and help us to acknowledge human similarities.

But one of the things that makes us unique, we would argue, is the *difference* between us all. Every one of us has experienced the world differently and these differences started as soon as we were born into our family and its culture – its customs, practices, rituals and heritage. Just as we acquired our first language unconsciously, so we unconsciously acquired our home culture.

Our language, or if we were lucky, languages, mediated that culture, helped us to develop a sense of, and mark out, our individual selves as well as our connections to those around us. There is a central role played by language, culture and family in forming personal (and social) identity and, indeed, in helping children to develop the multiple identities that most of us need to function in contemporary society. Certainly, we would want all children to be confident and secure about themselves. We suspect that, given a happy and secure home life, most of them are, at least until they encounter the first long-term setting outside home.

We would also hope that each child would see, in their early years domain, something of the home life to which they could connect and that their individual experiences, however different from those of the adults around them, would be accorded the recognition, respect and esteem they deserve.

Positive relationships

If each child is unique then it follows that every family is unique too. Each one has its own ways of 'doing things' and its own ways of expressing different feelings and ideas. Undoubtedly, children thrive in a loving, secure home where their personal and emotional development is nurtured and they begin to establish a wider range of social relationships with family members and friends.

We would hope that whatever early years provision the child goes to s/he will experience, as far as possible, a replication of the best of the relationships of home life. By this we mean that the adults/key person working with the child will be able to offer her/him a similar quality of contact and support. It also means that the 'professional' adult must avoid judging the child's family life if it is markedly different from their own. It is all too easy for those of us in the West to assume that 'our' ways of doing things (e.g. child-rearing) are the right ways; we must try to bear in mind that there are other, equally valid ways of bringing up children.

'Positive relationships' refer to those between the early years workers and the families as well as between professional and child. Many early years providers are very successful in establishing good relations with families – the Centre we visited was, we felt, exceptional in this respect.

'Positive relationships' also refer to those between children. We no doubt want them to develop friendships, become caring, respectful of and concerned for, others. We want them to enjoy learning about each others' languages and cultures. We also probably want them to start learning how to manage their own feelings of anger, jealousy and sadness and to help other children who may experience similar emotions. Do we also want them to develop a sense of fairness and justice, of feelings of indignation when fairness and justice are ignored?

Enabling environments

We would suggest that in working with young children and providing for their PSE growth, as well as the other areas of learning, practitioners could extend this to pay more specific attention to the impact of children's environments on their development. This has to be done, sensitively, of course. As with 'positive relationships', it is all too easy to fall into the trap of 'measuring' different environments using some idealized setting (usually one's own) as the yardstick, or making ill-informed judgements based on little real knowledge. This is where the making of (invited) home visits can bear such good fruit and enable staff, particularly in discussion with parents, to identify features of home that could be replicated in the early years setting and to find out as much as possible about the languages that may be in use or that the children are familiar with.

All practitioners and adults working professionally with young children should look carefully at the 'environments' they set up and decide whether these adequately reflect the lived environments the children come from. Displaying different artefacts and features from a variety of homes not only helps strengthen and support the cultural identity of individual children; it also enlarges the knowledge and experiences of them all. Needless to say, this should be done with tact and care and individual differences borne in mind.

> No group of children or any individual should be treated as having a homogeneous experience with others of their 'type'. (Siraj-Blatchford, 2010)

Even if home visits are not possible, then, at the very least, all practitioners should be aware of the expectation that they are as professional as possible in their approach in these matters and do their best to provide an environment that welcomes all the children, makes their languages visible, provides a variety of familiar artefacts and offers more than an English monoculture.

Learning and development: Emotion and knowledge

Here is what a more recent psychologist, Margaret Donaldson, in her book *Human Minds* (1992), has to contribute to our exploration of children coping with their understanding of the world and with emotional experiences:

> We can know in different ways. Some of our knowledge is explicit, out in the open. We know that we know it. We can give an account of what we know, and sometimes of how we came to know it or how we would justify the claim that it is 'knowledge'. But we also have knowledge that is to varying degrees implicit, in the dark – not spoken of, sometimes not able to be spoken of.
>
> We like to 'take control'. Typically we try to manipulate what we encounter. We try to change the world to suit our purposes. These purposes are often powerful and passionate. And reality often resists them.

> In much of human functioning, knowing and thinking are interfused with
> emotion. This means that they may be interfused with happiness but also,
> not infrequently, with distress and pain. (Donaldson, 1992, pp. 24–5)

While some of this may be aimed at adult knowledge, it may be helpful
to think about this in relation to children. Donaldson's earlier book *Children's Minds* (1978) provided some fascinating insights into children's
conceptual development and the problems associated with 'disembedded' learning. If children are given activities to do that are too abstract
and therefore meaningless, the learning process may well be threatening
and uncomfortable and the emotions connected to that learning be, as
Donaldson says, those of 'distress and pain'. As we see the early years
curriculum move increasingly away from what should be its founding
principles, we are likely to see young children apparently 'failing' to succeed. As we have already suggested, the content of CLL, for example,
and the current emphasis on crude phonics teaching is one way in which
the linguistic knowledge of bilingual children is undermined.

Statutory Framework – additional materials

There is a vast amount of additional, non-statutory material accompanying the Statutory Framework. This includes 'Practice Guidance' and
'Principles into Practice' cards (in these the four 'themes' seem to have
been transmuted into principles). In the additional materials are many
more explicitly helpful ideas and suggestions for staff to meet children's
needs and to support bilingual learners. Unfortunately, we suspect that
busy staff and other early years providers will tend to read the statutory
requirements of the Framework and give less attention to the non-statutory materials – of which there are a great many! This is a shame since
they will find in these materials much more to think about when addressing PSED in relation to language and culture. However, they often seem
to read as a list of recommendations or instructions for the adult rather
than place children at the centre.

Statutory assessment – the early years profile

Earlier we discussed the CGFS 'stepping stones' which were a way of
tracking children's progress in the areas of leaning and experience.
Assessment in the Statutory Framework is necessarily statutory too and

comes in the form of the early years profile. This obliges early years staff to allocate children a numerical *score* recording their progress across the six areas of learning and development. The Profile is thus a summative report that should be produced for the use of Year 1 teachers and for parents/carers to see.

Although the writers of the Framework stated that all six areas of learning and development are equally important only *three* of them are scored.

These are PSED, CLL and PSRN, which gives some indication of departmental or governmental priorities and concerns and links the Foundation Stage to the primary school SATs in English and Maths.

We wonder what message this gives about the supposedly equal importance of Knowledge and Understanding of the World, Creative Development and Physical Development? We would not wish to see a points scoring system extended to the other areas of learning (in fact, we don't wish to see one at all) but government commitment to all six areas would have been more convincing if they had all been included in a more 'child-friendly' system of record-keeping and assessment.

The points system

There are 9 assessment points on each of the 13 scales for the 3 assessed areas, making a total of 117 potential scores for each child in any setting.

We might query here the thinking that requires numbers to be used to identify apparently successful learning and progression and which fails (or appears to fail) to foresee that numbers imply ranking and implicit, or even explicit, failure as well as success. Add to this the stipulation that there is an 'average' score that children are expected to reach (6 points) at the end of Foundation Stage and it is easy to see how this form of assessment begins to disadvantage certain children. It then becomes very easy for teachers and others surveying the scores to see failure in those who do not reach the 'required' score. Personal and anecdotal evidence from schools and governors' meetings suggests that these scores have a profound impact on staff and governors alike, with the inevitable corollary that lower scores indicate if not failure, then a 'problem' of some kind that is apparently located in the children.

Scoring PSED – some of the problems

If we do not take into consideration the child's circumstances, family background and home situation, we may well not be making a fair assessment. For many reasons, a child may have difficulties forming friendships, playing co-operatively or expressing feelings and may need longer than other children to settle into the life of the nursery or setting.

The technology that now enables schools and local authorities to analyse data can certainly assist in identifying 'gaps' in assessed attainments. We should bear in mind that data is open to a variety of interpretations and that we must look for reasons for apparent gaps. Particular groups of children may appear to be scoring below their peers – who might these be?

Children from refugee and asylum seeking families

One such group might be children who are from refugee or asylum seeking families who may well have had disrupted lives and witnessed events that most of us are fortunate never to have encountered. They may well find it hard to talk in their home language about such things, let alone try to employ English. In such cases, the provision of emotional support and a secure, non-judgemental friendly environment in which the children can gradually recover is essential. Such children, indeed all children, need time to settle, establish friendships and then flourish. If their scores for PSED and CLL are lower than children who have not had similar horrific experiences should we be surprised? Is it their 'fault'?

The reader is recommended to research the evidence into the situations of these children and their families as they arrive here and attempt to settle. The Refugee Council is an excellent source of information and statistics which can be used to counter the many ignorant and discriminatory accusations made about refugees and asylum seekers.

Children with EAL

Many children who start in preschool provision at the age of 3 will be fluent in their home or first language/s and will be starting to acquire English. They are likely to have experienced different exposures to English in which case the nursery or EYC (or any other provider) that receives them should be aware of this. In Chapter 5, we shall discuss multilingualism in more detail but we cannot overstress the importance of staff having knowledge of first and second language acquisition and bilingualism. Armed with such insight, staff can support young emergent bilinguals appropriately and provide their own record of the children's English language development to set alongside the PSE and CLL assessments.

Gender

Gender is another obvious example. If more boys than girls have a lower score for aspects of PSED (as seems to be the case nationally), adults might be in danger of assuming that there is something inherently 'wrong' with small boys that leads to their apparent failure in certain types of behaviour (this can lead to 'pathologizing' certain children and their families). While gender differences certainly should be investigated, so also should adult (in early years settings the majority of adults will be female) attitudes, expectations, behaviours, the level of provision and the quality of monitoring all these.

Ethnicity

Simplistic analysis of the achievement of different ethnic groups may lead the unwary into making unjustified assumptions about those from various minority ethnic groups who score below the required number. This brings us back to the 'deficit' thinking of the 1970s and 1980s which is proving so difficult to eradicate and the 'pathologizing' of groups we referred to earlier. This is partly why monitoring by ethnicity is often challenged as being inherently racist; however, it seems to us that any racism probably lies elsewhere. It may be that some minority ethnic groups are generally more subject to racist behaviours and attitudes than others: that stereotypical, negative assumptions may be made about these groups and that, conversely, stereotypical, 'positive' assumptions may be made about other minority ethnic groups. Interpretation of data that does not attend to the contexts in which all ethnic groups are operating can contribute to mistaken judgements. However, monitoring by ethnicity is pointless if it is not followed up with appropriate action.

There is a subtle interplay between all the above factors, children's observed behaviours, adult interpretations of these, adult expectations and adults' understanding of the ways in which their own prejudices may unconsciously affect their judgements. It is more constructive for staff to examine their own practice and principles to find out if they are, however inadvertently, themselves relying on stereotypical expectations of different groups of children and thus creating a 'disabling' environment.

As Bettelheim (1961) suggested, the effect of different environments can be profound. As an intelligent, articulate adult he found himself at various stages of his life struggling to cope with places that were either hostile or unfamiliar (and these included a year in a German Concentration camp in the Second World War as well as trying afterwards to settle in America). How much more might very young children, moved from a familiar setting to an unfamiliar one with cultural practices, routines and expectations that differ from their known ones, struggle to 'find their feet', learn to adapt, begin to use a new language, make friends, and so on? If the adults are tuned into the potential difficulties for the children and understand how important it is for them to nurture their charges, giving them time to adapt, well and good, we hope. But if the adults are preoccupied, not with genuine support and observations, but with embarking on scoring the children's progress, it is only too possible for some children to be deemed to be 'failing'. And do we really want to make such a judgement of children who have not yet reached statutory school age?

The Tickell Review of the EYFS (2011) analyses responses made to this form of assessment in chapter 4 ('Assessing Children's Progress'). Problems associated with recording information for assessment are noted in para 4.15 and dissatisfaction with the 117-point scale is noted in para 4.22. However, there seemed to be a widespread agreement that summative assessments are important for different transitions, not just that from Foundation Stage to Key Stage 1.

> Children can experience many changes in the early years, including moves between different settings. While the EYFS Profile is the only compulsory summary of assessment in the early years, some practitioners would like more information – sharing between settings, recognising how challenging these transitions can be for children. Fifty eight per cent of respondents to the call for evidence said that there should be a summative report to support transition.

> Of respondents' views on the timing of assessment to support transition, 35% said it was needed at all transition points, for example between settings, from setting to school, and from nursery to reception. Other transition points were also identified and 19% of respondents chose transfer to school – for example, nursery/pre-school to reception year. Eighteen per cent said a summative assessment must take place before any transition. This would enable practitioners to prepare for a child's individual needs and put in place any additional provision before a child moves.

At the time of writing, the government's response to this review is unclear.

The news that children in Year 1 are to undergo a phonics test (for that is what it is) in the summer term indicates to us that any concerns expressed about the EYFS are falling on deaf ears. We can only hope that early years practitioners and particularly Reception teachers, will hang on to their principles and not take this test to mean that they must drill phonics into the children at an even greater rate. Our observations in the two Reception classes suggest to us, unfortunately, that the pressure may be very hard to resist.

So what did we see in the two Reception classes?

PSED in the Reception classes

As we have already noted, life in the two Reception classes was markedly different from the EYC. We have commented on the emphasis on the narrower aspects of CLL; we also saw a reduced attention to children's PSED. Where, for instance, in the EYC there was a remarkably close relationship between families and centre staff, this relationship appeared to change in the Reception classes. Parents were welcomed at the start and end of the day but the quality of the contact seemed to us to be weaker. In the Centre, activities and resources were all set up, indoors and out, with the arrival of children, parents and younger sisters and brothers all seen as part of the day's routine. Time was given to exchange information and time was also given to the children to settle.

By contrast in the Reception classes the expectation was that for the children the day started on the carpet waiting for the register to be taken. This might then be followed by assembly (a non-existent feature in the EYC and in early years provision outside of primary school) or by the ubiquitous phonics, or similar, session. Under such a regime, there was very little scope for the parents and teachers to exchange much information or for parents to take a more active part in the day's routines. The end of the day offered more opportunities for conversations but it often seemed that despatching the children took priority.

This is not to say that there were not positive relationships between teaching staff and parents in the Reception classes; rather that they were more formal, perhaps slightly impersonal so that the balanced relationships between child, family and school were changed. It should also be borne in mind that as children get older and more independent, there will be a loosening of the contact between families and teachers.

Nevertheless, there was a marked contrast between the ways in which the EYC incorporated and celebrated the children's home languages and cultures and the way in which these were far less prominent in the Reception classes.

In one of the schools, the display titled 'multicultural class x' remained on the wall all year but never included all the children. In the other, there were more positive attempts to incorporate cultures and languages via Chinese New Year, foods from different countries, stories such as 'Handa's Surprise' and some bilingual notices. Even here, though, there appeared to be very few instances of these things being linked *directly and explicitly* to individual children and groups so that personal knowledge and experience was not acknowledged publicly. It is not possible to judge whether any of this had an overt detrimental effect on the children; what we ask our readers to consider is what might be the effect on the children if Reception classes continued the practice of the EYC? Going further, what of continuing this throughout the primary school?

It is disappointing that so many government documents, guidance and, indeed, legislation report do not explore the powerful, emotional role of language in children's personal and social development nor highlight the nature of the connections between language, culture and ethnicity. It is disheartening that such major aspects of early childhood are still not accorded a central place in government thinking.

Indeed, there often appears to be a perverse determination to ignore the research that has been carried out in relation to language, bilingualism and identity and to focus instead on narrow, rather insular concepts of spoken language development. There is still a rigid adherence to a hierarchy of languages with English at the top, a few European languages next, followed by all the rest. But our own cultures and identities do not stand still; if we think back to what we were in childhood and compare that with what we are now, all of us can see how we have changed, adapted and added new features to our identities.

The children we teach are just setting out on this adventure. Siraj-Blatchford (2010) says:

> Staff (also) need to find resources and a shared language with which to work with dual-heritage children and their parents to support a strong identity. But it would be even better if staff worked with all children to make them aware that they all have an ethnic/racial identity and that they all have a linguistic, gendered, cultural and diverse identity. Surely this is the way forward? In being sure of one's own identity as multifaceted, it must be easier for children to accept that others are exactly the same – even when the combinations are different! (p. 154)

Summary

In this chapter, we have revisited aspects of the political, social and educational history that addressed PSED and introduced some 'new' figures whose ideas, thinking and research have helped educationalists define and implement PSED. We have looked further at the Statutory Framework for the EYFS and its requirements and raised questions about the validity of attempting to make a measurable assessment of PSED. Underlying this is our concern that all children, especially in the English education system, are in danger of being judged largely through numerical scores and that bilingual children especially are in danger of being underestimated and their language capacities undervalued.

Reflective activity

1. What is your attitude to PSED? Is it important or not? Why?
2. Since it is a statutory requirement, how does your workplace provide for it?
3. What personal experiences of your own childhood might help you to help the children you work with explore and cope with different emotional challenges?

5 Multilingualism: Key Issues and Debates

In the previous chapter, we looked at PSED and the ways in which it links with matters of linguistic and cultural identity. In this chapter, we will discuss the misconception about multilingualism and multiculturalism in the United Kingdom and its consequences in practice, specifically in early years contexts. We discuss this in relation to the use of children's first languages as part of their learning environment. We argue that utilizing children's first languages in early years settings will greatly enhance children's acquisition of English and positively affect their social and emotional development.

In the United Kingdom what we say we understand by the term *multiculturalism* and how we interpret its meaning in schools are often contradictory. Successive government policies and major reports (Plowden, 1967; Bullock, 1975; Swann, 1985) have all endorsed multiculturalism as a positive aspect of modern Britain and stressed the importance of children's mother tongues for maintaining their culture and identity. More recent government documentation such as the Department for Children, Schools and Families (DCSF) (formerly the Department for Education and Skills (DfES), 2006) document *Excellence and Enjoyment: Learning and Teaching for Bilingual Children in the Primary Years* also echoed similar sentiments for children's bilingualism and the role of the first language in the development of identity. However, these documents do not go beyond a mere acknowledgement; failing to put forward practical strategies to utilize positive links between the first and the second language development. We only need to look at research carried out in the past 60 years in the United States, North America, Australia and more recently in Europe (including the United Kingdom), to see the academic as well as psychological benefits of bilingualism (Beardsmore and Swain, 1985; Cummins, 2000; Bialystok, 2001).

In Britain, we often associate multiculturalism only with 'celebrating children's different cultural' practices. Often this is shown in the form of displays of colourful artefacts, maps and other visually stimulating materials representing all children attending the nurseries/EYCs. At other times, we see hastily prepared displays of religious festivals and other events often produced without much input from the children. Such work can only be described as tokenistic. This often suggests that multiculturalism is not being thoroughly embedded in thinking and practices of some schools. Rather it is seen more as something that needs to be done because 'that's what schools are required to do'. Clearly there are whole school issues around collective thinking and training for staff relating to this area.

We often forget that the term *multiculturalism* also implies *multilingualism*. This particular confusion is partly related to our misconception about the term multilingualism, associating it with *teaching* rather than *facilitating* the use of languages. With the former the *teacher* is the expert, with the latter it is the *child*. When one of the authors of this book (TI) was delivering a session on multilingualism to a group of PGCE (Post Graduate Certificate of Education) students, he faced the following question from one of the trainees: 'It's all very well but how are we expected to teach 8–10 languages in the same classroom environment?' This question reflects a commonly held view among some student teachers, teachers and even some headteachers. One of the reasons for this misconception is related to confusing multilingualism with bilingual education where the medium of instruction is in two languages (for further examples of bilingual programmes from Europe and North America see Baker (2006)).

Multicultural Britain

Britain is truly multicultural and our school population in the United Kingdom reflects this. Below we present some statistical information to support our claim:

UK population

- Out of the UK population of just under 54 million, 7 million residents are born outside of the United Kingdom (11.6% of the total population) (Office for National Statistics, 2010).
- 222 countries are represented in this number.
- There are more than 300 languages spoken by children in London Schools making the capital the most linguistically diverse city in the world.
- Statistical information suggests that the number of children who have EAL is actually increasing as shown by the recent Department for Education (2010) data:

Proportion of children with EAL (English as an Additional Language)

- In primary schools it has increased from 8.4 per cent in 2004 to 16.0 per cent in 2010.
- In secondary from 8.6 per cent in 2004 to 11.6 per cent in 2009 (DfE, 2010).

The other misconception about multilingualism is that the term is sometimes synonymous with English language support for children who are from ethnic minority backgrounds. Support for these children is covered by funding directly from the Central government under the Ethnic Minority Achievement Grant (EMAG). The Grant's main focus is supporting children's access to the National Curriculum where the development of language competence is indexed to learning of specific subject related concepts and vocabulary. The introduction of the EMAG has complicated the issue of ethnic minority support further. Although the EMA teams employed are experienced specialist teachers in schools, due to the nature of the programme organized, these teachers were spread too thinly across the school making it difficult for them to have a real impact on pupils' levels of achievement. This has caused further misconception of the roles between the EMA and class teachers where the latter began to see issues which are to do with ethnic minority children to be mainly the responsibility of the EMA teachers and not theirs. This has resulted in the compartmentalization of support for EMA. Presently, the situation is even bleaker: at the time of writing of this book, the EMAG services in most schools and LEAs has been severely cut by the government leaving the support of ethnic minority pupils in the hands of mainly undertrained classroom teachers.

Despite such worrying developments, some innovative schools still manage to provide good support for their ethnic minority children through effective collaborative teaching programmes between class and EMA teachers. In these schools, the EMA staff are actively involved in the planning process delivering sessions jointly with class teachers. In other times, they carry out specialist support to less able pupils through differentiated work. Such excellent practice supports EMA teachers' specialist status alongside other professionals in the school.

Supporting children's linguistic and cultural experiences in early years settings: Some theoretical perspectives

According to Vygotsky (1962) language is produced as a result of a series of historically contextualized cultural experiences which mark one's identity. What this implies is that when young children start nursery school the language they have, hear and respond to in their family and/or community contexts is the language through which concepts are formed. In thinking along Vygotskian lines, these young children are interacting with adults and peers in their home environments while developing conceptually. With guided learning and planned facilitation such experiences can be utilized to extend children's thinking when they start nursery. 'A child first seems to use language for superficial social interaction, but at some point this language goes underground to become the structure of the child's thinking' (Vygotsky, 1962).

What Vygotsky is implying here in relation to bilingual children is that when children do not appear to be competent in communicating in English on starting the nursery, this need not be taken as indicating that they are not thinking. Given the opportunity there is a strong probability that they will be able to do their thinking in their home languages. Here we would particularly like to mention the importance of memory both as a central to information processing theories as well as its role in collective meaning making. Like Vygotsky, Kuhn (2000) emphasizes memories arising out of social and cultural contexts. Bilingual children's social and cultural experiences arising out of their collective construction of their local realities need to be perceived as linguistically charged and culturally enriched 'raw materials' waiting to be enriched further by new learning. Let us develop this important link between children's (early) cultural experiences from a socio-cultural developmental perspective and explore possible influences on the development of emotions and thinking.

The role of the home languages in learning in school: The debate

The problematic interpretation of the home language as the main factor contributing to ethnic minority children's lack of educational attainment is not new. The assimilation policies and practices of the 1950s and 1960s – mainly imported from the United States – were to ensure that ethnic minority children would rid themselves of the 'influence' of their home languages which was perceived as interfering with learning of English. In the United Kingdom, English reception centres were set up mainly for teaching newcomers English. Some children were bussed to other schools to receive such instruction (Issa, 1987). Similar problematic views of the home languages are still with us today. For example, the Organization for Economic Co-operation and Development (OECD) Programme comparing International Student Achievement (PISA) in different countries (Stanat and

Christensen, 2006) claimed that in both mathematics and reading, first- and second-generation 'immigrant' students who spoke their first languages at home were significantly behind their peers who spoke the school language at home. This suggested to the authors that insufficient opportunities to learn the school language might be a causal factor in students' underachievement. 'These large differences in performance suggest that students have insufficient opportunities to learn the language of instruction' (Christensen and Stanat, 2007, p. 3). Esser (2006) went further and argued on the basis of PISA data that 'the use of the native language in the family context has a (clearly) negative effect' (p. 64). He also argued that retention of the home language by immigrant children would reduce both motivation and success in learning the host country language (2006, p. 34). Nushe's (2008) study report explores the process of 'internationalization (p. 13) as he assesses the contribution of the migrant labour force to the demands of the domestic skills market and the growth of the tertiary education systems in the host countries.

According to Cummins (2009), the unspoken logic here is that total immersion of immigrant students at a very early age in the host country's language will ensure cultural and linguistic assimilation and get rid of the 'problem' of children's home language. Cummins goes on to argue that no mention was made of bilingual education as a credible or legitimate option in the report. Cummins also argues against the findings of the OECD report stating that no relationship was found between home language use and achievement in the two countries where immigrant students were most successful (Australia and Canada). In addition, Cummins claimed that the relationship disappeared for a large majority (10 out of 14) of OECD-member countries when socio-economic status and other background variables were controlled (Stanat and Christensen, 2006, table 3.5, pp. 200–2). Cummins concludes in his response to such negative reports by stating that:

> The disappearance of the relationship in a large majority of countries suggests that language spoken at home does not exert any independent effect on achievement but is rather a proxy for variables such as socioeconomic status and length of residence in the host country. (Cummins, Keynote Presentation, London Metropolitan University, 20 June 2009)

If we briefly pause to try to make sense of all this research, we can say that there are still a lot of misconceptions about the role of the home language in many parts of the world. Some authorities and their educational 'allies' appear to be keen to stigmatize the use of home language on educational attainment where often other (social as well as individual) factors work. Here in the United Kingdom, successive government policies have largely seen the use of home language alongside English as inconceivable. In this part of the chapter, we turn back to look at some of the developments in United Kingdom.

The European Commission (EC) Directive and the 'mother tongue' debate

The Bullock Report (1975) generated some positive discussion on the role of mother tongue education but it was left to the individual LEAs to put forward programmes of mother tongue teaching and endorse bilingual education initiatives. Some LEAs employed bilingual teaching staff to work within mainstream schools and alongside classroom teachers. The ILEA and Birmingham were such progressive authorities. But as these LEAs were not getting extra funding for this, their resources were insufficient to address all the needs of the bilingual communities they were serving. Many communities decided they had to run and finance their own supplementary schools, the earliest of which went as far back as 1930s serving the Chinese community (Ng Kwee Cho, 1968).

As we mentioned in Chapter 1, the Labour government's changed interest in the mother tongue debate came with the European Community Commission (ECC) Directive in 1977. The Directive was the outcome of the work carried out by the Council of Europe formed primarily for the unity of the European Community. As the numbers of migrant workers' children began to appear in European schools, it became concerned with the educational needs of their children and subsequently established a subcommittee on the education of migrant workers in 1966. Between 1966 and 1980, it had passed a number of resolutions and a project which ran for five years (Wittek, 1992). These resolutions and activities enabled the ECC to issue a Directive and this was eventually adopted in 1977.

The Directive represents what could be termed the standard model for 'National Educational Policies': Article 2 requires reception arrangements, in particular for teaching of the official language of the receiving country, and specialist teacher training. Article 3 requires support for the teaching of the language and culture of origin. The Commission's suggestions, which recommended that equal weight should be given to each article were watered down by the representatives of the Member States with reference to support for the mother tongue and culture (Boos-Nünning and Hohmann, 1986).

Britain reacted to the Directive by pointing out the differences in status between the minorities in Britain and the workers in other European states. The argument seemed to be on grounds that the minorities in Britain were settled and had no particular desire to go back to the countries of origin of their parents. This argument was not wholly true. First, there was no statistical information on the minorities' aspirations for the future. Secondly, there were some (not a large number) of migrant workers who were in Britain under the work permit scheme that was part of the regulations applied after Britain entered the European Community. Britain's response seemed an attempt to remove the mother tongue clause from the programme rather than the development of a more coherent programme. Despite criticism about the way it was prepared and presented (Khan, 1980; Brook, 1980), the EEC Directive helped put the mother tongue issue on the agenda in Britain. The many projects established around the country facilitated contact between the educators, researchers and teachers and helped mother tongue teaching gain support around the country. New projects set up in different parts of the country assessed the role of mother tongue in learning English. A National Council for Mother Tongue Teaching was established and this became instrumental in building contacts between all the relevant bodies. The Mother Tongue and English Teaching Project (MOTET, 1978–80) was formed to promote the status of children's first languages and English. The Schools Council Mother Tongue Project (SCMT, 1981) was established to promote the awareness of language diversity and bilingualism and to develop materials for the teaching of the mother tongue.

There was however, one significant study backed by the central government into the language development of children in Britain. The Report of the Committee chaired by Sir Alan Bullock (Bullock Report, 1975) not only emphasized the importance of language development of all children but also highlighted the importance of bilingualism. This report was the first official document into the language development of children that openly endorsed children's bilingualism:

> The importance of bilingualism, both in education and for society in general, has been increasingly recognised in Europe and in the USA. We believe that its implications for Britain should receive equally serious study. When bilingualism in Britain is discussed it is seldom if ever with reference to the inner city immigrant populations, yet over half the immigrant pupils in our schools have a mother-tongue which is not English. (Bullock Report, 1975, p. 293)

There were some central government-backed projects as well. The Bedford Mother Tongue Project (1978–81) was to assess the first language use of Punjabi and Italian and was funded by the DES. The Bedfordshire Project was funded by the European Community and ran for four years (1976–80). Both projects were based on regarding the contribution of the mother tongue as positive rather than a hindrance to the second language learning.

The projects helped to create genuine multicultural approaches in some schools. There was backing from some LEAs, which appointed advisors and inspectors for multicultural education to oversee policy developments and to develop practice in their schools (Blakeny, 1981; Matthews, 1981). A few authorities such as Lambeth, Berkshire and Bradford had developed policy documents. Genuine enthusiasm and individual efforts by teachers helped create examples of good classroom practice. The need for a whole school transformation of the curriculum required a lot of work and needed expert backing and financial support. Nevertheless, there remained a large group of professionals who still believed that success for minority children depended upon their exposure to English. There were also some regions where the issue of minority education was debated not because there was a small proportion of minority children in their schools.

The situation in most schools was that they were only prepared to do a limited amount without the backing and support of central government. In practice, spending on education was reduced because of the economic uncertainties of this period. The period that followed, however, was characterized by massive spending on urban regeneration programmes. It was also the preparation period for the most significant education bill since the 1944 Education Act: the introduction of the National Curriculum. But in neither of these radical moves was there any acknowledgement of the need for bilingual provision in education.

Educational initiatives at local and national levels were described in reports that seemed to endorse the government's provision for minority education. The first major study on the education of minorities was undertaken by the Committee chaired by Lord Swann (DES, 1985). This provided an in-depth study of minorities and their language use in the United Kingdom, and put the educational developments in policy and practical levels into context. The report provided a climate for healthy debate on the education of the minority communities. However, its position on the role of English was viewed with scepticism by some members of the minority communities. The Report's overall emphasis was on raising achievement levels of minority pupils under the 'unifying' (Swann Report, 1985, p. 385) function of the English language. The report had a carefully drawn agenda within which bilingualism was not acceptable. The report conveyed the government's position on the issue of bilingualism: 'We find we cannot support arguments put forward for the introduction of programmes of bilingual education in maintained schools in this country' (Swann Report, 1985, p. 400).

As these developments were taking place in the United Kingdom, there was an increasing amount of research emerging from Europe and North America that pointed to numerous advantages of bilingualism.

Bilingual children and metalinguistic awareness

In early years contexts young children's spoken language is the most effective tool for communication. Wells (1986) points out that as children are learning *through* talk and learning *to* talk, they are also learning and thinking *about* talk. When children reflect and talk about language this is called metalinguistic awareness. Young children display their knowledge and reflection about language at a very young age ('yes! I speak my language!'). Research shows that bilingual children have a particular advantage with respect to metalinguistic awareness. Robson (2006) points out that particular ways in which children switch and borrow between languages as they speak allow them to manipulate language as a formal system (2006, p. 112). Encouraging young bilinguals to experiment and reflect on their language use in this way not only allows them to develop their linguistic skills, it also enables them to defuse some of their anxieties in monolingual learning environments; in addition, allowing young learners to capitalize on their linguistic skills has a positive impact on their cognitive and emotional development. We discuss this in more detail further on in this chapter. First, we would like to develop our point about the relationship between children's socially and culturally accumulated thinking which Vygotsky calls *socio-historical* and Bourdieu describes as *cultural habitus* (Bourdieu, 1990) and the development of children's emotional well-being.

Socio-cultural perspectives in children's emotional development

Building on the ideas of Vygotsky (1962), Rogoff (2003) defines the development as a 'sociocultural-historical process through which humans develop through their participation in the socio-cultural activities of their communities which also change' (2003, p. 11). Here Rogoff's idea of culture as a dynamic concept is a useful one to mention particularly when we think about bilingual newcomers in early years settings. The children's culturally acquired thinking embedded in the home language can develop and change with the new experiences they encounter. Children will try and make sense of their new worlds constantly by evaluating new information in relation to their existing culturally oriented experiences. This is when children's thinking starts to adopt a new bicommunicative mode; that new experiences negotiated to them in the language of the nursery (i.e. English) will start to develop at a faster rate than the home language as the medium of thinking. This does not necessarily suggest that the home language will cease to function as a tool for thinking; rather, it is to be used less frequently particularly as the medium for negotiating new skills and knowledge in different learning environments. It will be confined to environments which are largely outside mainstream schools (e.g. supplementary schools, after school language clubs). Children's social worlds will effectively be separated into two: the home and the school.

As children begin to make less use of their home languages in a more formalized learning environment of the nursery school, some negative processes may begin to emerge which affect bilingual children's cognitive and emotional development.

Emotional and cultural consequences of monolingual development in bilingual children

Smith et al. (2003) carried out a range of studies which showed that children who grew up on a farm, for example, may have a better understanding of life and death at a much earlier age than children growing up in a city. Similarly, some of the bilingual children in Issa's (2005) study showed a more sophisticated understanding of primary school children's socio-economic concepts such as cost, money, buying and selling than children whose parents did not own small shops. The study showed that these children often visited their parents' shops and frequently experienced customer/shop owner transactions and related conversations in their homes. The study also showed that children's thinking and understanding about such concepts were embedded in their use of Turkish at home.

Dunn (1996) points out that children often display their most advanced reasoning in situations that have the most emotional significance for them. Donaldson (1992) also explores this in her work. Mac-Naughton supports the view that emotion and cognition are connected and that 'pleasure, desire and emotions are powerful motivators of learning' (2003, p. 53). Furthermore Eliot (1999) suggests that children's social experiences – and their interpretations of their social worlds – are central to emotional development and the growth of emotional self-regulation. What this suggests is that when a young bilingual learner begins to develop both emotionally and intellectually through social interaction, the very essence of those feelings and emotions are stored in the 'two almond shaped structures in the brain called the *amygdala*' (Robson, 2006) 'acting as the gatekeeper of the emotional brain' (Eliot, 1999). Rogoff (2003) argues that there are cultural variations in children's emotional experiences and their interpretation (and therefore expression) of cultural values. However, as Eliot argues 'emotions influence every aspect of children's thought' (1999, p. 294).

If we are to bring a Vygotskian perspective into this we need to mention the role of language not merely as a useful tool through which children think and learn, but as a powerful tool through which young learners display their feelings and emotions. Vygotsky calls these 'cultural tools', which he described as human cultural and historical activity. Pea (1993) stresses the important association between cultural tools and intelligence and how such practices represent the individual's association with their community and social practices.

In the case of young bilingual learners entering early years settings, these complex processes take place through the child's home language. Dweck (2000) points out that not allowing the expression of emotions as part of everyday experiences affects children's development of self-efficacy, self-competence which develops at a young age. Equally, if we perceive bilingual children's emotional experiences as 'culturally embedded' verbal and non-verbal expressions, Dweck's points become clearer. He concludes by saying that these play a significant part in the development of young learners' attitude to learning.

There is no doubt that what Dweck describes relates to all children. What we are trying to explore in this book are some of the negative consequences of not exploring young bilingual learners' existing cultural (and linguistic) experiences fully.

So, if we agree that children's expression of their emotions are crucial not just for their psychological but also for their cognitive development then there is a need for adults to facilitate children to do this in early years settings. This is often where the confusion sets in. Most adults working in early years settings wrongly assume that they will need to speak children's home languages in order to do this. Although we would point out that learning some common phrases such as greetings, key words of praise are always useful for maximizing interaction with bilingual learners, it is learning how to facilitate *children's use of their home languages* which we think is more important in this case. We devote the remaining part of this chapter to this point by exploring some practical ideas for early years practitioners. We also hope the examples we will share with the reader will help contextualize the theoretical perspectives put forward so far in the book.

Drury (2007) suggests that in order to support bilingual children's language and learning effectively in a school environment educators working in early years settings need to have a 'holistic socio-cultural approach' to their learning (p. 49). Drury goes on to point out that such an approach is necessary to meet the varying needs of children from different cultural and linguistic backgrounds who often arrive with very little or no English.

Issa and Öztürk (2008) support Drury's point by stating that first educators need to uncover crucial aspects of children's individual learning at home and that discovering children's routine activities often involve conversations with parents, grand parents, playing with siblings or friends from the same community. They add that although English is understood in most bilingual households, it is often the case that the language of interaction takes place in the child's home language. Issa and Öztürk explain this as a desire to maintain and transmit the cultural and linguistic traditions of the communities concluding that for a young bilingual learner the concept formation often occurs in the child's home language.

Drury suggests that 'tapping into' children's learning experiences at home may also reveal valuable insights into their learning in preschool settings and form an extension to their home environment. Drury (2007, p. 4) describes how Samia, a 4-year-old girl from Azad Kashmir province of Pakistan 'played school' with her brother using *Kahari* the language of the region which illustrates a powerful point about how concept formation, cultural experiences and language are important and closely associated aspects of early bilingual child's formation of self. Home contexts often provide unique insights into parents' views on education. Drury gives us an example of a useful response from Samia's mother: 'Samia is an intelligent girl. She is learning very quickly. Hope she do well, providing she gets enough help, because I cannot help her' (2007, p. 11).

Here Samia's mother clearly associates 'learning' with 'learning in English'. She also implies that it is Samia's teachers who know best how to teach her daughter. Samia's mum speaks little English. Situations such as this can be used to explain to parents who often think that learning a second language can only be achieved through total immersion in the language (i.e. English) and its rapid replacement with the home language as early as possible. This is closely related to the perception that academic success can only be achieved through learning English and that children need to learn English as soon as they enter the nursery. The process as to *how* this is to be done is not often realized by all parents and teachers.

Issa and Öztürk (2008) point out that bilingual children's early learning and language development takes place in community schools as natural extensions of their home environments. The majority of children's early development takes place in their home languages. This includes the development of early reading and writing. Kenner's (2004) perceptive study explores how children's familiarity with their own writing systems helps them to develop their understanding of the English writing system. She points out that children study their community languages only a few hours a week compared to learning English every day in their primary schools. Kenner suggests that 'Language awareness develops quite quickly if children have the chance to encounter other writing systems' (2004, p. 55). To support this Kenner mentions children's experiences of early writing which help develop a flexible and comprehensive approach to the act of writing pointing out that learning each script 'gives young learners expanded range of possibilities as writers' (2004, p. 104). She gives the example of how learning Mandarin can be applied to learning detailed observational drawings.

Facilitation of children's use of their home languages in the classroom through play is crucial for its association and transfer into English. Finding out about children's familiar cultural experiences embedded in their use of their home languages can only be done though information collected from their home environments. Home visits are used for talking to parents about their role in developing their children's home languages through interaction and modelling.

We will return to the topic of home visits when we discuss how the staff at the EYC use home visits to find out about these crucial family practices and routines. In the remainder of this chapter we would like to explore some practical implications for developing children's listening and speaking skills.

Wyse et al. (2008) explore excellent speaking and listening strategies for young learners in early years settings. They refer to Tizard and Hughes (1984) and Wells (1986) to highlight the positive influence of the home language in developing children's ability to use English effectively. They also quite rightly point out how the quality of social experiences and interaction of young children will vary when they arrive at the nursery, pointing out the need for teachers 'to be aware that some children will arrive at school appearing to be confident articulate masters of the English language' (Wyse et al., 2008, p. 151). While agreeing with Wyse et al.'s analysis whole-heartedly we would also like to point out that teachers should also be aware that some children will arrive at the school equipped with similar confidence with the use of their home languages. The difference here of course is that teachers may not be aware of this as these children may not get an opportunity to articulate their confidence. We agree with Wyse et al. (2008) that early years practitioners need to understand about language and diversity and have a more holistic approach to language diversity recognizing that language is deeply rooted in social and cultural experiences (i.e. including the family).

They then propose a number of useful practical activities they call 'purposeful language situations' (p. 152). In the case of bilingual children one of the useful way to start such activities would be to prompt children to talk about things which are directly related to their home experiences. The questions need to be devised according to the level of English language competence of the children. For those who are at the early – and most anxious – stage of English perhaps starting with 'one word' questions accompanied by actions: 'happy?' to develop into more complex sentences, for example, *what do you like to eat when mummy or daddy cooks at home? Can you tell me how s/he cooks it? Where do you get it?*

Such culturally relevant questions very much tap into children's everyday experiences; however, they may not always provide adults with all the detailed responses they would hope for. This is when the value of home visits can be seen, when a more real picture of a child's home life

Table 5.1 Invisible learning – Mete Can

| | At nursery | | | At home | |
Activity no.	Transcript title/activity	Learning strategy	Activity no.	Transcript title/activity	Learning strategy
15	*Very hungry caterpillar*	Procedure in a recipe	20	Lets make lahmacun (Turkish pizza)	Procedure in a recipe
16	*Handa's surprise*	Names of fruit	21	Guess the fruit Basket game	Names of fruit
17	Song – Head and shoulders, Knees and toes . . .	Body parts/ language game	22	*Baş, omuz, diz ve parmaklar. . . .* (Turkish version)	Body parts/ language game
18	I spy . . .	Turn taking/ word game	23	*Gözüm Gizli birsey görüyor . . .* (My eye sees something hidden)	Turn taking/ word game
19	Lets play shops	Extending cultural experiences	24	Visit to Uncle Mehmet's shop	Extending cultural experiences

Source: Issa and Öztürk, 2008

can be obtained. If this is not possible, talking to the child's mum or dad when they come to the nursery may be another way of gathering useful information provided practitioners take care not to be too intrusive.

The summary table below shows how children's home experiences can be linked to activities in the nursery. The child's individual profile is drawn following the home visits. Here particular home activities, for example, cooking *lahmacun* (Turkish pizza) which the child enjoys participating (or eating) is then matched with a corresponding activity at the Centre to consolidate relevant associated concepts and vocabulary.

Summary

In this chapter, we looked at some of the misconceptions and the key debates about multilingualism and multiculturalism in the United Kingdom and its consequences in practice. We discussed this in relation to early years contexts and argued that utilizing children's first languages in early years settings will greatly enhance children's acquisition of English and positively affect their social and emotional development. To support our claim we used some theoretical and practical considerations for inclusive practices and as well as some research that highlighted a socio-cultural perspective in young children's emotional development.

Reflective activity

1. In what ways have the discussions presented in this chapter shaped your understanding of multilingualism/multiculturalism?
2. Are you using any of the practical strategies suggested in this chapter? If so which strategies are you using?
3. In view of some of the theories presented here, do you think there are more things you can do to support young children's first and second language development in your own setting?

First and Subsequent Language Acquisition: Key Issues and Debates

6

In the previous chapter, we explored the key issues around multilingualism. In this chapter, we will explore the debates around first and subsequent language acquisition with particular reference to bilingual children who are exposed to a second language at home or school. We explore these for two reasons: first, we believe that it is important to make a case for the benefits of bilingualism in the context of multilingualism. Secondly, by exploring the debates around bilingualism will help our readers to contextualize some of the policy initiatives by successive governments we discussed in the earlier chapters.

In the second part of this chapter, we explore practical strategies used to support children's language acquisition and bilingualism by referring to our findings at the EYC. We do this by highlighting the particular ways children's bilingual development is supported through effectively planned daily routine interactions.

Bilingualism: The debate

Traditional views of bilingualism perceived it as negative and harmful for the developing child (Laurie, 1890). This early perception, which continued to be held by many in the United States and Britain throughout the twentieth century, was the outcome of assumptions that bilingualism was a burden on the cognitive processes, which would lead to mental confusion, inhibit the acquisition of the majority language and might even lead to a split personality. The influence of these professionals on the general public was great. The following quote from Laurie clearly illustrates this:

> If it were possible for a child to live in two languages at once equally well, so much the worse. His intellectual and spiritual growth would not thereby be doubled, but halved. Unity of mind and character would have great difficulty in asserting itself in such circumstances. (1890, p. 15)

When children used home language in school, the punishment might be that they had their mouths washed with soap (Isaacs, 1976) or were beaten with a cane (Baker, 2006). The common anxiety of professionals (teachers, doctors, speech therapists and school psychologists) was that the use of the two languages would seriously hinder the functioning of the brain. It was believed that the learning of the second language would be at the expense of the first, hindering the development of thinking skills (see Baker, 1996). Consequently, it was assumed that people who learned another language suffered serious intellectual disadvantages. Research up to the 1960s was used to support this negative viewpoint, linking poor test performances to low intelligence (Saer, 1923; Darcy, 1953). Research during the 1980s and 1990s concentrated on intelligence as the key concept in assessing bilinguals (see Nanez et al., 1992). In a typical study, bilinguals and monolinguals would be given an intelligence test. When their IQs were compared, the result usually showed bilinguals scoring lower than monolinguals. For example, research by Saer et al. (1924) suggested that university student monolinguals were superior to bilinguals: 'The difference in mental ability as revealed by intelligence tests is of a permanent nature since it persists in students throughout their university career (p. 53).

But from the 1960s onwards this belief about bilingualism and intelligence was challenged by further studies in this field (Peal and Lambert, 1962; Jones, 1966). Two major arguments were used against the earlier research. First, it was claimed that these had been class biased, that is, once children's socio-economic backgrounds had been taken into account, there were no differences between monolinguals and bilinguals (Cummins, 2009). Secondly, when parental occupations were considered, the differences between the two groups diminished considerably.

The major turning point in the history of bilingualism was the realization of the relationship between bilingualism and cognition. Peal and Lambert's (1962) study in Canada suggested that bilingualism not only did not hinder intellectual development but also had certain cognitive advantages. Bilinguals outperformed monolingual pupils in tests administered during this study. Further research after Peal and Lambert also strengthened the argument that there were cognitive advantages in bilingualism (see Cummins, 1976, who explored the effects of bilingualism on cognitive growth; Cummins, 1984, for assessment and pedagogical approaches; Diaz, 1985, on research on cognitive advantages of bilingualism). These findings on bilingualism prompted some investigators to look more closely at bilingual cognitive processes.

Bilingual cognition

How does a bilingual mentally reproduce two languages? What processes lead to such a representation? The central issue is the extent to which two languages function in bilinguals whether independently or interdependently. Early research attempted to show that early (compound) bilinguals who had become bilinguals at a young age were more likely to show interconnections in their two languages than late (co-ordinate) bilinguals who had become bilingual at a later period in their lives. In the 1960s, this was redefined in terms of memory storage (Kolers, 1963). A separate storage hypothesis suggested that bilinguals had two independent language storage and retrieval systems with the only channel of communication between them being a translation process linking the two separate systems. A shared storage hypothesis suggested that the two languages are kept in a single memory store with two different language input channels and two different language output channels. Later studies supported an integrated model involving both these hypotheses on mental representation through dual coding approaches (Paivio, 1986; 1991 also Heredia and McLaughlin, 1992 on bilingual memory; Keatley, 1992 on collection of research on cognitive psychology; Hummel, 1993 on storage to processing issues). What are the cognitive advantages and disadvantages of bilingualism?

The essence of the question was whether bilinguals and monolinguals differed in their thinking styles. Were there differences in the way they process information? Did having two languages create differences in thinking about language? (Baker, 2006). It was held by some that the ownership of two and more languages increased fluency, flexibility, originality and elaboration.

Research has compared bilinguals and monolinguals using a variety of measures on divergent thinking (Cummins, 1976, 1977). The research was international and cross-cultural: from Ireland, Malaysia, Eastern Europe, Canada, Singapore, Mexico and the United States, sampling bilinguals using English plus Chinese, Bahasa Melayu, Tamil, Polish, German, Greek, Spanish, French, Ukrainian, Yoruba, Welsh, Italian or Kannada. As Lauren (1991) notes, such research has mostly taken place in additive bilingual contexts. This is where both the languages are given supportive environments to develop equally.

The research findings largely suggested that bilinguals are superior to monolinguals on divergent thinking tests. It was also found that balanced bilinguals, whose two languages are developed to an extent to enable them to be used fairly equally by the speaker, were superior in fluency and flexibility scales of verbal divergence, marginality on originality when they were matched to non-balanced bilinguals. The matched monolingual group obtained similar scores to the matched bilingual group, but scored substantially higher than the non-balanced group. Generally, the differences in this particular research, between matched groups of balanced bilinguals and non-balanced bilinguals were suggesting that bilingualism and superior divergent thinking skills were not necessarily related. This however must not be taken at a face value as Cummins (1977) cautiously proposed: 'There may be a threshold level of linguistic competence which a bilingual child must attain in order to avoid cognitive deficits and allow the potentially beneficial aspects of becoming bilingual to influence his cognitive growth' (p. 10).

The difference between balanced and non-balanced bilinguals thus suggested the existence of a threshold. Once children have obtained a certain level of competence in their second language, positive cognitive consequences could result from this. Similarly, if competence in a second language was below a certain threshold, there might not be any cognitive benefits.

Overall, it could be argued that 'bilingualism is actually good for one's brain' (Cummins, 2009). Ellen Bialystok et al's (2006) work looked at the age of onset of dementia (e.g. Alzheimer's disease) in a population of elderly people in an old people's home in Toronto, Canada. Interestingly, they found that for bilinguals/multilinguals the age of onset of dementia was four years later than for monolinguals.

Bilingualism and metalinguistic awareness

The research on bilingualism and divergent thinking tentatively suggested that bilinguals might have some advantages over monolinguals. Ownership of two languages may provide additional insights into the way language relates to thinking. Studies in this field also concentrated on the processes of cognitive functioning rather than the products of it (Kardash et al., 1988; Bialystok, 1991; Harris, 1992; Keatley, 1992; Hummel, 1993). Metalinguistic awareness is defined as: 'The ability to reflect upon and manipulate the structural features of spoken language, treating language as an object of thought' (Tunmer and Herriman, 1984, p. 12).

Donaldson (1978) suggested that metalinguistic awareness is a key factor in the development of reading in young children. She mentioned homes where the awareness of the spoken word is encouraged and parents *talk* about words to their children. Donaldson regards this as the key in children's understanding of speech as being broken up into units, and words existing as separate units. She talked about the importance of context related activities which is often lacking in children's first encounter with language:

> For many children the earliest encounter with the written word is indirect, arising in the situation where a story is read aloud by an adult. This is already in a sense language freed from context; but the experience of

hearing a story is not so likely to enhance awareness of direct grappling
with words on a page. (Donaldson, 1978, p. 9)

It is argued that the interaction between the child and the environment
supported the role of children's cultural experiences in linguistic development. According to Bruner (1975) children initially talk to themselves
and direct their talk at themselves. This he called egocentric speech.
This is developed further through children directing new language,
encountered during their social and co-operative encounters with other
children and adults, towards themselves. The Russian psychologist
Vygotsky (1978) argued that children also learn by turning round and
reflecting on their thoughts when using language, and came to see things
in a new way. This is related to the analyses of language, produced in a
variety of contexts. The so-called product research has concentrated on
the accumulation of previous research on cognitive functioning and
bilingualism. It has also focused on metalinguistic awareness in bilingual children.

Marian and Kaushanskaya's (2009) work on English–Mandarin and
English–Spanish bilinguals can be shown as an example for bilingual
superiority in metalinguisitic awareness compared to monolingual speakers. In their study, bilingual speakers who had learned both languages
prior to schooling were compared to monolingual English speakers in
how well they mastered words in an invented language that bore no resem-
blance to English, Spanish or Mandarin. The bilingual participants 'mastered nearly twice the number of words as the monolinguals' (*ScienceDaily*,
www.sciencedaily.com/releases/2009/05/090519172157.htm)

Having looked at relevant research on the benefits of bilingualism, let
us now look at the process of language acquisition and possible ways it
can support children's social, emotional, linguistic and cultural
development.

First and subsequent
language acquisition

Some of the children in the United Kingdom, especially those from language communities often start school having been exposed mainly to a
language other than English at home. Department for Education

Table 6.1 Annual school census: Language data collection (England) number of children with a first language other than English

Year	2008	2009	2010
Primary	14.3%	15.2%	16%
	(466.420)	(492.090)	(518.020)
Secondary	10.6%	11.1%	11.6%
	(349.04)	(364.280)	(378.00)

Source: Department for Education (DfE), 2010

Table 6.2 The top 15 languages spoken by pupils whose first language is other than English

Language	Number	Percentage
Punjabi	102,570	1.6
Urdu	85,250	1.3
Bengali	70,320	1.1
Gujarati	40,880	0.6
Somali	32,030	0.5
Polish	26,840	0.4
Arabic	25,800	0.4
Portuguese	16,560	0.3
Turkish	16,460	0.3
Tamil	15,460	0.2
French	15,310	0.2
Yoruba	13,920	0.2
Chinese	13,380	0.2
Spanish	10,000	0.2
Persian/Farsi	8,510	0.1

Source: Department for Education (DfE), 2010

statistics supports this showing a modest rise in numbers in primary and secondary schools across England (DfE, 2010).

Some children have access to two languages from birth. This happens when both parents are different nationalities such as the case of Selma in our study whose parents were from Italy and Egypt. This would imply that when children start learning English in a school environment many would already have developed mechanisms for decoding and classifying language and began developing concepts in their home language/s.

It is a widely held belief among parents, educators and politicians that acquiring two languages from birth is detrimental to the child's language growth, especially if this language is different from what is learned in school. It is still assumed that simultaneous acquisition, that is, children being exposed to two languages at home or within their communities will muddle the mind and/or retard language development (Baker, 2006). Research supports the opposite, that babies are biologically ready to acquire, store and differentiate between languages from birth onwards (Meisel, 2001; Genesee, 2007). Infant bilingualism (or multilingualism) is shown to be normal and natural and typically beneficial. There are social, cultural, emotional, cognitive and communicative benefits. These studies show that infants are able to differentiate and successfully store two or more languages for both understanding (input) and production (output). Such studies show infant multilingualism as viable (Deucher and Quay, 2000; Genesee, 2004, 2008; Meisel, 2001).

Memory of language sounds begin operating at the foetal stage which suggests that the process of language acquisition begins before birth (De Boysson-Bardies, 2001). Upon birth babies immediately prefer their mother's voice to any other mother. There appears to be an immediate language differentiation in the newborn babies particularly to intonation (Genesee, 2004). Maneva and Genesee (2002) have found that in the babbling stage, a child who is exposed to two languages has the tendency to bubble in the stronger language demonstrating language specific babbling features in each of the languages. We know that very young children can easily switch languages and differentiate between them; however, there are variations between speakers. Deucher and Quay (2000) have found that a bilingual child as young as, 2 years of age uses two languages in contextually sensitive ways. In bilingual children, the ability to use appropriate language with a particular person occurs very early. Social awareness of 'one parent – one language' routine appears to encourage awareness of translations equivalents and to separate language systems.

Types of early childhood bilingualism

Drury (2007), Romaine (1995) and Piller (2001) have carried out in-depth studies of early childhood bilingual acquisition. Their studies tell us that there are broad categories based on the language or languages spoken by the parents and the language of the community. De Houwer (2005) suggests that the most typical input pattern that a bilingual child receives is a combination of hearing some people only speaking one language plus hearing other people speaking both languages on a regular basis. In one person–one language acquisition at home each parent speaks their own language to the child but tend to speak one language to each other. It is often the case that the language spoken by one of the parents is the dominant language as can be shown with an example from United Kingdom where one of the parents who is English speaking and the other parent who is a speaker of Mandarin. Here the child has access to both languages but English remains the dominant language as the language of the society at large. In delayed introduction of the second language, the parents consciously delay the introduction of the dominant language of the wider community. This is to ensure sound foundations for the home language – for the preservation of cultural and linguistic identity – until the dominant language as in the case of English in the United Kingdom are introduced. This probably explains a rather ironic situation in the United Kingdom, that despite successive government claims of a decrease in numbers of children with a language other than English starting school, evidence from one of their own sources appear to suggest that this is not the case (CILT, 2005). The point of concern of this chapter and indeed the whole of the book is one of diminishing status of home languages in schools which is happening at an alarming rate. Baker (2006) talks about subtractive bilingualism, operating within individuals and communities where the home languages are marginalized and not allowed to be part of the mainstream learning environment in schools. Piller (2001) rightly points to the social class aspect of this stating that lowering of status of some languages masks the social class factor. His analysis rests on the assumption that middle-class families will tend to value their home languages consequently supporting their maintenance resulting in additive bilingualism, whereas for lower social groups this develops in the opposite direction resulting in subtractive bilingualism. Clearly, there is also a case of power relations between languages that needs to be considered here. As Bourdieu (1990) advocates, schools operate to perpetuate the cultural capital of their pupils.

Having looked at the debates around bilingualism we now turn to some findings on teaching strategies which support positive outcomes of bilingualism and enhance bilingual children's learning. We think these strategies are worthy of our attention as they are closely linked to some of the approaches of the EYC. We share these with the reader in the remaining part of this chapter.

A growing body of research appears to support the validity of co-operative learning strategies as: 'Extremely valuable instructional strategy for promoting participation and academic growth in culturally and linguistically diverse classrooms' (Cummins, 1996, p. 82).

Co-operative learning strategies involve small groups of pupils working together for a common objective though activities based on interdependent co-operation (Abrami et al., 1995; DeVillar and Faltis, 1991; Holt, 1993; Kessler, 1992). One of the effective programmes of research on the levels of achievement in collaborative programmes was carried out by Garcia (1991) on Latino speaking pupils in the United States. The instruction was organized in a way to facilitate maximum pupil interaction. Heath and Mangiola (1991) show how peer tutoring can result in academic gains for both children. Heath (1993) highlights how concentrating on another child's learning helps children to 'decompose what is involved in learning language' (p. 188).

It is useful to remind ourselves that there are aspects of children's home backgrounds, for example, family run businesses, business related talk at home and certain characteristics of speech patterns used. It is argued that because culturally specific talk takes place in the child's home language, it is useful to look at children's interaction in bilingual home language – English medium. Children's cultural experiences need to be looked at in informal settings as there are opportunities for children to use their naturally occurring language and work collaboratively to meet the challenges presented to them.

Cummins' (2009) more recent work on using learners' home language for bilingual literacy development can be shown as an example. He demonstrates how allowing children to articulate their linguistic and cultural experiences through their first language results in highly motivated individuals and high quality work in English. As Cummins talks about Tomer's – new arrival from Israel – 'Identity text', *Tom Goes to Kentucky*, he provides useful insights into his feelings about using

Hebrew in the classroom. 'The first time I couldn't understand what she [Lisa – his teacher] was saying except the word Hebrew, but I think it's very smart that she said for us to do it in our language because we can't just sit on our hands doing nothing.' Cummins goes on to talk about how allowing Tomer to express his emotions in Hebrew enhances his thinking and subsequent written work in English. Similarly, Cummins shares the experiences of Madiha, Kanta, Baswa and Sulmana, four children who have recently arrived from Pakistan. They provide a touching account of their departure from their country, talking about how hard it was for them to leave Pakistan and adjust to a new way of life in Canada. The children produced an impressive account of their experiences in Urdu and English.

Earlier on in the chapter we mentioned social, cultural and cognitive benefits of bilingualism. Let us explore these further in relation to early years contexts.

One of the important aspects of promoting multiculturalism in early years is its creation of a cohesive learning environment and helping young children to understand about 'each other'. This helps children to start to move away from their own egocentric world, beginning to see the values and the cultures of others as different but equally enriching as their own. Here the values of the mainstream English society are promoted equally as all the others: focusing on 'English' cultural and linguistic values as other communities. One of the most visible aspects of the EYC in our study was its promotion of children's culture and languages as 'something to be clever about'. Children as young as two and a half were openly talking about their own languages as well as that of their friends in the Centre. Different scripts colourfully displayed around the Centre were readily identified and associated with particular children by their friends. Everyone proudly talked about their own families, their languages and customs at home in their own books titled '. . .'s book' preceded by their name. 'Here it says Aysha can speak Turkish' Aysha proudly informed us. English was also promoted alongside other languages as an equally useful language to learn. Furthermore, it was accepted by all as the language everyone was going to learn before starting the other school. The explicit message given was that all languages were equal and part of who children were, part of their developing identities.

Exploring the role of the home language in second language acquisition: Some psychological considerations

It would be a wrong assumption to make if we were to claim that schools are discouraging young children to value and develop their home languages in the early years contexts; however, it may be fair to say that not all of them are actively involved in promoting them alongside English. One of the reasons for this is the commonly held belief among some policy makers, senior managers and practitioners that children starting school need to learn English as fast as they could in order to catch up with their peers. For this reason, any attempt to explore and develop their home cultures and languages will be detrimental to this. We have already explored the benefits of maintaining young children's home languages and cultures in earlier chapters. What we will explore in this part of the chapter is the impact on young learners' emotional development of not supporting the natural development of the home languages.

We mentioned in earlier chapters that despite successive government claims young linguistic minority children start school with having been exposed mainly to their home languages. This would not imply that these children are conceptually inactive because of their lack of English, but they have already developed concepts as the result of their home experiences. It is useful to bear in mind that conceptual development occurs in relation to children's particular cultural experiences and such experiences are embedded in children's home languages. If we accept the findings of research on second language acquisition that the second language does not develop independently but *in relation* to the first language, we would expect the facilitation of the use of the first language by adults working in early years settings. The important question is how this to be done. There is a big debate around this area.

The first of such debates defends a view that this can only be done effectively if the language of the child is spoken by the adult working with the child/ren concerned. Having a bilingual member of staff working with targeted children is an excellent strategy; however, we do not live in an ideal world and although the number of bilingual adults working in early years settings is increasing, the present day early years settings are linguistically enriched environments where up to 10–15 languages can be represented by children attending them. Our project Centre had 22 languages represented by its intake including English.

Another view on this looks at the role of professional adults working in early years settings as *instigators* of language use. The main thrust of this argument is its claim that one does not need to have the knowledge of a particular language in order to facilitate its use. This requires further attention as this was the positive practice we saw taking place at the EYC. Positive language use was actively encouraged by monolingual English speaking staff. For example, we frequently saw staff uttering odd words in children's home languages which seemed meaningful and acted as a good starting point for interactions.

Children were happy not only talking about their own languages but the languages of others including some adults around them. Morning greetings in different languages were a familiar sight. Children responded positively to this. Staff frequently chose a particular word that fitted the social reality of the learning context. For instance, when TI was talking to Selma about her book, the word *torta* (cake) was mentioned by Selma. Andrew, a member of staff who happened to be passing by joined the discussion briefly by saying 'torta – I know that word, it means cake. I also know it in Arabic but I will tell you later.' From his response we were not sure whether Andrew actually knew the Arabic equivalent of *torta* but it was his contextualization of the learning environment that is worthy of a mention here. Selma was tuned in to what seemed to be a worthwhile learning experience that had herself at the centre of it. Children were frequently allowed to develop their imagination by exploring their previous experiences further. A 'reflection tent' is where children could see their own reflections in the mirror and pretend to be anything they wanted to be. It was here that we found children's creativity in language use at its best. Children role-played and experimented with different language varieties quite happily as shown by the following example by Selma pretending to be one of the adults in the household informing the other adult that she was 'going to a meeting'.

Johnson and Newport (1989) point out that between the ages of 2 and 5 language learning is effortless with young children. They also call this the 'critical period'. We explored this in the earlier chapters and talked about the process of laterization in the child's brain where the left hemisphere becomes adapted to support language processing. The view here is that provided young children are exposed to appropriately stimulating linguistic environment they are more than able to master two or more languages. There is no reason to suggest – as claimed by those opposing bilingualism – that using languages is confusing to children. In fact, we could argue that if the child's home language is ignored when they begin the nursery only to be picked up later on their primary years for the sake of recovery, the opposite occurs: the child finds it difficult and confusing to accommodate the home language. This is called *subtractive bilingualism* where the dominance of the majority language may result in the loss of or very little use of the home language (Baker, 1993). However, the so-called the critical theory has been discredited by Birdsong and Molis (2001) who argued that age still remains an important factor after puberty and learners can still become native like after this period. They also found that different first languages influenced the learning of the second language.

We have briefly looked at the physiological aspects of the young bilingual brain that favours maintaining and learning of new languages. Let us now explore the psychological aspects of a young brain that enters the nursery with the home language different to that of the nursery.

As part of the induction programme, we organize language learning sessions for our students on our teacher training course at the university. As a starter activity, we deliver lessons in different languages which are unfamiliar to students and are delivered by specialist teachers in that language. At the end of a 40-minute session, students are asked how they felt about the experience. Some of the responses we get from them are: 'Anxious, bored, frustrated, fed up, desperate'.

Students are also asked about their feelings when the teacher or someone else accidentally used English during the session. Their responses were often summarized with one word: 'relief'.

If this is the reaction of grown-up mature student with teachers then we can imagine how young bilingual children feel when they first start the nursery. As adults it may make perfect sense to rationalize the need to learn English in order to pass exams and be successful in the education system. However, to a young bilingual learner starting an early years setting having been exposed mainly to another language can be quite traumatic. Of course, we are not suggesting that adults working in early years settings actively discourage young children from speaking their home languages. We know that we have come a long way in preparing our teachers for working in early years settings. However, walking into a new learning environment can be challenging enough for any young child, starting a predominantly English speaking setting can be pretty daunting if not catastrophic for a young bilingual learner. It creates a negative self-concept – what's wrong with my language? Our colleagues working in early years settings may recall a period of silence when a child does not speak for several days even weeks. The reasons for this may be complex, however, we should not rule out the anxiety factor as one of the causes for this. Adults need be actively encouraging children to think and use their home languages in relation to all purposeful talk which takes place in English. Failure to do so will give out wrong signals to an already worried young bilingual mind, leading to further anxiety and more serious consequences.

Summary

In this chapter, we explored the debate surrounding bilingualism and arguments for and against it. We discussed the benefits of bilingualism particularly the role of the first language in second language acquisition and bilingual development. In the final part of this chapter, we concluded the debate on ethnic minority education by exploring the physiological and psychological aspects of a young bilingual mind and shared some examples of good practice from the EYC.

Reflective activity

1. Which collaborative activities do you use in your early years settings?
2. Can you comment on their effectiveness?
3. Have you had a young bilingual child going through a period of silence in your early years setting? Were you able to find out the reasons for this?
4. Do you have children who started your early years setting with mainly speaking the home language? If so what strategies do you use to utilize this to support their development in English.

The Role of Home Languages in Supporting the Development of Purposeful Talk in Early Years Settings

In the previous chapter, we looked at the key issues and debates in the area of multilingualism. We also explored some research findings that supported the role of the home language in developing children's bilingualism in schools. In this chapter, we will discuss the role of the first language in bilingual development further by focusing on the maintenance of children's home languages in early years settings. We support our ideas with examples from the project schools, that is, the EYC and two receiving primary schools.

First we start by looking at the development of the then called 'mother tongue' debate by providing a short historical account on Europe and North America. We follow this by exploring the developments in the United Kingdom and conclude the chapter by discussing the role of the home language in supporting young children's verbal interaction.

The mother tongue debate: Research from Europe and North America

Europe

We have mentioned the EEC Directives and other initiatives in previous chapters. We begin by exploring the so-called mother tongue debate in Europe and discuss how such developments affected some of the bilingual programmes in North America (mainly the United States and Canada) before turning to the United Kingdom once again.

The expanding Western European economy during the 1950s and 1960s needed a work force from underdeveloped countries. These were mainly young men who left their families behind with the intention of making enough money to eventually return. As these intentions did not materialize, the workers were joined by their families. Similar to the pattern we have seen taking place in Britain, the first immigrant children began to appear in European schools from the early 1960s. Initial programmes were assimilationist and involved teaching the language of the host country as a second language. There was a similar pattern of provision throughout Europe through separate provision for immigrants. Equality of access to schooling for EEC member states has been a legal right for children of citizens of other member states since the Council of Europe Education Sub-Committee was formed in 1966. The Education Sub-committee supported migrant workers' children in the school system and the maintenance of their cultural and linguistic links with their countries of origin (ECC Directive, 1977).

By 1975, some countries, for example, Sweden and Finland, began to see the importance of the immigrants' mother tongues as their right in maintaining their identity. The Swedish Parliament gave ethnic minorities the right to study their mother tongue (Issa, 1987). The EEC Directive was interpreted differently in many countries. Some responded through direct intervention by central governments, where there was a positive influence on local government bodies, and there was little effect on others. Germany was an example of a state where discrepancies could be seen in the practices of different *Lander*. Some countries used the mother tongue clause to try to facilitate the return of minorities to their countries of origin. The positive outcomes of bilingual programmes were seen first in countries where there had been positive initial responses to the recommendations of the EEC. Germany and Holland did this during the mid-1980s (Issa, 1987). In more recent immersion programmes children were instructed in the language of the host country during an initial part of the project and this was then balanced by the use of the mother tongue at later stages. In Belgium, there were bicultural programmes in the Dutch Language school (Leman, 1993), in Denmark there were programmes on the German minority children (Byram, 1993) and the European School model in Brussels (Beardsmore, 1993). All of these programmes reinforced the validity of bilingual education as alternative models to be considered for minority children.

Research from North America

Research evidence from the United States and Canada significantly contributed to the field of bilingual education in Europe. But although there were many individual research findings from the 1960s onwards, they did very little in changing the State or Federal policies (see published papers on the International Symposium on Bilingualism, 1997). The response of the US Federal government to such developments was dramatic: the advocates of bilingualism were seen as part of a conspiracy to create a separate Hispanic State within the United States. Regular attacks against bilingual education in the media made an impact on public opinion and government legislators (Cummins, 1996). A study by Collier and Thomas (1997) strengthened the argument for the maintenance of the first language and actively showed the contribution of the first language to academic achievement.

The French Immersion programmes in Canada began operating during the 1960s. These were all different types of programmes but each has been successful in strengthening evidence for the role of bilingual programmes in enhancing academic achievement (Lambert and Tucker, 1972; Swain and Lapkin, 1991; Cummins, 1989; 1996). Although smaller in number, there were also studies which challenged the validity of some of the claims made by such studies (Schlesinger, 1991).

The developments in the United Kingdom

Despite the evidence from this growing research from Europe and North America, the UK government's position on the education of the minorities remained largely unchanged and similar to those previous periods. In previous chapters, we talked at 'some length about the numbers of children with EAL showing a steady increase each year across England. We argued that the Bullock Report (1975) generated some positive discussion on the role of mother tongue and bilingualism. We also mentioned that it was left to the individual LEAs to put forward programmes of mother tongue teaching and endorse bilingual education initiatives. Some LEAs employed bilingual teaching staff to work within mainstream schools and alongside classroom teachers. The ILEA and Birmingham were such progressive authorities. But as these LEAs were not getting extra funding for this, their resources were insufficient to address all the needs of the bilingual communities they were serving. Many communities decided they had to run and finance their own supplementary schools, the earliest of which went as far back as 1930s serving the Chinese community (Ng Kwee Cho, 1968). Despite such restrictions many positive initiatives were implemented by such authorities. The ILEA is worth of our mention in this respect.

ILEAs multicultural policies were largely engrained in progressive practice. It had established highly experienced advisory teams that had firsthand experiences of multicultural teaching in schools. Bilingual Under Fives (BUF) team was made up of practitioners who were fully engaged with early years practice and produced materials that supported inclusive approaches in early years settings. The team was instrumental in changing some of the old and ineffective practices. For example, the team argued that withdrawal of young children from the nursery environment for specialist language support created resentment and divisions among children and this practice was soon abandoned by most nurseries. The team's emphasis on doing and talking through active encouragement of children's bilingualism provided a firm basis for planning in early years settings. The team also produced numerous materials in dual language such as videocassette programmes and story books.

One such programme titled *Early Days at School* looked at four children in different stages in their growth as bilinguals. One of the strengths of the BUF team was working alongside practitioners, offering support as they developed their own practice. Equally there was effective work carried out by ILEA primary advisory teams. *The Primary Language Record* produced in 1985 was compiled by the steering group made up of teachers, headteachers and inspectors. Their task was to devise a more effective system for recording children's language development in primary schools. Series of working parties drafted and redrafted the proposals finally producing a version that was comprehensive and workable in meeting the needs of children from diverse backgrounds. Children's language development was seen from a holistic perspective with equal emphasis given to their first *and* second language development. Such initiatives were so successful that other institutions began to follow ILEAs work. BBC's *Mother Tongue Song and Story* published in 1989 was broadcasted regularly on Radio 4. In addition, there were numerous studies – some written by ILEA inspectors and advisors – that provided a theoretical and practical rationale for supporting multilingualism in schools (Wright, 1982; Hester, 1984; Wiles, 1985).

We have already discussed in the previous chapter that the Labour government's changed interest in the mother tongue debate came with the ECC Directive in 1977. The Directive was the outcome of the work carried out by the Council of Europe formed primarily for the unity of the EEC. As the numbers of migrant workers' children began to appear in European schools it became concerned with the educational needs of their children and subsequently established a subcommittee on the education of migrant workers in 1966. Between 1966 and 1980 it had passed a number of resolutions and a project which ran for five years (Wittek, 1992). These resolutions and activities enabled the EEC to issue a Directive and this was eventually adopted in 1977.

There were some central government-backed projects as well. The Bedford Mother Tongue Project (1978–81) was to assess the first language use of Punjabi and Italian and was funded by the DES. The Bedfordshire Project was funded by the European Community and ran for four years (1976–80). Both projects were based on regarding the contribution of the mother tongue as positive rather than a hindrance to the second language learning.

As we mentioned in Chapter 4, the projects helped to create genuine multicultural approaches in some schools. There was backing from some LEAs, which appointed advisors and inspectors for multicultural education to oversee policy developments and to develop practice in their schools (Blakeny, 1981; Matthews, 1981). A few had developed policy documents (e.g. ILEA, 1981). Genuine enthusiasm and individual efforts by teachers helped create examples of good classroom practice. The need for a whole school transformation of the curriculum required a lot of work and needed expert backing and financial support. Nevertheless, there remained a large group of professionals who still believed that success for minority children depended upon their exposure to English. There were also some regions where the issue of minority education was debated because of a small proportion of minority children in their schools.

Having looked at some projects related to the home language maintenance, we now discuss its role in the development of thinking and learning in young children.

Hearing children's voices: Exploring the potential of home language use in children's talk

There are various ways in which children's potential as talkers and learners can be utilized effectively in early years contexts. One of the strategies we are going to consider in developing young children's purposeful talk is setting up of productive environments for collaborative learning. Crook (2000) describes collaborative learning as a process where children are provided with opportunities to explore the dynamics of a given task by discussing, questioning and learning from each other. He talks about the role of adults in facilitating a medium of productive interaction. Let us explore this further by considering various factors that affect children's understanding as they interact and mediate with their partners during tasks. In talking and learning together one of the first things that practitioners need to consider in planning for collaborative interaction is the selection of the 'topic of interaction'. Children will respond to a topic of discussion which enables them to draw upon their existing experiences from their home and community. For bilingual children, it is reflective of their cultural practices which often develop in a medium other than English. What this implies is that the process of conceptual development occurs in the home language and this forms the basis of children's thinking. As children are asked to verbalize various aspects of a 'thinking task', they first 'activate' their existing cognitive systems which are often reflected in egocentric speech before being shared with others. Young bilingual learners develop and activate their cognitive systems in similar ways except the medium through which this is activated may differ depending on who they are communicating with. In the home environment, this often occurs in the child's home language. In the nursery environment, the process is more complex.

From the first day of having arrived at the nursery, young bilingual learners become aware of the existence of a different medium of interaction than their own, that is, English. When children are given opportunities to play and think about various activities, their cognitive systems activate their linguistic device/s and the egocentric speech that follows is usually in the child's home language which lends itself as a more natural and 'automatic' process as shown in Table 7.1.

As shown in Table 7.1 (with the activity, *learning of fruit names in English*) the adult tries to activate the learner's cognitive systems by appealing to her existing vocabulary in the home language. It is useful to remember that the adult does not know what is already 'planted and growing' in the child's cognitive 'garden' as she does not know the child's

Table 7.1 The processes of smybolic activation in adult–child interaction (Issa, 2012)

Proactivator (adult)	Reactivator (child)
(Shows and tells) *apple*	(Sees and symbolically activates in Turkish) *elma*
(Shows and tells) *banana*	(Sees and symbolically activates in Turkish) *muz*
(Shows/tells/models)	(Unsure – tries to contextualize by visual and auditory cues)
I like apple	Ben (I) elma . . . **like**???
I don't like banana	Ben (I) banana . . . **don't like**??
(Shows/models/tells)	(Visual and auditory cues strengthens symbolic conceptualization)
I like *apple* (not the banana)	Ben (I) like?? . . . elma don't like *muz*?
(Shows/models/asks)	(Symbolic conceptualization achieved.
Do you like apple or banana?	Corresponding vocabulary in Turkish activated)
	Like *elma* . . . **like** *muz*
	Like . . . like . . . like . . .
	Ahhh . . . like . . . sevmek . . .

language. By making it visually supportive and using repetitive language, the adult activates the child's linguistic systems through scaffolding the available information as shown below:

In the reality of an English speaking nursery, children catch on pretty fast to the existence of a different communication system than their own that is, English and may subconsciously become reluctant to allow their existing systems to work naturally. There are contextual (and practical) factors that play a part in this:

- Children often think that they will not be understood if they spoke in their home language and this will lead to confusion.
- Sometimes there is an element of anxiety that if they speak in their home languages they will be made fun of by other children.
- There may be a possibility that they would have heard one of the adults trying to instil 'the rule of speaking English only' at the nursery.

One of the likely consequences of the scenario we have described above is that young bilingual learners become accustomed to use the only available *verbal communication channel* open to them: English. If we remember the limited linguistic resources available to young bilingual learners in English, we can then begin to understand the anxieties faced by some of these children as they begin to grapple with the demands of the routine activities of the nursery. Of course, we are not suggesting that the monolingual conditioning of bilingual learners would result in catastrophic consequences with no learning taking place; however, focused learning strategies need to be implemented in order to maximize bilingual children's language and learning experiences.

The role of the adults is crucial in this respect. We have mentioned in the earlier chapters that supporting children's home languages needs to be *facilitative* in nature and can be implemented successfully without the extensive knowledge of children's languages. We would like to share with the reader, the multilingual training programme we have been involved in for our Post Graduate Certificate in Education (PGCE) early years students at London Metropolitan University.

The aim of the programme was to raise awareness of trainee teachers' own linguistic and cultural skills, knowledge and experiences that could be drawn on for their teaching. We also wanted to raise student's awareness of languages and multilingualism as future early years teachers to utilize, in their teaching across the curriculum, a range of children's linguistic, cultural knowledge and experiences. Although the university is highly diverse linguistically, the majority of our students enter the PGCE programme feeling fairly insecure about tackling language and diversity issues in their settings. Many are monolingual English speaking. The challenge we faced in the programme was how to raise student expectations about their own abilities as language teachers in inclusive early years settings. Overall, we taught four sessions for each group. In these sessions we covered the following areas:

- range of adult roles: in reacting situations for facilitating children's use of their home languages
- theoretical perspectives on language and literacy acquisition: language, culture and identity in a multilingual context
- planning for language learning across the curriculum using a thematic approach.

At the end of the programme we asked students to fill in an evaluative survey followed by focus group discussions. We were interested in finding out the impact the programme had on their perception of their roles as language teachers and facilitators. The survey revealed positive outcomes relating to students' own learning. They felt that the session had positive impact on their thinking in the following ways:

- positive attitudes to language teaching in early years contexts
- clear shift in perceptions of their roles and responsibilities as language practitioners in early years contexts
- aware of living in a multilingual world and having a natural approach to language learning
- topic-based approach – contextualizing the language in a topic helps language learning
- positive about being early years practitioner and supporting specialist teacher
- links to language awareness, multilingual approaches.

Students' evaluations from their school practice showed that overall they felt more confident about their roles as facilitators in utilizing children's linguistic cultural experiences which they mentioned as crucial in supporting their identity development.

Our findings from the project schools echo the feelings of some of our students' experiences on the programme mentioned above. As seen in the examples taken from our project schools, speaking a few words often acted as a catalyst in securing 'one-to-one' rather personalized interaction between the adults and the children. The headteacher and most of the adults we spoke to at the EYC were quite aware of the importance of their role as facilitators:

Headteacher:	Getting children to speak their languages is not really that easy as children are often quite shy about using their home languages when they arrive at the nursery.
TI:	How do you instil this confidence in them? What happens after this initial period of shyness?
Headteacher:	This is to do with our ethos as an early years centre I feel.
	We put in a lot of effort to show our multilingual/multicultural ethos to children as well as to the parents. This is done through policy of active engagement of everyone involved. (Field notes, TI: 27 March 2008)

What the headteacher is saying was clearly visible throughout the Centre. In addition to a welcoming, friendly and calm atmosphere, language awareness featured highly on the Centre's agenda. Displays featured signs and captions in different languages. The welcome sign in different languages at the Centre entrance contributed to the whole ethos of the Centre as did photos of some of the families with captions describing the use of home languages. There was a notice board giving information about various Centre activities available for parents and children during each week, for example, parents and toddlers singing sessions. Children were constantly building on previous experiences relating to themselves as well as others in their environment as demonstrated in the following example:

During an arranged visit to Selma's home we noticed that three languages were actively used there. As her mother informed us, Selma's parents made a decision to speak to her in their first languages to develop her language skills and as they put it 'to ensure the maintenance of our linguistic and cultural identity'. Selma regularly visited her grandparents in Egypt and Italy. It was to be Arabic to dad (his first language) and Italian with mummy. Selma seemed to be quite happy with practising this rule. In turn it was decided that 'the language of the home' was English. As Selma's mum commented:

Mrs Kouneri: Our decision to use all three languages interchangeably proved to be challenging to start with but once my husband and I decided to stick to the rules and insist upon the use of our own languages with Selma it eventually paid off. When she spoke to us in English we simply answered back in our own languages. After a while Selma started to follow the rule. Now we seem to be doing ok.

TI: How do you solve the issue of which story/which language/how often?

Mrs Kouneri: Well. We alternate between Italian and Arabic each night but English *on* every night.

It was a moving moment when we observed Selma reading her Italian book when she came over to her mum to ask the meaning of an Italian word in English, clearly using the vocabulary bank of her stronger language (i.e. Italian) to learn new vocabulary in her developing language (i.e. English).

Parents we have visited at home have commented how their children's language awareness was reinforced by the centre's positive attitude towards languages. The role of the staff was particularly significant in this respect: Heidi, talking to us about her daughter Helen who is one of the children with special educational needs told us the positive attitude of the centre staff to languages during our home visits.

> **B:** Yes they try so hard as well to learn like different language, like M. M's French is so bad but he tried so hard to speak French with all the children. When he learned the children there speak French he try as well. All the staff like 'bonjour Helen', everyone is trying to speak, they're really involved and respect. They see someone doesn't understand they put everything together to empower us and to be inclusive.

Belinda went on to explain how the centre used her expertise as a French speaker, enabling her to have a closer link with the centre:

> sometime they need somebody to translate. Like one time I was there they asked me to translate for one mum and it makes me really happy as well. They try everything. It's a really, really good nursery. Because sometime you send a child to school, people there they're not really open, even if the law says that the child needs to be in this school but you need to be open as well to say that ok this child need to learn maybe English and give them time. . . . sometimes it doesn't happen in all the schools I know that I recommend (the nursery) to all parents . . . if they've just arrived to England. . . . I don't know what to say but they are really, really open.

The Ramos family we have visited commented on how much their son Petro has benefited from being at the nursery as it highlighted children's different backgrounds and talked about them in a positive way. For their son Petro, the nursery was a 'happy environment' where all children felt welcome. They commented that as parents they were welcome to stay with their children as long as they liked and the free flow approach helped children to pick up English; the setting up of different things, such as the home corner becoming a hairdresser's, gave vocabulary to the children. Much was learned through play, especially for children whose first language was not English. Petro's mum Mary mentioned the importance of music and songs, noting how Martin the EMA teacher taught the children a Bangladeshi song and how he used Spanish and how French was being taught to the children (by one of the parents). Petro was very attached to Matthew because of his use of Spanish and, probably, because he is male. Mary also commented on Martin's ability to speak some words in many of the nursery's languages. She also referred to a teacher who also spoke Spanish and a teaching assistant, now on maternity leave, who spoke Italian. The nursery helped children to count in different languages and encouraged parents to use their home language with their children. All of these according to the Ramos family were 'good ingredients for a healthy (language) learning environment'. (Notes: 12 November 2008).

The attitude to languages in the receiving schools

We managed to obtain permission from two of the receiving primary schools where some of the children went after finishing the nursery. Both shared similar characteristics as ethnically and linguistically diverse schools and had obtained excellent reports from OFSTED.

Otter primary school

The school catered for 295 children between the ages of 3–11. The second school, Palace Manor also catered for 224 children from the same age range.

Otter was a large school situated in a culturally, socially and ethnically very mixed community. Some areas had very high levels of social deprivation. Close to a half of all pupils received free school meals. Most pupils came from black African heritages. The next largest groups included those from white British, Bangladeshi and black British Caribbean backgrounds. A high proportion of pupils spoke English as an additional language. Over 35 different languages were spoken in the school. A high proportion of pupils had learning difficulties. These were largely linked to moderate learning difficulty and problems with social skills, behaviour and speech and communication difficulty. The proportion of pupils who joined and left the school at unusual times throughout the school year was very high. The school had gained the Arts Mark Gold and the London School Environment Award at the gold status level. OFSTED report described the school as: 'An outstanding school where pupils' achievement is excellent. Pupils are thoroughly prepared for their future lives. Pupils benefit from a very rounded and enjoyable education.'

On the staff it reported: 'All staff work hard to help pupils to enrich their language and ability to communicate with others. The rigorous drive to improve pupils' understanding of letters and sounds is quickly helping them to read and write.'

Children's attitudes to languages

As expected we found that children's attitudes to languages continued to be positive; however, it was disappointing for us to see that in Otter the children's experiences were not made visible in the classroom. The children we were following from the EYC already had particularly broad competence in a variety of languages. At the EYC, children's cultural and linguistic experiences were prominently displayed throughout the building and these constituted a large part of the activities planned for the children. During the course of our school visits to the school, we failed to see any resources or displays that reflected children's linguistic and cultural backgrounds. In the case of Selma who could speak Arabic, Italian and English and was very conscious of her skills, (as we found at the EYC) no opportunities appeared to be provided for her to share and celebrate her skills. This was also the case for Emilie who could speak German, French and English. Although French was being introduced in the school as an additional or modern foreign language, no account appeared to be taken of French and the many other community languages represented in the classroom.

It was interesting to note that Selma who was very confident and articulate at EYC was described as having 'a processing delay' and 'a bit anxious' by the class teacher.

During one of the activities the children were decorating a drawing of a fish. TI asked Emilie what she liked doing at this class. Selma joins in the conversation.

> **E:**   I like drawing and reading, she replied.
> **TI:**   Do you read French books here?
> **E:**   No, Mummy reads them to me at home.
> **S:**   My mum reads to me in Italian. My dad speaks and reads to me in Arabic.

Parents' attitudes to multilingualism

During one visit we managed to speak with Emilie's parent who was the French teacher at the Otter school. She commented on how little language work was being carried out at the school. She said that despite this she was confident that Emilie would still continue to extend her linguistic experiences at home. We noticed that when we visited Emilie's home this was indeed the case. For example, we noticed a large collection of story books in German, French and English. Mrs Kinsky used all three languages interchangeably with Emilie who responded accordingly. What was interesting was that there was no acknowledgement to the richness of her linguistic experiences at the school.

Palace Manor primary school

Palace Manor is an average sized primary school, serving a diverse community. The proportion of pupils entitled to free school meals is well above the national average. The majority of pupils are black African and Caribbean origin, and the remainder are mostly white British or of Asian minority ethnic heritage. There are more girls on roll than boys. Children are admitted to the Nursery class in the EYFS from 3 years of age, and move to the Reception class in the autumn term of the school year in which they are 5 years of age. A high proportion of pupils have learning difficulties and/or disabilities, including moderate or severe learning needs and autism. Well above average numbers of pupils speak English as an additional language. The proportion of pupils moving in and out of school other than at the normal time of admission is high. Extended services are provided on the same site, including a Saturday school and family learning programmes. Also, there is after school care managed by a private provider.

OFSTED findings

The 2009 OFSTED Report states that Palace Manor is:

> An outstanding primary school. It provides a caring and loving environment for each pupil, seeking to ensure they are happy members of the school family, who enjoy learning and leave school with the knowledge, skills and attitudes relevant to the changing world in which they live.

> From very low starting points in the Nursery, pupils make excellent progress and attain average standards by Year 6.

> There is an excellent focus on developing skills of communication and language, as many children speak English as an additional language. Staff have high expectations of their progress. They provide practical examples by role-modelling answers for children in the Nursery, but

children are encouraged to speak in sentences by the end of the Reception Year. Overall achievement is outstanding. By the end of the Early Years Foundation Stage, many children reach expected goals in their personal and physical development, and all are close to national expectations for their age in other areas of learning. Leadership of the key stage is excellent.

Pupils' spiritual, moral, social and cultural development is outstanding. They show very good respect for different cultures and beliefs.

Under the Effectiveness of Early Years Foundation stage all categories were assessed as outstanding. (OFSTED, 2009)

Children's attitudes to languages

Although there was an emphasis on play and discovery learning there appeared to be little overt recognition of children's linguistic and cultural experiences. As we saw with Otter primary school, the teacher appeared to be under some pressure to concentrate on the Literacy component of the CLL area of learning to the detriment of the areas. Due to this there were very few opportunities to collect relevant data from the children.

Parents' attitudes to multilingualism

Parents of the children who transferred to Palace Manor school were not available to take part in the project. Although we believe they were as supportive of home languages as our research group, it was not possible to collect data to confirm this.

Summary

We started this chapter by exploring the so-called mother tongue debate with research from Europe and North America before turning to the United Kingdom. We then developed the discussion on the home language use in early years settings by discussing the importance of setting up careful planned activities for encouraging children's development of purposeful talk. We mentioned two useful points to be considered by practitioners:

1. The development of oral skills is a social activity: collaborative learning need to be planned where young bilingual learners can interact with monolingual children as well as with other bilinguals.
2. The development of oral skills in English need to be explored in relation to young bilingual learners' home language which may be in more developed 'stage' due to the child's home experiences. For this reason adults need to facilitate the use of children's home languages in order for them to meaningfully contextualize the use of English.

We went on to discuss the educational justifications by describing the process of activation of children's home language experiences to overcome the initial anxiety of being in an English speaking environment. We argued that although speaking the child's home language is a great advantage, the adult could help the learner activate her home language systems through the process of facilitation. We showed how monolingual English speaking teachers can do this effectively through the examples from the EYC. We argued that sadly an inclusive ethos of the nursery environment somehow was not maintained in the two receiving schools.

Reflective activity

1. In your own settings, what strategies do you have in place for the development of young learners' oracy skills in their home language?
2. What systems do you have in place for facilitating the use of home languages in your settings?
3. Are there any activities you do which promote the language awareness in your settings?
4. Have you or any other staff in your setting received any additional training on inclusive practices in your nursery environment?

Supporting Children's Language Development: The Role of Parents, Carers and Other Adults

8

Mā mātau e raranga te wā matauranga.
Together – let us weave the threads of knowledge. (Maori proverb)

In the previous chapter, we explored the role of the home language in bilingual development and discussed its use for supporting purposeful talk with examples from the EYC. In this chapter we shift our focus from children's development in early years contexts to their home environment; not least because it is to be regarded as separate from children's overall development mentioned in the previous chapter but because it is an integral part of it. We present parents' views on the ways in which good early years practice can foster children's personal, social, emotional, linguistic and cultural development. We draw particular attention to parents' views that home languages should be recognized and supported in early years settings. We also explore the professional relationships that can be promoted between adults concerned in young children's overall development.

First we begin by giving a brief account on policy initiatives and debates around parental involvement.

Rumbold and other policy initiatives

Looking back at relevant policy initiatives and publications on parental involvement, successive government perspectives have mostly focused on a deficit model of parenting, with a mission of 'educating' parents to 'fulfil' their roles in bringing up their children to 'succeed' in the schools' system. Early years education is presented as a crucial step in achieving this. One of the earliest reports that mention parental involvement in early years settings appeared in the 1933 Hadow Report. It notes that effective cooperation between parents, teachers, doctors and school nurses has resulted in 'a marked improvement alike in the health and cleanliness of the children' (Hadow, 1933, p. 176). The report urges that such cooperation should continue. Parental roles were very much seen in the context of maintaining healthy youngsters. Despite this Hadow was surprisingly progressive for its time with its emphasis on 'a community of old and young, engaged in learning by cooperative experiment' (Hadow, 1931, p. xvii). The subsequent reports were more geared to shape the organizations of schools than any radical programmes for facilitating parental involvement. Consequently the 1938 Spens Report became primarily concerned with tackling the inequalities in accessing secondary education (the percentage of primary school children attending the secondary schools was mere 10%). The report recommended three types of schooling to tackle the issue: Grammar schools, technical schools and secondary modern schools. The 1943 Norwood Report followed on from Spens by supporting a provision that perceived children as having 'three types of mind' and therefore advocating an educational system that supported organization of schools along these lines. The coming of the Second World War did not stop the publishing of two further reports. McNair and Fleming reports both published in 1944, were more concerned with teacher education (McNair) and the public schools and the general education system (Fleming). The Plowden Report (1967) echoed most of the principles of Hadow highlighting the social deprivation model of education urging the authorities to compensate for the disadvantages caused by such deprivation. In fact it is in this report where we see the role of parental involvement highlighted as an important factor affecting educational achievement. Closer co-operation between schools and parents were called for. The parental participation has continued to be stressed as important to educational success in subsequent reports during the 1970s and 1980s. However, it is with the publication of the Rumbold Report in 1990 that we begin to see a call for an active participation of the parents in their children's education. Governments' planned intervention to offer guidance to parents to take an active role in the education of their children took off with this report. Here with the 'compelling need to address the issue of quantity the committee urge those who make provision to recognize: "The extent to which demand outstrips supply, and to secure a continuing expansion of high quality services to meet children's, and their parents', needs"' (1990, p. 1).

In fact a significant number of reports commissioned by the government after its publication echoed the findings of the Rumbold Report. One such study commissioned by then DfES has set out to explore possible relationships between parental involvement, parental support and family education on pupil achievement and adjustment in schools. One of the report's significant findings focused on 'good parents at home' and its positive effect on children's achievement and adjustment shaping attainment (Desforges and Abouchaar, 2003). Others point at particular social and economic factors in evaluating parental involvement in schools. One such report commissioned by Local Government Improvement and Development Agency draws our attention to lack of home resources, low levels of literacy among parents of children from working-class backgrounds and ethnic minority communities, high levels of separation and high levels of movements around the country.

The Labour government's agenda since the early 2000s was to drive the *Sure Start* programme, and place more emphasis on parental involvement which was one of the main items on the agenda at the National conference organized by the Preschool Learning Alliance in 2003, the largest voluntary sector provider for early years education. At the conference, Charles Clarke, the then Secretary of State for Education and Skills, set out to explain why the government's commitment to early education, childcare and family support was essential to ensure all children got a sure start in life: 'Parental involvement is at the heart of our work to support families. As well as encouraging parents to become more involved in their children's learning and development, Sure Start brings together a wealth of family support structures' (DCSF, 2008).

As successive governments preached for a particular model of parenting at home, their support for professional organizations continued and was seen as more 'in tune' with the needs of parents and the community. Parents, Early Years and Learning (PEAL) originated as the consortium project of the National Children's Bureau (NCB), Coram Family and London borough of Camden. Their work focused on training which supports all early years settings to meet requirements of the EYFS and Children's Centre Practice Guidance to work in partnership with parents to enhance children's learning and development. Supporting government initiatives was a number of researches carried out by organizations on support for early years education and parental involvement. Research published by British Market Research Bureau (BMRB) took place in May 2003 screening a total sample of 1996 interviews with adults aged 16+ living in Great Britain. It showed that 90 per cent of parents polled wanted more involvement in their children's early years education. This follows earlier research by BMRB in May 2002, which showed that 86 per cent of parents believed that encouraging parental involvement in early years education and care can help to prevent anti-social behaviour such as drug taking and crime in later years.

More recently a comprehensive government review into the early years provision (EYFS, The *Tickell* Review, 2011) although recognizing 'parents influence on children's learning' (p. 6) and the importance of partnership between parents and EYCs, appears to preach the 'deficit model' of parenting:

> The amount of time and energy that parents and careers invest in home learning varies greatly from family to family. For example, evidence shows that parents with lower qualifications engage less frequently in some home learning activities, such as reading, than better educated parents. Another example is the number of words experienced by a child by age 3: in the average professional family a child experiences around 45 million words, compared to 13 million in the average low-income family. These

differences in children's experiences of language at home impact directly on their subsequent development. (EYFS, 2011, p. 6)

The report makes generalizations about parental occupations, socio-economic backgrounds and the time and energy spent by parents on their children's learning. A more worrying aspect is the way 'a number of words experienced' by the children is seen as an indicator of the quality of learning by the children. In talking about children's experiences of language no reference is made to homes where children are exposed to vocabulary through experiences in other languages. More importantly no reference is given to how such skills can then be utilized for vocabulary building in English.

Such limited perception of parenting and the subsequent compensatory role of EYCs to 'remedy' the situation leaves some gaps in understanding more complex issues relating to parental involvement. These initiatives lacked a clear understanding of the needs of parents as they were based on the assumption of a 'deficit model'; that the reason why the parents were not involved in the life of their children's school was because there was something lacking in their home environment. It was evident that the home circumstances of the families affected their level of involvement in the life of their children's school however this was not the main reason why some schools were unable to manage a high level of involvement among their parents particularly those from working-class and ethnic minority communities. Also it doesn't explain the differences in the rate of involvement among schools who are serving communities from similar socio-economic backgrounds. Our findings relating to the EYC in our study is an example of how this can be achieved. The difference has to do with the way some EYCs plan, develop and implement their parental involvement initiatives. Next we explore some of the thinking behind multicultural perspectives on parental involvement in early years settings. We then follow these with examples from the EYC in our project.

There is research from different parts of the world which states that there is a passive correlation between parental involvement and children's level of achievement in school. One such study from the United States found that there were positive correlations between students' level of achievement and parental involvement regardless of parental occupation and the family structure (Coddington, 2003).

Nationally driven policies of parental involvement initiatives are highly effective in New Zealand. The National Network of Partnership Schools (NNPS) is a government-backed project that offers a number of supportive models at organizational, professional levels at school districts and national levels. These involve a multitude of organizations, professional networks that assist schools with the development of their parental involvement strategies. They propose six types of parental involvement initiatives that facilitate partnerships in schools. These are parenting, communicating, volunteering, learning at home, decision making and collaboration with the community (Epstein et al., 2002).

In Europe the parental involvement initiatives have been developed as part of compensatory education programmes in the United States and United Kingdom, placing an emphasis on a more active role for the parents in the educational achievements of their children(Bakker and Denessen, 2007). From 1980s onwards similar to the situation in the United States parental roles in Europe were essentially seen as one of fund raising. The European Commission Directive (EC, 1993) on parental involvement that was adopted in 1995 mainly focus on fair leave and childcare arrangements for the parents and procedures for active involvement of parents of children from migrant families (BIS, 2009).

So far we have explored various policy initiatives on parental involvement in the United Kingdom with some references to Europe and other parts of the world. We now turn again to the United Kingdom exploring the developments of multicultural perspectives in parental involvement in education in general and early years education in particular.

Multicultural (parental) perspectives in early years settings

In our review of literature on multicultural perspectives on the involvement of parents, it was surprising to see very little relating to early years settings. Those we found were either relating to some of the earlier policies and practices of pre-Thatcher era, BUF project of ILEA or those that echoed similar views expressed by successive government rhetoric: 'equipping' and 'enlightening' parents of the benefits of multicultural approaches to the curriculum while 'educating' them against the dangers of negative depiction of ethnic minority communities (Ramsey and Derman-Sparks, 1992). Some focus on teacher–parent partnership efforts encouraging parents to gain confidence in 'modelling' and 'teaching' roles (Swick, 1993) while others relate to classroom study teams, school advisory groups and multicultural planning sessions are some avenues that assure parents' input in policy (Ramsey and Derman-Sparks, 1992). It is quite clear from the evidence we presented above that more recent studies on parental involvement on multicultural issues were mainly focusing on the monolingual English speaking parents, to equip them with dealing with the multicultural 'other'. The emphasis appears to be supporting parental understanding of cultural practices which is not the same as those practised by the mainstream culture. There is hardly any mention of the benefits of the linguistic diversity and the benefits of incorporating multilingual experiences of parents into the English speaking environment. Equally surprising is to see the absence of discussion around language, culture and multiple identities and incorporating these into coherent strategies for parental involvement. We note, rather disappointingly that the trend appears to be moving backwards rather than forward with no progress from some of the inclusiveness policy and practice initiatives of the 1980s.

Looking back at ILEA documentation to schools we see a number of guidelines on policy initiatives, anti-racist education, parental involvement and classroom practice. One such document titled *Education in a Multi-Ethnic Society* prepared by the then chief inspector for ILEA, M. Birchenough, lists a number of strategies for schools for involving parents and their communities through appropriately phrased questions:

- Does the school actively seek the views and perceptions of parents about their children?
- Are these taken into account in the school's provision for each child?
- What particular provision is made to communicate with parents whose mother tongue is not English? (1981, p. 15)

These questions have made some impact on the way schools planned and implemented their parental involvement strategies. Those that took them seriously reported positive outcomes in their work with parents.

Examples from the EYC

In this part of the chapter we turn our focus on the EYC exploring some of its strategies used for parental involvement. We also present a selection of data from the parents' meeting and our visits to children's homes.

In the small lobby area of the nursery, a large panel with pictures of children and their parents reading books in their home languages as well as English was clearly visible. 'Me and my dad are reading a Portuguese Book' said one. The other was the picture of another parent reading a story from Nigeria in Yoruba and English. Walking around the EYC one would hear something with reference to a language or a word uttered by somebody in a different language. The staff was incredibly proactive with regard to this. Almost all the staff knew a word or two in another language. These were learned either from the parents or from the children themselves. Greetings were the most commonly used among the staff.

There was a positive atmosphere in the Centre. Walking around the nursery we could see a variety of activities with clearly planned outcomes for language development – *all* the language varieties help create an 'affinity group' *a* term Mackay (2007, p. 2) uses to describe users with different styles of language brought together through a common experience of talk. His ideas that echo Gee's (1996) theory on second language learning suggests that learner discourses are the result of many social, cultural and situational expressions of experiences which make up learners' linguistic identities.

In the EYC, on one occasion we noticed more than a dozen yellow 'post-it' notes stuck on different sections of the nursery. When we looked at them more closely we saw handwritten information about individual children that each member of staff wanted to share with the rest of the team. These were either information from home or a particular development relating to a child's learning they have noticed during over the past few days. This was a collaborative team effort that produced excellent staff results for this team.

In another part of the Centre there was a parent toddler group having a singing session in French and English. This was a good-sized group with nearly 20 parents from different backgrounds in action. The staff said that most of the toddlers would end up attending the nursery. The group appeared to serve as a good base for *acculturation*. It appeared that the parents were not just there for the signing toddler group. A number of advisory services from the local council visited the school on similar days. These provided advice on general health, family planning, adult courses as well as information about local schools and admissions procedures.

Table 8.1 shows the timetable for the activities of the Centre in a specific week.

During our visits we noticed a selection of 'profile books' produced by the children titled 'My activity book' where children stuck pictures of themselves doing various activities at home, in school, in outings accompanied by explanatory sentences in different languages. In every picture the knowledge about and use of languages were noticeable. This did not only refer to children's own languages but also to languages of their friends in the nursery and their family members. Ayse, who came from a Turkish and English speaking home (mother Turkish, dad English) appeared in the album of another child in the nursery with the caption 'This is my friend Ayse, she speaks Turkish and English at home.' Under another child's picture was the caption 'Jayden can say hello in Spanish' the writing *ola* clearly visible under his picture. In

Table 8.1 The timetable for the activities of the Centre in a specific week

Monday	Tuesday	Wednesday	Thursday	Friday
8.45 a.m.–9.30 a.m.	9.30 a.m.–11.15 a.m.	10.00 a.m.–12 noon	9.30a.m.–12 noon	9.15 a.m.–9.45 a.m.
Toy library	Parents and toddler group	Introduction to NVQ	Childminders group	Book library
10.00 a.m.–12 noon	With Amy, D., Tanya, Cathy and Amy, R.	With Teri		10.30 a.m.–11.30 a.m.
Parents				Parents and toddlers signing group
Make and take				
With Tracy				With Valery
1.30 p.m.–2.45 p.m.	1.00 p.m.–3.00 p.m.	1.00 p.m.–3.00 p.m.	Hair and beauty workshops	1.00 p.m.–3.00 p.m.
Toy library	Sewing group	ESOL group	Dates available after Easter	Early literacy workshops
+	With forever	With Andy		For parents and carers
Stay and play				(details to come)
Speech, language advisor				
With Amy, D.				

almost all of the albums we have seen, there were references to children's parents engaging in a variety of activities with them at home or outdoors and explanatory notes about each, often in more than one language. Some of the photos of the parents were taken during their visits to the Centre, either reading a story or engaging with the children during a session. One of the parents taught French to the children once a week for half an hour.

Meeting with parents

Parent A mentioned that the nursery showed children that it was good to be different. She also went on to say that the school encouraged all children to work together and accept each other's languages. Other parents talked about how unsure they were about the importance of maintaining the use of their home languages until they had seen a variety of activities involving children's own languages. Parent B who spoke Italian and English at home, noted her child singing in Bengali and how pleased that with two languages at home her daughter was picking up a third at school. She also went on to state that children can cope with three or four languages noting the similarities between Spanish and Italian. Another parent who spoke German and her husband English at home mentioned that in order to instil different language competencies in children you needed to pretend as if you did not understand the language: 'If children realise you understand the language they use it with you. Or pretend not to understand English with my daughter, who is now speaking more English than German' (German/English speaking parent).

She expressed some anxiety about this since her younger child was also using more English than German. The same sentiments were echoed by another parent who spoke Italian and was married to an Arabic speaking person. She noted the differences between her younger child and the one at nursery – the younger one was using English more than Italian. She stated that adults should stick to using one language each with children and not mix them. This was one of the families we visited at home. Readers will find the details of this visit at the latter part of this chapter.

The parents went on to explain how their anxieties about their children's use of English were quickly dispersed by the staff at the Centre, assuring them that children's existing knowledge of home languages would support the development of English. This appears to have made an impact on parent's attitudes towards the use of the home languages:

Parent C commented on how her two children not wanting to speak Twi when they first started at the Centre were taking more interest in using Twi at home and in the Nursery. Parent D who had a child with cerebral palsy who understood English and some French – but could not speak either yet – commented on the support her daughter received at the Centre: 'Oh my God, I'm really lucky'; the nursery provides 'great support'. She mentioned that she spoke French more confidently than English and at first thought that child would not understand both but was advised by the doctor and the nursery staff that adults could use many languages with children up to the age of 3. Parents also commented on how their children were using words and phrases from other languages. An English speaking parent explained the joy of hearing his son arrive at home and uttering phrases in French – his child is taking part in learning French sessions in the nursery and how the Centre is giving his son other languages (he cites Chinese): 'Its good here with languages'.

Home visits

Following our meeting with the parents we managed to arrange home visits with some of them to follow up on some of the ideas raised during the meeting. We were also curious to see existing provision at home. We present a selection of extracts from the conversations we had with parents during these visits. First is from the visit by Tözün Issa (TI) made to Selma's home. One of the immediate concerns of the parents appeared to be related to Selma's 'level of English compared to her Italian which was more advanced'. The concern was whether this would hinder Selma's English Language development. Here the Centre appears to have alleviated that concern.

Selma's father began talking about how anxious they were with Selma's level of English when she started attending the Centre.

Mr Ali:	No I am sorry because we asked the teacher at school, 'how has her English been?' and she said, 'Absolutely normal'. And since we got that answer from her I am a bit relaxed about her English. I am not worried about her English at all, because what's her name – Elaine?
Mrs Ali:	Elaine yes (Selma's key worker)
Mr Ali:	. . . because when we had the meeting with her to ask how Selma was doing at school she said, 'absolutely normal'.
TI:	Were you are worried about something?
Mrs Ali:	I am worried because I know how fluent she is in Italian. I can talk to her almost like I am talking to you, and I can see, when we are in a situation where she speaks English, that her English is not the same level as her Italian. I know that is something we discussed with her Arabic. My worry is she could begin to get frustrated, because she can express very complex things in Italian, and she is very aware that, in English, she can't do the same. She is even more aware that, in Arabic, she can't do the same. That was what worried me in the sense that it could affect her confidence.
TI:	Yes.
Mrs Ali:	I just need to wait and see.
TI:	There is research – could it be . . . I have a feeling that it could be to do with the fact that she started using English in a kind of official sense very recently, hasn't she, compared to how she uses Arabic and Italian with you? I guess the process must have started much earlier because she started hearing Italian and Arabic much earlier, from birth, whereas the English language she uses only became official fairly recently when she started the nursery.
Mrs Ali:	Yes, yes.
TI:	So I have a feeling that the input you have given her in Arabic and Italian is actually going to strengthen her English, as she gets older.
Mrs Ali:	Yes. My only worry is how she can express and how she is used to talking in Italian. The fact that she can't yet repeat that in the other two languages.
TI:	Sure. I think it's a process. She is developing a system that will translate what she already knows – her extended vocabulary in Italian – into English.

It was interesting to hear from Mrs Ali that Selma has already started using her stronger language (i.e. Italian) to make sense of new vocabulary in the target language (i.e. English).

Mrs Ali:	What is lovely – what is really great about her is that more and more often she is asking me for translations. 'How do you say this in English?' or 'Mummy, how do you say this in Italian?'. She is asking me more and more and more.
TI:	That is a positive sign, isn't it?
Mrs Ali:	Very often. . . . It was really amazing. It was more than a year and a half ago that she actually translated a song. You know, we said, 'how can we sing this beat?' And she did it for me, which was lovely.
TI:	That is really exciting.
Mrs Ali:	(speaks to Selma in Italian).
TI:	I can give her some paper if she wants.
Mrs Ali:	(Continuing to speak to Selma in Italian. Selma starts to write on the paper some words in Italian) Oh they know where it is. In fact that is why you see all the paper there.

TI talked about their recent visit to the nursery and mentioned how the nursery staff commented on Selma's growing ability and confidence with tasks and how happy she was when they walked in four weeks ago.

Talking to both parents it was evident they were investing a great deal of time and effort supporting both of their children's language development:

Mr Ali:	I will tell you what is good. I spend a lot of time with them every day I am at home from 2.30 and 3.30.
TI:	Yes When she asks you, 'how do you say this word?' is it usually, 'how do you say it in English?' or 'how do you say it in Italian?'

⇨

Mrs Ali:	She asks me in Italian. She would ask me, 'Mamma come se dice tree – not tree. *Come se dice canarino in Inglese*?' (How do you say canary in English?') So English words come.
TI:	So that's how words come.
Mrs Ali:	Oppure '*come si dice yellow bird in Italiano*'.
TI:	Is there routine story telling?
Mrs Ali:	Loads of it. Loads of it actually. I mean I've . . . I was very good. I was very very good before Amina (their younger daughter) arrived. We'd read any time. Whenever she picked up a book. I mean I love reading so for me it is something I am very happy to do.

For Mrs Ali it was important that adults in the nursery provided good role models for using English.

Mrs Ali:	Then there was the summer break, and then we moved her to (inaudible) nursery. I think Vivienne (Selma's teacher) did a fantastic job. It was a very small nursery – Montessori but probably not very structured – very white middle class. One of the reasons I chose it was that Vivienne – her English was impeccable. It was just so beautiful, and for Selma that is quite important.

It was evident that parenting was a hard job especially when one realized the importance of supporting their children's home language development. For Mrs Ali this was challenging, when she realized that she had to start developing *her* own Italian language skills first.

Mrs Ali:	I used to find it quite draining.
TI:	Parenting – yes.

⇨

Mrs Ali:	Because also what happened – I had to relearn Italian in a sense. Because, having been here for so many years, I always used to feel when I went back to Italy that I had lost my fluency, and it would take me a couple of days to get back into the language. And so it was a bit hard, maybe at the beginning, talking and talking and talking because I knew that is what I had to do.
TI:	Yes
Mrs Ali:	But now it has become quite natural.
TI:	Yes of course
Mrs Ali:	. . . and because we always talk a lot. It was only me that she could talk to so I always had to be listening. We used to be very tired. Now it has become . . . (Talk with child) And what is lovely is that, so far, they are still talking Italian to each other.
Amina (Selma'syoungersister):	*Per favore*
Mr Ali:	*Per favore.* She used to shout at me, 'computer'. I said, '*Mamma, posso avere il computer, per favour? Grazie. Prego*'.
TI:	Wonderful. You have all these three languages going. Amazing.
Wife:	She wants her tea. I am going to . . . (talk with the children) When Mrs Ali left to attend to Amina, Selma approached TI with a book in Arabic.
TI:	When you look at the Arabic book, and when you are reading an Italian book, you know which page to turn first, don't you?

⇨

Selma:	Yes
TI:	Which page do you turn first with the Arabic one?
Selma:	(pointing to the right side of the book) Not this one. This one
TI:	I see. So you turn it this way do you?
Selma:	No actually . . .
TI:	How do you turn the Arabic book, when Mummy reads to you in Arabic? Daddy, sorry.
	(. . .) So would you open this book for me, to show me how Daddy would open it for you? . . . (Selma showing it to TI) Absolutely, yes. So he does it from here, yes?
Selma:	Yes
TI:	That's the first page, isn't it?
Selma:	This is the . . . (not clear)
TI:	What is happening with this doggy, do you know?
Selma:	Yes
TI:	Do you know what this story is called? What is it called?
Selma:	'The Dog'
TI:	'The Dog' How do you say 'dog' in Arabic?
Mr Ali:	No. No No (something in Arabic) The story called '*Oh My Stomach*', but it is all about this dog called *Esmoye*. Tell him. Tell the gentleman.
TI:	What happens to the dog. Does he eat too much? What does he eat?
Selma:	He eats all of these, and . . .
TI:	All of that
Selma:	And then his tummy hurts.
TI:	His tummy hurts – no wonder. What sort of things does he eat then? Bones?
Selma:	Bones
TI:	Anything else?
Selma:	He just eats bones and fish.
Selma:	Bones and fish.
	(Mr and Mrs Ali say something in Italian and in Arabic in turn.)
	⇨

Selma:	I know what these names are.
TI:	Do you? What are they called?
Selma:	On mine this is Fifi.
TI:	Fifi What about your Italian? Which is your Italian book? Which Italian book do you like? Which one is your favourite one?
Selma:	Mmmm.
TI:	I know it is a difficult question maybe. You wouldn't be able to tell me, but pick one that you like.
Selma:	I just like the best of all, but these are the best.
TI:	These are the best.
Selma:	But the best of all these. This.
TI:	Oh this one. You actually like this Arabic book about the doggy. Okay. Which ones. . . . These are English or Arabic?
Mrs Ali:	Yes but, as I said, I read all of them in Italian. (She said a number of titles of books in Italian, for example, *La Bambola Saggia*.) Oh yes, this is an Italian one actually she picked up. (She spoke to Selma in Italian, and picked out a book.)
TI:	This is about. . . . I think I know this story. What is happening to Ahmet in this story?
Mrs Ali:	Speaks in Italian to Amina, and then says, *La Storia per Scegliere* – you know – the 'you choose the story'. She loves this one.
Selma:	It is all just pictures. (Something indistinct.)
TI:	Is that the sun or the moon?
Wife:	. . . about words. One we have been reading a lot is this one for example (showing a book in Italian). If I change . . . If I say a word and then I say later???? is a better word, they actually find it really annoying, and they tell me, 'no Mummy. That is not what you say. You say this. So I find it quite important to actually stick to er . . .' (inaudible)

⇨

TI:	To stick to the message.
Mr Ali:	To what you say.
TI:	Yes
Mrs Ali:	To the actual story word by word, because . . .
TI:	Because she is developing that kind of knowledge about the words and the concepts, isn't she?
Mrs Ali:	And they imagine as well – it is not just about listening – they imagine . . .
TI:	They imagine the actual??? That is absolutely the case.
Mrs Ali:	But what we are doing as well. You have been telling them stories just without any images and that . . . I have been reading from this book. I have just been reading to them. I mean obviously there is more here for Selma than for Amina. Just so that they can concentrate on the language, and we use CDs now as well in both languages, both in English and in Italian, because I think that should help her.

The visit to Selma's home proved to be highly informative particularly relating to the ethos of the home environment. It was evident that both parents – encouraged by the EYC – started to develop the home languages (Arabic and Italian) alongside English. Both children having established the link between the language and the parent, children were to speak to their dad mostly in Arabic, to their mum in Italian and used them freely in the household. English remained the *lingua franca* of the household. As shown in the transcripts all three languages were supported by a variety of resources available to children. There were no strict rules about their use. At bedtime children heard stories in at least two languages, English always included with parents alternating between the other two. This most exciting aspect of this particular household was to witness the actual use of the three languages in real-life contexts and to witness children's attempts to grapple with the related concepts as they enthusiastically tried to form associations between different vocabulary, sounds and meaning.

Summary

In this chapter we focused on children's development in their home environment. First we began by giving a brief account on policy initiatives and debates around parental involvement. We then presented parents' views on the ways in which good early years practice can foster children's personal, social, emotional, linguistic and cultural development. We drew particular attention to parents' views that home languages should be recognized in early years settings. We also explored the professional relationships that can be promoted between adults concerned in young children's overall development.

Reflective activity

1. What are the strategies used in your early years setting to support parental involvement?
2. To what extent parental experiences are utilized in your early years setting.
3. Are your current parental involvement strategies used in your early years setting working? If so what is it that makes them work? If not, why not?

The Development of Communication and Oracy

Chapter Outline

In the previous chapter we looked at parents' views on the ways in which good early years practice can foster children's personal, social, emotional, linguistic and cultural development. We showed that the development of communication and oracy in young children at home makes a significant contribution to this process. In this chapter we look at this in more detail. First, we revisit the EYFS Curriculum in the light of previous discussions and consider how it could be extended further in relation to children's language and identities. We draw on existing research that highlights the importance of communicative competences, speaking and listening as forerunners to becoming literate. In the final part of the chapter we return to the CLL area of learning and development drawing from current practice and suggest ways this might be made more responsive to children's languages. First we start with a brief historical account of oracy development in the United Kingdom.

The studies of oracy development in the United Kingdom during the 1970s and 1980s were dominated by the so-called deficit model which was based on the assumption that children mainly from working-class and ethnic minority families did not have sufficient enriched communication experiences with their parents. This was reflected in the studies of Bernstein (1971) and Tough (1976) and to a certain extent with the Bullock Report (1975) although Chapter 5 highlighted the importance of language development in the early years placing an emphasis on the talk facilitated by parents at home. The only major work which challenged such ideas was conducted in by Wells (1981) with the Bristol Language Study. Similarly Tizard and Hughes' (1984) influential work focused on the role of parents in developing children's thinking through logical discussions at home. Through the evidence provided from conversations from the home environments the authors demonstrate how parental influences can play a crucial role in developing children's thinking through oral communication. Previously the ORACLE project (Galton et al., 1980) mainly targeting talk in the primary school also relevant to the aims of this chapter, exposed how very little interaction prevailed in primary schools and how much teacher-dominated classrooms were the main features of the primary school.

We can conveniently link the principal findings of the studies to Vygotsky's (1962) main thesis on the role of language as an important tool for communication. In applying it to learning satiations we can see how Vygotskian scholars see collaborative and group-based activities as crucial in the development of oracy in young children.

We have covered some aspects of EYFS in the previous chapters. In this chapter we develop these further in relation to the focus of this chapter. The EYFS is the document that provides the Statutory Framework for all maintained/independent schools or registered early years providers in the private, voluntary and independent sectors, caring for children from birth to 5. It enables young children to learn through a range of activities (www.direct.gov.uk/en/Parents/Preschooldevelopmentandlearning).

EYFS is guided by four overriding themes which facilitate effective practice: *A unique child, positive relationships, enabling environments* and *learning and development*. Each of these themes is designed to promote various aspects (both social and physical) of the early years environment and the children that attend them. The Framework also stresses the importance of equality of opportunity:

> All children, irrespective of ethnicity, culture or religion, home language,
> family background, learning difficulties or disabilities, gender or ability
> should have the opportunity to experience a challenging and enjoyable
> programme of learning and development. (2008, p. 10)

It is quite clear from the statement that the Framework values supporting and developing children's cultural and linguistic experiences and
recognizes the need to support these in early years settings. Although
statements such as 'to ensure positive attitudes to diversity and difference' 'removing or helping to overcome barriers' and 'to value diversity
in others' (p. 9) show that the focus of the Framework is on the right
lines, it is tokenistic in the absence of adequate practical guidance to
support them. Looking at the *Practice Guidance for Early Years Foundation Stage and Supporting Resources* – (CD pack – practice cards 1.2)
under *a unique child* theme, we find a number of statements which support a positive allegiance to inclusive education practices rather than
specific activities to utilize linguistic and cultural experiences of young
children:

> Children should be treated fairly regardless of race, religion or abilities.
> This applies no matter what they think or say; what type of family they
> come from; what language(s) they speak; what their parents do; whether
> they are girls or boys; whether they have a disability or whether they are
> rich or poor. (2008, p. 7)

Similarly under *positive relationships* (card 2.1) there is a stress on the
importance of building up of positive relationships between young children and professionals working in the same environments. It highlights
the importance of respecting each other's cultures and languages and it
is interesting to note that under the guidelines of *effective teaching* it
proposes that: 'The more practitioners know about each child, the better
they are able to support and extend each child's learning.' A statement
anyone would hardly disagree with. However, the question remains as to
what is the advice given to practitioners in terms of how are they to
achieve this? Here we can hear the reader asking the question: 'But isn't
the guidance talking about the value of assessment'? Of course the
answer to this question is a definite 'yes', however, when we look at the
Assessment section of the practical guidance document there is hardly

any strategy that incorporates children's home languages and cultures as part of this process.

In the first instance we see a number of good points about tracking children's achievements through a variety of assessment procedures. The document also explores the values of Common Assessment Framework (CAF) for children with 'additional needs' (p. 21). If we accept for the sake of argument that young children from diverse cultural and linguistic backgrounds can be seen as having an additional need, nothing is mentioned about this in the document. Interestingly under 'reflection on practice' section it is appropriately pointed out that practitioners should 'consider' *all* the factors that affect children's 'development and learning' but home languages and cultural experiences are not mentioned at all. There appears to be an implicit assumption that practitioner would either 'understand' what is implied by these statements or would simply 'know' what to do.

Looking at the six areas covered by the Early Learning Goals and educational programmes, a similar picture emerges. We have already discussed these in Chapter 2.

The Framework stresses the importance of each of these areas. It also states that none of the areas are to be seen in isolation but as 'depend(ing) on each other to support a rounded approach to child development' (2008, p. 11). For the benefit of the reader – and the focus of this chapter – we explore CLL and discuss its key components in relation to the points we raise in this chapter.

First, the Framework outlines its main approach under the stated educational programme for the CLL area.

> Children's learning and competence in communicating, speaking and listening, being read to and beginning to read and write must be supported and extended.
>
> They must be provided with opportunity and encouragement to use their skills in a range of situations and for a range of purposes, and be supported in developing the confidence and disposition to do so. (p. 13)

The points summarized under the main approach above are then used as basis for setting out the Early Learning Goals for CLL, the stage young children are expected to reach at the end of the EYFS. Again, we have already said much of this.

As Boys (2008) rightly points out, the first two categories *Language for Communication* and *Language for Thinking* are both related to the social nature of oracy development (p. 69). She also outlines a number of contexts for facilitating children's communication in collaborative settings. As children interact with each other they negotiate the rules of their interaction. In the Early Learning Goals for CLL, turn taking is shown as an important skill to be learned by the children as they engage in conversation. Their thinking also develops and leads on to new areas of learning. In the same document such collaborative activities are crucial for the development of children's linguistic skills. The whole notion of interaction and communication of ideas and feelings contributes to the development of emotions, another crucial aspect of the developing child. So if we are to summarize briefly what we have just shared with the reader: providing opportunities for young children to develop their language for *thinking* and for *communication* are the two essential ingredients for oral language development and emotions.

It's a perfectly reasonable thing to expect children to 'enjoy listening, using spoken language' and 'interacting with others and negotiate plans and activities', but how do you provide opportunities for children to 'enjoy something using spoken and written language' if the child is new to English or started an early years settings with a home language which is not English. Here there is not only a clear lack of guidance for the practitioner; there is an implicit assumption that *all* the children in the early years settings have English as their home language. The notions of 'attentive listening, responding to what children have heard' are equally vague and taken at face value when we know that children come with a multiplicity of experiences from a variety of linguistic and cultural backgrounds – including monolingual English speaking homes. The principle to be adopted in exploring such diversity needs to be based on the principle of exploring such experiences with the children 'as experts' and then sharing these with other children again through the narrative of the bilingual child. We provide a number of examples relating to this strategy in the final part of this chapter when we share our observations from the EYC with the reader. We will stress that such effective facilitative strategies were all the result of collaborative teamwork planned and delivered by a group of dedicated practitioners who, with the exception of a few, were all monolingual.

Looking at the statutory document more closely we are immediately struck with the absence of practical strategies put forward to be used as models for practitioners, particularly those who may be in the early years of their professional careers. It is a perfectly reasonable claim as suggested in the document, to use children's spoken and written language as basis for developing their learning through play. What kind of interactive approaches are needed to utilize children's spoken language? When we are talking about 'spoken and written language' are we referring only to English? In cases where some of the children who are exposed to a language other than English at home, can this be used to provide a useful link for developing children's language in English? Questions such as these largely remain unanswered in the document.

Another missing focus from the *Early Learning Goals* relates to a lack of awareness about the close association between language and culture. There is hardly any mention of the selection of topics that would reflect children's cultural experiences which are embedded in the use of the home languages. The importance we would like to place in embedding such experiences in culturally specific events is its very relevance to young children's emotional development. This means that, provided children are given the right encouragement through stimulating activities they will have things to say about themselves. And once young children start talking there is no stopping them. We will return to this point later on in this chapter when we share examples with the reader from the EYC.

The internal processes of bilingual thinking

Children who are exposed to another language at home often have developing vocabularies and phonological awareness associated with that language. This makes the transition of already familiar sounds (in the home language) into English relatively smoother for the bilingual child. Here we can talk about a process of *association* where the young bilingual learner begins to form 'internal links' as he/she begins to 'regurgitate' new sound experiences – both existing and newly acquired – in their developing sound system. Now, we are pretty sure that the child begins to do this through what Vygotsky (1978) called 'inner speech' before things finally 'emerge' into the surface as sounds/words. It may seem rather complicated but the young bilingual brain does this almost subconsciously: it incorporates the new system (English) into an existing one (home language). We hope our practitioner colleagues will agree with us when we make the claim that young children cannot make such associations by themselves; and that they need assistance from adults who would facilitate this through carefully selected activities where children are given opportunities (here we are talking about picking out relevant sounds in both languages as they ask children to 'teach' them a new word in the child's home language and forming that link in English) to use two languages alongside each other in meaningful contexts. We have made several claims relating to the importance of developing communicative competences in young children. It would be useful to share a number of research studies that support our claim.

Communicative competence is a term used to describe 'an inner mental representation of language, something latent rather than overt. Such competence refers usually to an underlying system inferred from language performance' (Baker, 2006, p. 24).

In earlier research on language use Gumperz and Corsaro (1977) talk about how the socio-ecological environment of the nursery school provides specific socially defined opportunities for interaction and talk. Others explore its clear association with the development of socialization in young children (Schieffelin and Ochs, 1986). They point out two areas of socialization: socialization *through* the use of language and socialization *to* the use of language. The former relates to the use of language as a tool for socialization where the latter is more concerned with socialization to facilitate the use and development of linguistic skills.

We found ample evidence of research which supported the higher mode of communicative competence in young bilingual children compared to their monolingual counterparts. Genesee et al.'s (1996) study on young French/English bilingual children found them making accommodations that were linked to the monolingualism of the stranger. Equally Gertner et al.'s (1994) work explored the positive relationship between communicative competence and the social acceptance among peers in young learners.

Supporting communicative competence in young children

As we seem to agree on the vital importance of supporting the development of communicative competence in young – monolingual and bilingual – children how can we go about achieving this? Research is also plentiful in this respect. The first of such studies we would like to share with the reader is that of Dickinson and Tabor (2001). In their extremely accessible book they 'take' the reader by the hand and travel into the homes and schools of more than 70 young children (ages 3, 4 and 5) from diverse backgrounds and observe parent–child and teacher–child interactions. They report on how families talk to their young children during everyday activities like book reading, toy play and mealtimes. One of the most convincing aspects of these interactions relates to the bilingual learners as the authors unpick topics of interactions that reflect the culture of the home environment. We use the word 'culture' synonymously in a 'micro' as well as 'macro' sense. The former relates to topics specific to everyday aspects of the home environment which includes routine activities and interactions of the family members and can relate to any household (monolingual or bilingual) whereas the latter is used to imply the very same things also carry particular community-based attributes that facilitate interactions that are more community related such as customs, language and religion. The authors emphasize how vital such interactions are for the later development of literacy skills in children. Similar studies also point out to the vital importance of purposeful talk for the development of communicative competence and the development of literacy.

Uccelli and Paez's (2007) account of the exploration of oral language skills of bilingual children is also interesting. They look at the spoken interactions of young bilingual Spanish/English children in two language mediums focusing on the development of vocabulary and narrative. They demonstrate how children's oral skills in two languages form the firm foundations of literacy development. Hart and Risley's (2005) highly perceptive exploration of the development of 'quality talk' in young American kindergarten children is fascinating. They intricately demonstrate how adults can usefully draw upon 'quality features'

(p. 112) of language which they show as present in their daily interaction with their children. They show that the features of these quality interactions change with places and 'purposes of interaction' (p. 112). In describing one such interaction they talk about giving children freedom to express their views and interpretations of various classroom situations (p. 85).

Having explored some useful research in this field, let us now reconsider CLL component of the Framework from a more inclusive perspective. As we do this we draw on some of the strategies we observed during our visits to the EYC.

CLL revisited

When we discussed some of the missing elements of CLL guidance earlier on in the chapter, we mentioned how little it offered in terms of practical strategies that utilized children's existing linguistic and cultural experiences. Our main concern related to the perception of children's home languages – and language varieties – as somehow invisible or different, even detrimental, to the communicative skills to be acquired in English. In the remaining part of this chapter we challenge this notion by unpicking its main components and sharing with the reader examples of good practice from our findings from the EYC.

We begin by pointing out that the success of the whole approach of the EYC was related to its holistic perspective, namely inclusive strategies inside as well as outside the Centre. We explore these in some detail under four themes:

1. Children's attitudes to languages
2. Parents' attitudes to multilingualism
3. Children's knowledge and understanding of the world
4. The ethos of the setting

Children's attitudes to languages

In children we observed positive attitudes to their own languages alongside their highly developed sense of identity. In the following example Nicole was looking at the pictures of watermelon and aubergine with captions in English, Bengali and Spanish. She listened as the researcher (AH) read the English, Spanish and the Bengali transliteration and then looked at the watermelon and pointed to the writing: 'That says watermelon'.

She then pointed at numbers on a cupboard in the technology room and said: 'Those are numbers'. She thus demonstrated an ability to differentiate between different symbolic systems.

Children were constantly building on previous experiences relating to themselves as well as others in their environment as demonstrated in the following example:

> Before the group set off to a local ecology centre Preeta showed AH the picture of herself and her parents in the nursery reception area. AH read the caption to find Preeta willing to acknowledge:

AH: 'We speak Yoruba at home. Do you speak Yoruba at home?' (Preeta nodded.)

During a later observation, children were inside the 'reflection tent' (a specially constructed space where children could be private or be with others looking at their images in the mirrors provided). Jeremiah (JM) burst out, looked at the researchers (AH) and (TI) and said: 'I speak my language'.

Language awareness appeared to be embedded in the ethos and everyday practice of the nursery. This was most visible in children's knowledge of their own and other languages as clearly demonstrated in TI's conversation with Ernesto's in the following extract:

TI: Ernesto, what language do you speak?
ER: Portuguese
TI: *obligado*
           Ernesto looked at TI and smiled.

Children's experiences were collated in individual profile books which contained pictures with captions featuring children's home as well as Centre experiences. Children were usually invited to choose and talk about the photos to be included; if children spoke a language other than English, this was presented side by side with English. Parents played a key part in this. In the following example, Selma was talking to TI about her book written in Italian, Arabic and English:

SE: Here I'm playing with my baby sister
TI: (Pointing at the picture of an umbrella) Is that your umbrella?
SE: Yes
TI: Ah, you have long hair in that picture
SE: Mummy cut my hair
TI: (Looking at the photo) Ah, I love cheesecake.
SE: Yes, I like it too
TI: (Looking at Italian version) How do you say cake in Italian then?
SE: torta
SE: (Looking at her name written in Arabic) Here is Selma in Arabic, these are Arabic, my dad speaks Arabic
TI: Do you know Arabic?
SE: I speak Arabic, Italian and English
TI: How do you say daddy in Arabic? Is it *baba*?

In another example Ayse, who came from a Turkish and English speaking home (mother Turkish, dad English) appeared in the album of another child in the nursery with the caption 'This is my friend Ayse, she speaks Turkish and English at home'. Under another child's picture was the caption 'Jayden can say hello in Spanish' the writing *ola* clearly visible under his picture.

In relation to this theme it can be said that through the active encouragement of the Centre staff, children were confident about using and discussing their own languages as well other children's. The languages were perceived by the Centre as being an integral part of children's lives and cultural experiences. As we have shown in the examples above, such an open and positive practice contributed to the children's sophisticated levels of understanding about language as an integral part of their worlds.

Parents' attitudes to multilingualism

During our conversations with some parents, we became aware of how children's linguistic and cultural experiences from home formed the foundation for further development in the Centre. Our initial findings of the first part of Phase 1 of the Project appear to support this. Our discussions with one group of 12 parents revealed that the children were exposed to and encouraged to use the following languages in addition to English at home: Arabic, Catalan, French, German, Italian, Spanish, Twi, Turkish and Yoruba.

There was general agreement that the use of greetings in different languages helped children to know that people speak different languages; they agreed that the Centre supported languages and took the use of greetings further than just as a welcome poster.

One parent noted that children associated languages with different parents and had heard the appropriate greeting *Ola!* being used to a Spanish speaking parent.

All agreed that it was good that children were introduced to languages at a young age and said that children found them easy. There was widespread agreement that the Centre showed children 'it's good to be different' (parents' terminology). They also felt that the school encouraged all children to work together and accept each other's languages. A comment from another parent who spoke English at home showed that her child knew about other languages and was also learning French. She added that in addition to this he was becoming very aware of other languages in the nursery. She gave Chinese as an example of this and said: 'It's good here supporting other languages.'

In a separate conversation at home with one of the parents, Francesca commented on the greetings in different languages on display at the nursery, about one of the mothers teaching some French at home to Oscar (her son) and also at the nursery. She went on to say that different parents used their own languages for greetings, providing different vocabulary for the nursery's use. She said that children were interested in languages especially with so many spoken now in schools.

In another brief conversation at the Centre AH talked to Katisha's Japanese mother:

AH:	Do you speak Japanese to her at home?
MO:	Yes, all the time
AH:	And her dad?
MO:	No
AH:	So he speaks English and you speak Japanese to her so she's got the two languages together. What about the writing?
MO:	Not Japanese writing yet
AH:	So do you think she'll learn to write English first, at school?
MO:	Yes, Japanese writing is difficult

As shown by the examples we used in this theme, parents had a strong sense of the value of and a commitment to the use of the home languages. This is in sharp contrast to the reported views of some multilingual parents who it is claimed, play down the role and the status of the home languages in favour of English. Parents in our study stressed that the use of the home languages was actively supported by the Centre.

Children's knowledge and understanding of the world

It was clear from our observations that the Centre ensured that the children's own experiences of the world were acknowledged and extended by the provision in place.

In one observation, Malcine (MA) was playing on the large model wooden train and talking to AH:

MA:	We're going to Barbados
AH:	What will you do there?
MA:	Play with the sand and the water
AH:	Where will you stay?
MA:	In the restaurant, in the hotel . . . have to go on the aeroplane . . . train to the airport . . . mum and Dad lived in Barbados when I was born.

It is useful to mention here that although Malachi was actually of Eritrean background his family was going to Barbados for a family wedding. During another observation in the outdoor play area Jeremiah said:

JM:	I was born in England
AH:	'In a hospital?'
JM:	'No in England'

Another interesting area related to children's awareness and use of different language varieties was demonstrated in the following example by Selma (the Arabic, Italian and English speaker).

In the outdoor play area, accompanied by a doll, a bag and a broom, she showed her facility with South London English variety when she said to her friend: 'Bye, darlin', I'm goin' to the mee-in' (meeting).

Here we can clearly identify Selma's receptivity towards language forms by her demonstration of facility with a non-standard variety of English; she had already shown her ability with a more standard form with TI.

Another observation showed how adults utilized children's knowledge of cultural and religious experiences by positioning them as 'experts' in order to extend their linguistic repertoires and enhance cognitive development. One observed episode involved the Deputy Head and Sadia as they looked at a book about Islam. Another non-Muslim child was listening.

DH:	. . . big place but on this map it's very small but this is a map of the whole world so Eritrea is a very big place isn't it?
SA:	This is not Eritrea (indistinct), Eritrea's very far from this place (?)
DH:	Let's have a look. Teach me about Ramadan
SA:	Well, they pray (DH: yeah) and Ramadan we celebrate, Muslims all celebrate (?), my dad at Ramadan he pray
DH:	Every day?
SA:	Sometimes he pray at home
DH:	(Looking at a photo in the book): What are they doing on this page? Why do they have to do that?

SA: Muslims always do that (she then went on to recite one of the Arabic prayers) All the time at pray time you do that. All Muslims do that (shows position of hands for prayers)

DH: Who can speak then?

SA: Then when you're finished . . . quiet when you.
(Discussion of language-) DH: It's English?

SA: When they pray on the carpet . . . my mum always did that . . . on the pray carpet – so we mustn't put . . . on it

DH: So you do fasting in Ramadan?

The children demonstrated a remarkable sense of place and association with the different varieties of language and the world around them. As shown by one of the examples above the children were able to move beyond their current locales and make links between different places and languages associated with these.

The ethos of the setting

The welcoming, friendly and calm atmosphere of the Centre was clearly visible. The headteacher and the Centre staff played a key role in establishing positive links with the parents.

Children's awareness of different languages was also associated with knowledge about different countries and places, as we have seen. We could see evidence of activities related to Knowledge and Understanding of the World (one of the areas of Learning and Development in the Early Years Statutory Framework). For example:

A display about journeys and visits was organized to tie in with Katisha's return from an extended holiday to Japan to visit her maternal grandparents. In the outdoor area Japanese music was being played to accompany dancing activities.

In addition to its welcoming, friendly and calm atmosphere, language awareness featured highly on the Centre's agenda. Displays carried signs and captions in different languages. The welcome sign in different languages at the Centre entrance is a familiar part of most educational settings but at the Centre it was taken further through the accompanying photographs of all the children and of many of the families with captions describing the home languages they used. There was also a notice board giving information about the various Centre activities available for parents and children during each week, for example, parents and toddlers singing sessions.

We also noticed that the Centre staff, although largely monolingual English speakers, made every attempt to learn and use inclusive multi-lingual practices in their daily interactions with the children. They used key phrases such as greetings, taught the children songs, provided resources, particular books and audio materials in different languages. The teacher responsible for EAL was particularly effective in establishing good relationships with parents. In our conversations with him we learned that his knowledge of each family was extensive, often giving us small details of each child's particular characteristics. He also made every effort to learn and use the languages of the families.

We had ample examples of children's awareness and use of different languages. Again, this was very much supported by the Centre and reflected positively in parents' attitudes. In the following discussion at home with a parent of a child with special educational needs, the Centre's inclusive ethos is clearly expressed:

> **AH:** So how do you think (the nursery's) helped her?
>
> **S:** A lot, a lot, given that when I was down there sometime you see that they have books in Chinese, they have books in Spanish, in every language. I know that Heidi, because of all the problems she has, maybe she didn't learn maybe some word in different language but I saw the children there trying to understand what this means in Chinese because they speak the Chinese languages . . . (pause)
>
> (The nursery) is really open, really, really open and do a really good job with her, like I always say that. These people have done so much, so much for Heidi. People can't understand that but me as a mum I know how Heidi developed at (the nursery). They give her so much confidence with everything really, so now Heidi is learning more. I was really lucky that Heidi went there. She learned a lot from (the nursery).
>
> **AH:** Do the staff use other languages?
>
> **S:** Yes they try so hard as well to learn like different language, like Mark (the Ethnic Minority Achievement Grant teacher). Mark's French is so bad but he tried so hard to speak French with all the children. When he learned the children there speak French he try as well. All the staff like 'bonjour Heidi', everyone is trying to speak, they're really involved and respect.

They see someone doesn't understand they put everything together to empower us and to be inclusive . . . sometime they need somebody to translate. Like one time I was there they asked me to translate for one mum and it makes me really happy as well. They try everything. It's a really, really good nursery. Because sometime you send a child to school, people there they're not really open, even if the law says that the child needs to be in this school but you need to be open as well to say that ok this child need to learn maybe English and give them time . . . sometimes it doesn't happen in all the schools I know that.

I recommend (the nursery) to all parents . . . if they've just arrived to England. I don't know what to say but they are really, really open.

AH: Would you say the parents all get on as well? There's lots of different families, lots of different backgrounds, lots of different languages and cultures.

S: Yes and the thing is the parents meeting room at the back of (the nursery) they have how to learn English there. One time I start to learn English there to do my computer course there. Like sewing, everything. We are so different people. Some come in for Somali, some come in for Nigeria, so many, even Chinese people, so many different language. They educate us as well. Before when I arrived here I didn't know nothing about computers. Today even if it's a small certificate one level, two levels, it was (the nursery) that gave me that. Heidi has achieved something there, my self as well and all the parents there as well. So after we finished the computer course there we went to Kings College, all the parents as well. They teach us as well as the children.

In another conversation with one mother (Francesca) we learned that she believed that children should be started on languages when they are young and that the EYC was good in relation to this. Oscar (her son) told Faye about the languages spoken at the nursery. Oscar mentioned Mandarin as a starter. There was a 'French-speaking mother' (Oscar's phrase) and Selma's father spoke 'Egyptian' (Oscar's word) and Bengali words. He was very interested in languages and often talked about the different languages that were spoken in different countries. She also said: 'If the Head is good, the staff will be'.

She noted that the staff at nursery incorporated activities such as cooking from other countries. At parents conferences the EMAG teacher (Mark) attempted to speak to Oscar's father in Irish and to speak to other parents in their languages.

At another meeting with Gina (Piero's mother) she commented on the way the Nursery highlighted children's different backgrounds and talked about them in a positive way. For Piero, the nursery was a 'happy environment' where all children felt welcome. Parents were welcome to stay with their children as long as they liked. The free flow approach helped children to pick up English; the setting up of different things, such as the home corner becoming a hairdresser's, gave vocabulary to the children. She stressed that much was learned through play, especially for children whose first language was not English. Gina mentioned the importance of music and songs, noting how Mark (the EMAG teacher) taught the children a Bangladeshi song, how he used Spanish and how French was being taught to the children (by one of the parents). Piero was very attached to Mark, because of his use of Spanish and, probably, because he is male. She commented on Mark's ability to speak some words in many of the nursery's languages and referred to a teacher who also spoke Spanish and a teaching assistant, then on maternity leave, who spoke Italian. Gina said the nursery helped children to count in different languages and encouraged parents to use their home language with their children.

Our research in the EYC and our conversations with the parents shows that the Centre has successfully managed to bring together different experiences of multilingualism, identity and culture through establishing an open and welcoming ethos. As we have shown, the outcome of this is reflected through the positive attitudes of the children towards linguistic and cultural diversity but most of all reflected in their overall communicative competence. We feel that the success of the Centre was not just due to the recognition and the high value they have shown towards children's linguistic and cultural 'capital' but creating practical opportunities and strategies for actively utilizing them. One of the key components of this success was clearly visible during a staff meeting we have attended as part of our brief for the research. The ownership and collective responsibility of the staff was very much in evidence. This was supported and encouraged by a very dynamic and enthusiastic headteacher who actively guided and supported her staff on the strategies to be adopted.

We feel that the key ingredient to this success is the conviction of the entire staff that this is not a problem; rather this is simply *how things are.*

Summary

In this chapter we discussed some of the missing elements of CLL guidance and mentioned how little it offered in terms of practical strategies that utilized children's existing linguistic and cultural experiences. Our main concern related to the perception of children's home languages – and language varieties – perceived as invisible or different even detrimental to the communicative skills to be acquired in English. In the latter part of the chapter we challenged such notions by unpicking the Framework's main components and sharing with the reader, examples of good practice from our findings from the EYC. Our observations mainly showed that the Centre managed to utilize young learners' linguistic and cultural experiences through effective team work and close collaboration with the parents.

Reflective activity

1. What kind of interactive approaches do you think is needed to utilize children's spoken language?
2. In your own settings, what strategies do you use to facilitate children who are new to English to enjoy something using their spoken language?
3. How relevant do you think embedding young children's experiences in culturally specific events is to their emotional development?
4. In your own settings do you do any activities that specifically explore children's languages and culture?

Making the Transition to Reception Classes in Primary Schools

10

In this chapter, we look at the evidence collated from our visits to the two Reception classes involved in the research and compare their practice with that of the EYC. We consider some of the challenges facing Reception class teachers and those facing children who make the transition from one setting to another. We query the apparent reluctance in the Reception classes to acknowledge and embrace openly the languages and cultural experiences brought to them.

First we take a brief look at the background to Reception classes and the school starting age in primary schools.

Historical background

As we said earlier in Chapter 1, the statutory school starting age was established rather arbitrarily in the Elementary Education Act of 1870 with the common result of very young children in Infant classes (or Standards as they were originally called) receiving a very inappropriate education. The Board of Education decided in 1907 to make it part of its policy to discourage the attendance of under fives in elementary schools (Plowden, 1967, para 264). This helped to stimulate an expansion of nursery schools and of nursery classes in elementary schools. There was also a history of Infant only schools for children up to the age of 7 – infants being deemed to be children of the ages 5 to 7.

During the 1980s, however, the policy of one single entry to Reception in September, while easing some of the problems of three-term entry, also led to problems of adequate provision for the youngest children – those who had their fourth birthday in August. David (1990) provides some analysis of this situation and queries what was then becoming the tendency to impose a more formal curriculum on children whose learning was best supported through a rich and varied play-based curriculum. However, the continuing economic pressures on parents to find work have also contributed to the expectation that there will be 'care' for young children in some form or another and that they will be in formal schooling as soon as possible.

Transition to Reception

We now move on to consider some of the issues surrounding transition to Reception classes. Fabian and Dunlop (2006) provide an extremely useful overview of research into the processes of transition into primary schooling in which many points pertinent to this book are raised. The reader is recommended to browse through this article; there is too much to include here but the following should give some indication of its relevance:

> Currently, educational transition is defined as the process of change that children make from one place or phase of education to another over time (Fabian & Dunlop, 2002). Changes of relationship, teaching style,

environment, space, time, contexts for learning, and learning itself, com-
bine at moments of transition making intense and accelerated demands
(Fabian & Dunlop 2005). Change can bring the excitement of new beginnings, the anticipation of meeting new people and making new friends,
and the opportunity to learn new things. There can also be an element of
apprehension of the unknown which can cause confusion and anxiety,
leaving an impression that may still affect behaviour many years later.
Page (2000) suggests that allowing children to experience discontinuity is
seen as part of the continuum of life and learning. If going through a
transition is a learning skill in its own right, it is therefore important that
children build resilience to change but are also given support to help them
mark, as well as to negotiate, change. (Fabian and Dunlop, 2006, p. 3)

We now move on to explore some of the links between the research
mentioned above and our own findings.

Moving from the EYC to Reception

We have noted in previous chapters the potentially damaging effects on
young children's emotional health and security if due attention is not
paid to the ways in which changes in their lives are managed. We have
asked our readers to think about the impact on children of moving from
a familiar environment to an unfamiliar one and possibly one in which
they see little or nothing that connects them to their homes and their
early experiences of life.

Things that are second nature to the adults (and some of the children)
in an early years setting may be a source of acute discomfort for other
children.

David (1990) refers to this too: 'to put children in a situation which is
totally different from their earlier experiences amounts to decontextu-
alisation; what we should be promoting is *recontextualisation* (Walker-
dine 1982), that is, building on previous learning.'

Fabian and Dunlop (2006) draw attention to the notion of 'resilience' – the personal qualities that can help children cope positively with
changes and summarize the possible roots of such qualities:

Factors of family, school or community which may influence outcomes
and help children to cope with life-stressors, of which transition may be
one, are believed to be caring relationships, high expectations and

opportunities to take part (Benard, 1995, p2). In terms of educational transitions the optimism engendered by a caring relationship with a teacher can promote a sense of self-worth (Kidder, 1990) and support the development of self-esteem, self-efficacy, autonomy and optimism, which are all critical features of resilience. (p. 6)

It is, we feel, vitally important that adults working with children in early years settings are able not only to empathize with the children in their care, but also to be imaginative and intelligent enough to think about the possible problems that their setting might pose, particularly to young bilingual children.

There are many questions that staff in a setting could raise, for example:

- If the language you hear is not the one you know and use at home, how do you communicate what you want? How do you cope with a barrage of unknown language (English)?
- If you are not used to large numbers of children around you, how do you react to them all?
- If you eat at home with your fingers, what do you do when confronted with knives, forks and spoons?
- If you cannot see any images or resources that connect with your family and culture what unspoken message might you be receiving about your family and culture?

These are just four possible 'scenarios' where young bilingual children might find themselves at a loss – you can probably think of many more. Whatever the situation, we cannot overstress the importance of the adults examining every aspect of their setting with a view to ensuring that it is open and welcoming to ALL children (and their parents).

We are of the opinion that the EYC we visited had indeed rigorously assessed its practice so that, as far as was humanly and professionally possible, it provided an environment that not only welcomed the children's languages and cultures but positively endorsed them, using them as springboards for extending social, emotional and intellectual development.

It is therefore not surprising to find that the Centre gave a great deal of thought to the older children's moves to primary school.

Leaving the EYC

Towards the end of Phase 1 of our research, the EYC staff started to implement the programme they had devised to help the children prepare for joining Reception classes in the autumn term. At this particular centre, the children were moving to a large number of different primary schools, some in the borough but several in other boroughs. This meant that in some schools only one child from the centre would be starting in Reception, in others perhaps two or three. The staff were very aware of the significance for the children of leaving the centre, leaving friends and embarking on new experiences.

One member of staff took the lead in this transition process, carrying out a range of activities to make the changes as positive as possible. On one of our visits, we saw how the Centre's approach celebrated the end of the children's time in nursery and the excitement of starting in primary school, but it did not avoid the inherent sadness in the changes that would mean disruption to friendships, farewell to familiar faces and routines and, for some children, the challenge of starting in Reception classes knowing no other children.

In celebration, there was a display in the entrance with captions letting everyone know what schools the children would be joining.

In more reflective mode, for example, the leaving children were all involved in contributing to memory collections where they talked and drew about what they would remember of the centre and what or whom they thought they would miss.

On more practical levels, receiving Reception teachers visited the centre to meet the children coming to their classes, the children already having visited their new schools with their parents. The leavers were also introduced through role-play to some of the more formal routines they were likely to meet in Reception-sitting on the carpet for registration, for example.

What were the children leaving behind?

Drawing from our visits throughout Phase 1, we would conclude that the children had been provided with a rich curriculum that did indeed give equal weighting to all six areas of learning and experience. The large indoor and outdoor spaces allowed children to play, investigate, explore, make friends, have quiet and noisy times and interact with many different adults. In addition, they could see themselves, their families and their languages represented in photos, displays, resources and practices. Knowledge of what young children require to thrive – stimulation, talk, responsive and sensitive adults, a safe and comfortable setting, respect, fair treatment, care for individuals and genuine interest in their concerns, for example, – formed the foundations on which the demands of the curriculum were balanced. In other words, it was the children who largely directed the curriculum, not the other way round.

That the children were given a secure and enriching start was reiterated by the parents we spoke to, as we saw in Chapter 8.

What were the children going to?

That the children were going to a number of primary schools meant we had to select for Phase 2 of our research. With the help of the staff we identified two schools to which three of the children were going in the following September and contacted the headteachers to discuss our research project and seek permission to continue in 'their' schools. Fortunately, they agreed and we then set up preliminary visits to the two Reception teachers to outline the project and agree on the number of visits during the year (one each half term, six in all).

In both schools, the Reception classes were in large rooms with one, School B, having a small outdoor area. Both schools had nursery classes with larger outdoor areas. The teaching team in Reception consisted of the class teacher and a teaching assistant with other occasional additional staff.

Immediately, then, there are marked differences in the provision for these under fives, with particular difficulties surrounding physical development where constant access to outdoor activities that match and complement indoor activities became almost impossible to achieve. (Access to suitable outdoor equipment and activities is a requirement of the Physical Development area of learning in the Statutory Framework but little has been done to help different settings and providers meet the requirement.)

Another contrast was the much smaller ratio of adults to children: in the Reception classes it was close to 1 to 15. The role of the teacher as the person 'in charge' was much more overt, with the teaching assistants taking a more subsidiary role. The recommendation in the Statutory Framework for all children to have a Key Person (see DfES, 2007b, p. 15) who was not just the class teacher, was not yet being implemented in the two schools we visited.

This led, perhaps, to an emphasis on behaviour management and 'crowd control' with constant reminders of expectations supported by systems of rewards for acceptable behaviour.

Classroom organization

Almost inevitably, perhaps, the organization of the Reception class was very different from that of the EYC. In the Primary sector of the British education system, the embedded practice is that of 1 class teacher to approximately 30 children. Inevitably this brings its own benefits and constraints for both children and teacher. Before the Education Reform Act of 1988 what were then termed Infant schools or Infant classes in primary schools were run on similar lines to nursery practice. With the establishment of Key Stage 1 and the National Curriculum this changed and the practice was pulled towards the secondary school subject content curriculum model.

Thus we saw in the two Reception classes a form of organization that straddled uneasily the play and investigative approach of the EYC and the six areas of learning and experience of the EYFS Curriculum and the demands of the National Curriculum, or more specifically, the dominance of Literacy and Numeracy. Thus, the children were taught more often as a whole class, were more teacher directed and began to be allocated to *ability*-based groups (note that these are usually decided through children's perceived abilities in Literacy and Numeracy and not other areas of the curriculum).

It should be emphasized, however, that Reception aged children are still part of the Foundation Stage, should still be receiving its curriculum and be moving towards the achievement of the Early Learning Goals not National Curriculum levels. Immediately, we have here one of the problems facing the Reception class teachers, pulled towards providing the children with the continuity which thoughtful transition from nursery education should offer and also being pulled by the primary school to contribute to the school's league table ranking by getting the children onto the National Curriculum levels as quickly as possible.

And as we have said, the levels that currently appear to matter are those for Literacy and Numeracy.

The ethos of the Reception classes

Otter school

During our first visit to Otter school in the autumn term, the Reception class, which we will call Class X, had a display with the caption 'Multicultural X'. This showed photographs of some of the children with accompanying statements about family origins, plus a map of the world. Both Selma ('my dad is from Egypt and my mum is from Italy') and Emilie ('my mummy comes from Germany'), children from the EYC, were featured.

There was also a circle of friendship display that had cut-outs of the children's hands; underneath was independent writing (e.g. IPPiSD – 'I playing in the sand'). There were also 'post-its' many of which had Selma's writing; some had Emilie's writing. Another display 'at the beach' had Selma's writing 'I been in Italy on the beach'.

Palace Manor school

The school's Reception area had a permanent display of photographs of school projects that reflected the cultural backgrounds of the children and families.

When we made our first visit to Palace Manor school's Reception class in the autumn term there were brightly coloured displays, most created by the class teacher. One display of 'superstars' had with photographs of the children and their 'dream' of Reception. There were also photographs of the children near the carpet with teacher instructions (sit still and look at the teacher, line up straight with your hands at your side). These emphasized the role of the Reception class in socializing the children into the required behaviours in primary school.

In Palace Manor, for example, the class teacher used routines for settling the children (counting down – 54321), repeated instructions calmly, noticed all kinds of behaviours and praised those who were doing the 'right' thing. Ticks, stickers and stars on wall charts were used to reinforce acceptable behaviours.

The emphasis on phonics

In both schools, the day usually started with a phonics session for the whole class.

In Otter school, we observed a session where the class was divided between the teacher and the nursery officer for a very specific programme of teaching. The teaching was carried out through a game approach and short specific activities with an emphasis on 'consonant, vowel, consonant (CVC) words (tin, dog, bed). In the class teacher's group, each child had a picture and had to find the corresponding word. There was a lot of practice of initial sounds; the teacher used comprehensible language but the activity was clearly not comprehensible to all. No use was made of children's names or alphabet charts on the wall, nor was any reference made to things that the children might find more familiar and might give them more clues about initial sounds.

Another activity in which the teacher made a 'bouncing ball' arm gesture in silence (supposedly indicating the initial sound of 'ball') was met with incomprehension and required a considerable amount of explanation from the teacher to help the children grasp her intention. The children spoke very little in this 15-minute session and were rarely invited to make their own contribution.

The children who worked with the Teaching Assistant were given a more interactive, 'game' approach to the phonics which, if it did nothing else, created a more relaxed atmosphere for learning.

This short session gave an indication that for the adults at least, the 'literacy' of CLL was perhaps considered to be more important than the other two components.

Palace Manor school also often started the day with phonics but as a class session led only by the teacher. In one observed session, the letter for the week was 'w'; this was emphasized via the phrase 'windy day' and language play such as 'w w wind, w w wiggle'. The children practised writing the letter 'w' in the air and the teacher used the whiteboard, asking children where to start forming the letter. There was great excitement when the teacher exploited the whiteboard's versatility to reveal a 'web'. The child whose name started with 'W' was not referred to in this session.

The teacher and children also sang a song about 'w' and its sound and then sang a short song about all the 26 sounds covered so far in the phonics session.

There was no doubt that the children were involved in this session and enjoyed its humour and its elements of play. All three components of CLL received some attention in this session.

In another observed session, the teacher was concentrating on combining sounds through the use of the Interactive White Board. However, breaking words such as 'going' into 'go + i+ ng' proved problematic (this is probably better defined as the onset and rime of 'go + ing'). Interestingly, as he taught he abandoned his original breakdown of 'going' into three sounds and reverted to go + ing, realizing, perhaps, that this is actually how it is pronounced and consequently made more sense to the children.

Problems with 'discrete' phonics programmes

We know that the current emphasis on phonics is government directed and, during the time of our research, was largely influenced by the 2009 Rose Report into Early Reading and Phonics. Much of this emphasis, we believe, stemmed from the obsession with measurability. It is easy to create phonics programmes and easy to show that these are being worked through systematically by the adults involved. But there is, as far as we know, no evidence that children acquire knowledge of sounds and their symbolic representation systematically.

In fact what we do know of reading development is that children require far more than phonics to become successful and eager readers (which current national and international research suggests they are not). The London-based CLPE (Centre for Literacy in Primary Education) has many practical and perceptive publications and other resources on the development of reading, support for bilingual learners and other literacy matters. We recommend our readers to investigate it if they are not familiar with it. It is worth remembering, too, that since Sir Jim Rose is neither an authority on the Early Years or on early reading development it was curious that he was asked to be responsible for a report specializing in young children.

To become successful writers, children really need opportunities to experiment. We know that many young children use lines and marks, then familiar letters (as in their first names) and then a selection of sounds (as in 'IPPiSD' above) in the early stages of independent writing.

What often seems to be missing in both reading and writing in school is the attention that is due to *meaning*. *We believe that meaning is as fundamental to reading and writing as it is to spoken communications.* Unfortunately, much current practice emphasizes the discrete features of reading and writing rather than the whole text.

It seems to us that most children demonstrate their growing awareness of sound/symbol relationships in their writing and that no amount of phonics 'drilling' will actually prevent them from inventing their own spellings based on their own interpretation of the sounds they hear. In Palace Manor school, an outing took place to a local supermarket to buy food to accompany noodles (this was part of the celebrations tying in with Chinese New Year). The children made shopping lists that showed their independent spellings – 'sossij' and 'sors', for example. One of the problems with simplistic phonics programmes is that they fail to take into account the irregular nature of the English language and try to fit it into a phonics straitjacket or coyly call irregular words and spellings 'tricky'.

How much more wise it would be to accept English for what it is, explore the relationships between its spoken and written forms and celebrate its diversity rather than problematize it. Since children are fascinated by language and obviously have a vested interest in their own names (which are meaningful), it is both surprising and disappointing that in neither school were names used as a way in to looking at how sound/symbol relationships work in reality. The variety of first and family names found in most urban settings provides genuine opportunities to investigate the variety of sounds represented by the Roman alphabet's 26 letters.

So we believe there are real problems in presenting young children with 'discrete' phonics sessions that are divorced from a thoughtful programme that addresses the development of language and literature in combination.

Young children are linguistically very adept and responsive to play with language as we have seen. As well as names, very little attention was given in either school to the languages the children had in addition to English. Much could have been made of comparisons between home languages and English both spoken and written (especially with languages written in different scripts). This would not only have given children more stimulating learning activities but also given more recognition to their personal and family situations. This was one area where the schools' approach was considerably different from that of the EYC.

It is also important to remember that young children are remarkably compliant and accepting, on the whole, of the situation they find themselves in. They are unlikely to comment on the lack of recognition of home language, family, cultures and customs; but they may well feel that, since the adults at school make no mention of them, then they had better not either.

Displays

In the best early years settings, considerable thought and time are given to the creation, maintenance and changing of displays. These will include 2D and 3D work on walls and on surfaces, in the entrance, corridors, indoor classroom and outdoors. There is little point to them unless they attract the children's attention, so one would expect to see images of the children and examples of their work and activities.

In the EYC, as we have already noted, there were photographs of the children and parents drawing attention to the family's home language as well as the close and loving relationships. These were a more permanent part of the entrance but there were also changing displays which reflected events in the lives of the children (the return of Katisha from Japan, for example). The classroom was full of children's work as well as artefacts to investigate and explore.

In the Reception classes there was far more of published material on display-lists of letters/sounds from the phonics programmes, numbers and teacher materials and messages (star charts, instructions for good behaviour, etc.). Because of the style of school building the classrooms had high ceilings with display boards quite high up; consequently much of the work on display was not directly in line with the children's vision.

In marked contrast to the EYC, the two Reception classes, as we noted in Chapter 4, paid minimal overt attention to the children's home languages and backgrounds. Otter school had its 'multicultural class X' wall display; Palace Manor had the children's 'dream of Reception'; both remained in place all year. The latter class, however, did include some aspects of different cultural events and practices by the marking of Chinese New Year and the food festival which led to a display about foods from around the world and a 'feast' shared by the parents and children. However, in contrast to the EYC, we did not witness during our visits any attention given to the individual children's own languages, backgrounds and cultures or any discussions about the specific, personal experiences the children could have brought into the classroom.

As we have mentioned, in Otter school the 'multicultural class X' display remained on the wall for the year but never included all the children. There were no references or images to do with the children's languages in the displays. Yet, in this class was Selma who we knew was very proud of her ability to operate in three languages (Arabic, English and Italian) and informed us that 'my mum still reads to me in Italian' and 'my dad speaks to me and reads Arabic'. We are not certain that the class teacher was fully aware of this linguistic competence; Selma was often described as being anxious and having a 'processing delay'. What language/s might she have been processing? Where was the teacher's appreciation of Selma's linguistic and cultural experiences? Was there evidence that the teacher thought Selma had a language deficit? If so, is it surprising that Selma may have come across as 'anxious'?

Play and investigation

As we have seen earlier in this book, play has gradually come to be seen as the most important learning mechanism for young (and not so young) children. Through play intellectual, emotional, personal and social growth can take place. Given the space, time, resources and responsibility they need children are perfectly capable of satisfying their own curiosity and directing their own learning. The key role for the adults in attendance is to watch, observe, note and join in only at the right moment – this is not easy. But all early years practitioners should try to pause before they question or intervene – it is always possible they might just get it wrong.

We saw countless examples in the EYC of the children playing independently and socially where the adults observed and allowed the play to flow with minimal intervention. Certainly, in the times that we visited there was a relaxed atmosphere – no doubt not always easy to achieve – where the children were largely given opportunities to move freely, use the (adult provided) resources and reflect their own worlds and create new ones, through play. That there was free flow between the indoor and outdoor areas clearly helped establish this atmosphere of enjoyment, concentration and purpose, as did the generous staffing ratios.

In Otter and Palace Manor schools, it was not always evident that play was valued in the same way. It was certainly more difficult to promote genuine free flow play with restricted physical space but, again, with the move into the primary school, also appeared to come the expectation that it was time for the children to undergo more formal and direct teaching. There are subtle shifts taking place here, we believe, in philosophy and pedagogy. In fact, it could be said that the Curriculum, as interpreted in the Reception classes and particularly in Otter school, acted as an obstacle to meaningful explorations of language, culture and identity. The play that did take place could have been enriched by greater adult attention to what the children themselves could contribute.

The role of the adults

As we have noted, there was a shift in the adult/child relationship when the children started in Reception. The apparent democracy and adult/child equality of the EYC was transmuted into a less equal relationship. Where the children of the EYC were extensively trusted to direct much of their learning, in the Reception classes it was the teacher who became the director, focusing on behaviour management and control, and, as we have said, Literacy and Numeracy. Interestingly, the relationship between teachers and support staff was also less equal, with the support staff appearing to be very much under the direction of the teacher too.

At the EYC we also saw very positive relationships with parents. There was a real sense that they and the EYC staff were working together for the children with tangible two-way contacts being made. As we have said, there were also many additional supporting groups and activities on site which provided further opportunities for the parents to be part of the life of the Centre.

Again there was a contrast between the Centre and the Reception classes. Parents were welcomed at the start and end of the day but again due to curriculum pressures, teachers were keen to start the day formally with the 'congregation' on the carpet. In Palace Manor school it was apparent that the teacher had considerable knowledge of the families and the complex linguistic backgrounds of the children, but this knowledge was not made evident in day-to-day interactions with the children nor, on the whole, in the classroom ethos and work. In School A, there appeared to be even less understanding or awareness of the children's home and linguistic experiences and, again, no recognition of these in the daily life of the class.

And yet, as we have seen in all government documents relating to early years learning, the role of the adults in stimulating, supporting and extending the children's experiences and activities is crucial. These experiences and activities must also include the children's languages, cultures and identities.

At the very least, all the adults working in a particular setting should endeavour to find out, with sensitivity, information about all the children they are in contact with. Where home visits are carried out, parents can feel in control of the conversation and information can be successfully gathered.

The following are some suggestions for what could be asked of parents:

- the languages the child has encountered before starting nursery/EYC or Reception, both spoken and written
- the child's strengths in the language/s of home
- the languages used by the parent/s/carers
- how the family adults use home languages with their child/ren
- if the family practice a particular faith and which special occasions are celebrated
- customs and conventions around food and diet

- ideas about games and play
- ideas about education and its purposes.

Many practitioners will already be finding out similar things but if the reader is a student teacher or teaching assistant or EYP (Early Years Professional), it might be worth asking yourself if you know the answers for the children you are currently working with. Armed with this sort of information there is much that can be done to ensure that ALL children's experiences can be recognized and planned for. The links between the above information and different types of display and resourcing are obvious.

It really is up to the adults to ensure that Language, Culture and Identity are not forgotten or regarded as unimportant if we are to see children growing up as secure, happy and confident people. It does not matter if the adults involved are mono-, bi- or multilingual; there are many ways in which they can create an inclusive, welcoming environment provided they have the knowledge, the understanding and the commitment to bring this about.

What did the parents say about transfer to Reception?

We were able to carry out interviews with the parents of six children at the EYC. While much of the conversation was concentrated on the EYC, we also had some discussion about the transfer to Reception classes. Extracts from three conversations are presented here; we feel that the points raised by the parents are probably fairly representative and certainly valid but readily admit this is a very small sample.

Heidi (French (Ivory Coast) and English background)

The conversation with Sara (Heidi's mother) took place during the summer holiday before Heidi started in her new schools. Heidi had a statement for her special needs and had been well supported at the EYC. Because of her specific needs, Heidi was going to attend two schools part-time: the local primary school and a special school. Her mother, Sara, was anxious about some aspects of the transfer but totally positive about the commitment of staff at the EYC and the ways in which they helped Heidi develop. She was an emergent French and English speaker.

> **Sara:** These people have done so much, so much for Heidi. People can't understand that but me as a mum I know how Heidi developed at (the EYC). They give her so much confidence with everything really, so now Heidi is learning more. I was really lucky that Heidi went there. She learned a lot from (the EYC).

She made some pithy comments on the ethos of some schools:

> Because sometime you send a child to school, people there they're not really open, even if the law says that the child needs to be in this school but you need to be open as well to say that ok this child need to learn maybe English and give them time . . . sometimes it doesn't happen in all the schools I know that.

Sara had concerns that Heidi's use of French might not be supported in the special school; she was pleased that the primary school was going to be able to help her daughter maintain her first language.

AH: I know this is a bit more difficult – but how do you see things changing when she goes to (special school) and (primary school)? Is this sort of thing going to continue?

Sara: I hope so, I really hope so. For now I think that I'm worried. . . . I went to (special school) once and the way they was working with the children I like it. They use sign language, Heidi doesn't really need sign language but the way they work actively with the children was good. The problem is nobody there speak French (A: I was going to ask you that). I didn't see nobody there speak French. So I don't know.

AH: Did you ask them about that? Or will you wait to ask them?

Sara: No, I will wait to ask them. We'll see how we go

AH: What about in (primary school)? French speaking?

Sara: Heidi is really lucky because the lady who works with Heidi speaks French, she is coming from France, so she will be doing both with Heidi that's why I'm not so worried that people didn't speak French there because she's a French speaker.

Overall, however, Sara had reservations about the transfer to Reception. This was taking place just as Heidi, it seemed to her and to us as observers, was making real progress at the EYC.

> **Sara:**   If I got my choice Heidi would not leave (the nursery) because I can relax when she's at nursery there. (Transcripts from recorded conversation)

Oscar (Irish, English and French Patois background)

His father, Ben, was Irish. Francisca (his mother) was from Jamaica/Cayman Islands. She spoke English and French patois. Ben came from near Dublin and spoke Irish, could get by in French and in other European languages. He was teaching Oscar a few words of Irish. Francisca spoke English with Oscar but Patois with her family. Oscar knew when his mother was using Patois and she thought he would learn it soon. When on holiday with the family he used Patois vocabulary. She believed that children should be started on languages when they are young.

The EYC was good in relation to languages she said. Oscar told her about the languages of the nursery – Mandarin, a French-speaking mother, the father (Selma's) who spoke 'Egyptian' (Oscar's word) and Bengali words. He was very interested in languages and often talked about the different languages that were spoken in different countries.

At the time of the conversation, Oscar had started in Reception.

He had settled in well. There were only 15 in the Reception class with a new intake in January that would bring them up to 30. Francisca had attended a parents' evening where she saw 3 folders of work from Oscar. She was very pleased with how much he had done so far and that he was making friends (the only one from the EYC to go to this school). They still met other parents and his friends from EYC.

The Reception class was not working on other languages yet – this would come in Year 1. Francisca was disappointed that there were no displays of the children and their families. This contrasted with the EYC where there was so much focus on languages and countries, family backgrounds and photos. She noted that the school did not ask about family background whereas the EYC did.

Oscar had been doing lots of reading and writing; the class teacher said he was very good. The EYC gave him the confidence to learn. There was also lots of outdoor play there which was much appreciated by his mother. The primary school was strong on discipline but did or could not provide as much outdoor play although Francisca believed this was still needed by Reception children, and children in Year 1 and Year 2. The Reception class had limited space. We discussed the implications of the 'new' EYFS and its emphasis on outdoor provision and how primary schools would struggle to meet it with limited space available. Francisca was also a childminder so she was very familiar with all the new requirements and the difficulties involved in meeting some of them.

Oscar was keen to go back to say hello to the nursery; this was something that the nursery encouraged although it was difficult to find times to do this when schools had the same half term.

We discussed the idea of Reception and nursery staff meeting to talk about the children once they had moved to primary school and agreed it would be a good thing to try to do.

(Taken from notes of the conversation.)

Piero (Spanish and Italian background)

At home, Piero's father tried to stick to speaking Italian with the children and his mother Gina to Spanish. If Piero used Italian to Gina she replied in Spanish (there are many similarities between the two languages). He was becoming aware of these and knew that there are many different languages. Occasionally, his parents used English if they didn't want the children to understand; this would become more difficult as the children became more conversant with English.

Piero was going to start in one of the two Reception classes at a local primary school in the spring term. There was a similar approach to EYC there and the school had a good reputation. Both parents had visited and the class teacher had explained the approach to teaching, much of which was play-based. They were interested in the school's careful approach to the use of ICT and its emphasis on good handwriting. They were confident that the school would support Piero's language development.

Gina commented on the role of Piero's key worker, Edith, at the EYC, in helping with the transition from nursery to Reception and that she had been at the nursery for 30 years, which indicated how content staff were working there.

(Taken from notes of the conversation.)

In summary, we could say that while Piero's family were happy with the ethos he would meet in Reception, the other two parents had some reservations. Sara was concerned that Heidi's needs, both linguistic and physical, might not be fully met, while Oscar's mother regretted the lack of interest shown in children's languages and families. These two seem to illustrate the point made by David (1990) about the discontinuity of practice between the EYC and the Reception classes. Indeed, it seems to us, based on our visits, that there was indeed considerable discontinuity particularly in relation to children's languages, cultures and identities. These became, to different extents in Otter and Palace Manor schools, largely invisible. This is a disappointing state of affairs since there is such potential for the Reception class teacher to build on the children's existing knowledge and develop it to more sophisticated levels.

The difference in staffing levels between the EYC and the Reception classes was very marked, with a ratio of about 15 children to 1 adult in the latter with the class teacher clearly carrying most of the responsibility (despite the recommendations of the Statutory Framework for Key Workers in Reception).

Dowling (2010) notes:

> Settings and schools are increasingly beginning to tailor-make a transition to meet each child's needs, rather than expecting every child to fit into one size of provision. Despite this, too often staffing ratios in reception classes remain inadequate. It is essential that, whenever children are newcomers to a setting, they are able to have easy access to an adult who will introduce them to the multiplicity of new experiences gently and informally and interpret new requirements for them. The close involvement of parents in this process allows children to feel emotionally supported while they learn. (p. 17)

We were also made very aware of the differences between the EYC and the Reception classes in their interpretation of the statutory curriculum. Both settings are required by law to follow the same curriculum and to give the six areas of learning and development equal status. But it was obvious that in the Reception classes, for various reasons we have already discussed, this was not the case. At times it seemed as though an entirely different curriculum was being followed.

> The greater the gap between the culture of the school and the culture of the early years nursery setting or home, the greater challenge to the child and the greater the risk of not being able to comply with understanding the requests of the teacher. A study by Brooker (2002) outlines how children move from 'child in the family' to 'pupil in the school' and how the values of home and school often differ. These include differences in the way in which play at home and play at school is perceived according to family and cultural values, and may cause emotional difficulties for children. (Fabian and Dunlop, 2006)

It is fair to say that we did see distinct differences of pedagogy and philosophy between the EYC and the two Reception classes and that while we may not have seen overt 'emotional difficulties', we remain uneasy about children such as Selma and Heidi, for example. In Selma's case the move to Reception led to a situation where her pride and facility in using three languages was not recognized and validated. For Heidi, it would seem that while the move fitted her chronological age, it appeared to disrupt the developmental level she had reached in the EYC and where she was making considerable progress.

For all the other children, and especially those who were bi- or multilingual, we believe there were significant gaps between the ethos and practice of the EYC and the Reception classes but that these gaps could easily be bridged by a more reciprocal partnership between the two settings. As well as the EYC staff preparing children for Reception, Reception teachers could spend more time visiting the EYC to ensure a far greater match between the two and prepare their own classrooms to be more like the EYC. Perhaps, too, closer links with parents and carers could be established in the Reception classes with staff showing willingness to learn from the parents as well as expecting parents to learn from them.

What we find frustrating is that none of this is new. As we have said, the Plowden Report encouraged the development of relationships between home and school and between child, parent/s and teacher. Over the following years, other reports and research projects have also shown the importance of these relationships and the importance of nurturing children's first languages as they move into and through the education system.

One such report was that of Blair and Bourne (1998). They and their research team carried out a project for the DfEE, as it was then, into successful multi-ethnic schools. While this project did not investigate early years settings, many of the factors which made certain schools successful were evident in the EYC we visited. For example, 'a strong and determined lead on equal opportunities (was) given by the headteacher' (p. 6). Successful schools 'created careful links with local communities' and 'tried to understand and work with the "whole child"'(p. 7).

> Students of all ethnic backgrounds and with all kinds of learning needs were treated as potential high achievers. (p. 8)

In addition, 'Effective schools were sensitive to the identities of students and made efforts to include in the curriculum their histories, languages, religions and cultures' (p. 8).

In relation to bilingual learners and specific groups successful schools had clearly articulated policies and practices. 'The use of the first language was used for "settling in" as well as for longer term learning' (p. 7) and 'Bilingual support staff had a clear role in alerting teachers to concerns about bilingual children, and care was taken to distinguish language needs from special educational needs' (p. 7). 'Schools which showed commitment to equality of opportunity for minority ethnic group students seemed to also embrace the needs of White students' (p. 7) and 'The particular history and relationship to the education system of African-Caribbean communities was recognised and this was taken into account in considering the education and welfare of these students' (p. 7).

We find it bizarre that successive governments, having commissioned such research, seem unable or unwilling to commit themselves to the outcomes and recommendations made by projects such as the one above. It is disappointing to have to come to the conclusion that governments have neither the political will nor a genuine commitment to understanding and implementing (or trying to implement) real equality. It seems essential to us that recognition of all children's family, cultural and linguistic experiences and their incorporation into the daily curriculum should, as a matter of justice and equality, be visible and tangible. This, surely, is a matter not of ephemeral standards but of enduring human rights.

Summary

In this chapter, we have drawn on evidence from our research visits to compile a portrait of the two receiving Reception classes as experienced by six of the children from the EYC. We have contrasted the practices between the three settings and have highlighted the changes in emphasis in curriculum provision, although in law, all three are governed by the statutory curriculum. We have raised concerns about the concentration on narrow aspects of literacy and numeracy, rather than CLL and PSRN, and the reduced provision for the other four areas of learning and development. We consider the effects of these changes on all children, monolingual and bilingual.

We showed how thoughtfully the EYC addressed the transition of the children to Reception classes and the strategies the staff used to help the children prepare for this change. We query continuing government reluctance to pursue genuine equality for all.

Reflective activity

1. How does your workplace prepare children for the move to Reception class?
2. How does your workplace manage to liaise with staff in the receiving school? How has this been achieved? Is there more you could do?
3. How do you involve parents in their child's transition to Reception?
4. How well do you think your workplace caters for all linguistic and cultural groups? Is there anything more you can do?

Conclusions and Recommendations

The Britain of the twenty-first century cannot simply be described as an increasingly multilingual and multicultural society. It has *always* been one. We supported this claim by providing some historical accounts of why Britain has always been a country that attracted people from across the globe. As a result, our focus in this book has been based on our conviction that the education system should reflect such diversity not just in principle but also in practice.

As we tried to identify good practice relating to inclusive learning, we looked at existing systems in place for facilitating the smooth transition of children from a nursery to a reception class. Our other interest in exploring the dynamics of such a transition was to see the extent to which the inclusive support children received at the EYC continued after they arrived at a reception class. We started our research by reflecting on the daily practices of a typical multicultural EYC in South London and followed some of the children in our study into Reception classes. There, we were not surprised to find teachers overburdened with the demands of the National Curriculum and its related frameworks, the National Literacy and Numeracy Strategies which we believe are prescriptive and narrow in their approach and content. We witnessed teachers trying to implement the requirements of phonics programmes and the very effects of such strategies on some of our focus children who appeared to have changed from confident, interactive and highly verbal to quiet and timid children. What we did see was a very limited interpretation of language (i.e. as English) with little or no acknowledgement of the other languages of the children and an underlying neglect of culture as well as language. It disappointed us to see assessment of children's overall progress in literacy based on evaluation of children's performance in the phonics programme. However, we also saw more innovative phonics programmes too where music and games were incorporated into the daily session.

What was so innovative about an EYC with 18 languages spoken by children in addition to English and with the majority of the staff mainly monolingual English speaking? How did this create an inclusive multicultural environment? As we set out to discover the inclusive practices of the EYC, we were excited to see the children's cultures and languages *actively* celebrated throughout the Centre. Their ethos were based on the commitment of all staff to equality of opportunity and the children's equal entitlement to respect for their languages and cultures. There were plenty of evidences to suggest that the Centre was very proactive in incorporating children's home experiences into their learning and discovery at the nursery. The staff appeared to be very knowledgeable about the children's individual home experiences. This was very noticeable when we first approached the Centre to identify the children suitable for our study. Each name was accompanied by information not only related to the observations in the Centre but also from the home environment.

On the subject of the languages it was not just the awareness but the celebration of everyone's linguistic experiences – including English – which formed the basis of the Centre's inclusive ethos. This is what the staff used as the crucial starting point for all learning. For example, the children and their parents were warmly welcomed by the staff who used greetings in the children's languages: As Yasemin came in with his dad, '*Günaydın*' said Steve (a member of staff) as he greeted them both in Turkish. '*Günaydin*' replied Yasemin. '*Bonjour*' said Selma joining the morning chores.

The crucial elements that made the EYC so distinctive in its work with the children and parents were based on a strong understanding of and commitment to PSE (and CLL) development and the best ways to bring this about. Conversely, the Reception classes, obliged to start implementing formal programmes of learning and pulled away from the Foundation Stage curriculum – which they should have legally obliged to follow – left teachers either unable or unwilling to continue the good work of the EYC and, perhaps, rather ignorant about language development/acquisition in young bilingual learners. In this book, we were critical of the demands made of Reception teachers' vis-à-vis the points scoring of the profile and the ways in which the role of the family was gradually diminished in primary education. It was disheartening to foresee the long-term effects of burying children's languages and

identities in the race for supposedly high levels of achievement and global prominence and the bureaucratic hurdles on teachers as they got lost
in the plethora of documents and their preoccupation with levels, results
and outcomes. Our concern and focus was actually on staff, not children
or families.

We discovered the crucial importance of home links to such richness
of information obtained by the Centre. For new arrivals there were pre-
paratory visits to homes and to the Centre by the parents in return.
Home visits were not only confined to new arrivals. It included everyone. Parents had lots of reasons for visiting the Centre. There were regular advice sessions such as courses on health matters, English language
classes, provided by the LEA. There were also a mother and toddlers
group. As the daily routines of the home environment were observed by
the visiting staff, some careful notes were made on children's daily routines of culturally relevant experiences. These were then used to plan
activities which facilitated a smooth transition of existing concepts in
the home language to English. For example, on one of the visits we
arranged to Selma's house we observed her favourite Italian stories read
to her by her mother. We were not surprised to see the English version
of the same stories at the Centre when Selma's mother told us that during a visit by the Centre staff they commented on the importance of
buying the stories for the Centre. We have also seen the extension of
Selma's home experiences in her other related work. Her own experiences she collated in 'Selma's book' we saw a lot of examples from her
routine activities which she did at home. Active encouragement and
support from the Centre staff was also clearly visible.

If we were to evaluate the biggest impact of the Centre to children's
learning we would probably say it was the support they have provided to
newly arrived children. At the time of our study, we noticed a significant
number of the newcomers who came from homes where children were
exposed to languages other than English. The main tool for communication used by these children was their home languages. The support
that the Centre staff provided to the newcomers was the facilitation of
the use of their home languages. We have seen ample evidence of interactions between the staff and the children where an adult would start
the dialogue with a question: 'Can you teach me about . . . (often requiring information about the child's religion, food, and customs)? Can you

teach me how to say . . . (often a word in the child's language)? These were not based on random topics of interest of the staff but were embedded in real experiences of the children obtained though home visits as well as information from the parents. These were skilfully linked to the themes explored in the Centre. One of the staff described this strategy as 'children as experts'.

It was the Centre's individualist approach to children's particular needs which interested us. Heidi, a child with cerebral palsy received specialist one-to-one support. She came from a French speaking home. Our own observations of Heidi and our conversations with her mother confirmed how happy she was for attending the Centre. Her mother also commented on her positive responses to the use of French words at home, which can be seen as one of the possible outcomes of the multilingual ethos of the Centre. The most revealing aspect of the Centre's support surfaced during our meetings with the parents. There was a clear message about the positive impact made by the Centre's staff on children's language awareness. This was further confirmed with our observations during our visits to the Centre. Many parents in the group – some of whom were monolingual English speaking – mentioned how their children came home practising words they have learned in other languages during the day. We have shared various examples of children's linguistic experiences in different sections of this book. There was a clear message that children valued languages at a nursery age. One parent's regular French sessions has also contributed to the positive ethos of the EYC.

On the subject of the use of home languages, the practice in the United Kingdom is still based on the so called the 'deficiency' theory. We still appear to think that in order for children to be successful learners they need to drop their home languages as soon as possible to avoid mental confusion. In this book, we set out to challenge this myth by drawing on some of the prominent research in the field of bilingualism and second language acquisition. Our aim was to show that far from interfering with their learning, the home language actually support the development of the second language. In the significant majority of schools in the United Kingdom, the role of the home language is either seen as interfering with the learning of English or is perceived in its supporting role to help with the learning of English. Our findings from the

EYC is worthy of mention here. Many parents we spoke to talked about their anxieties relating to whether they needed to continue with the use of learning materials in the home languages before their children started the Centre. Parents mentioned how quickly they were made to feel comfortable about supporting the development of the home languages by the EYC staff. During one of our home visits, we witnessed how the concepts in the child's home language were used by the parents to support their child's understanding of vocabulary and concepts in English. Parents told us how refreshing it was to be told that they were actually on the right track with their approach to supporting their children's bilingual development.

Our findings relating to all the inclusive practice of the EYC needs to be seen as the outcome of a highly professional and an effective team work co-ordinated by a dynamic and innovative headteacher. The ethos of the EYC was the product of her vision and commitment which filtered through to the rest of her staff. This was an ongoing, 'learning from experience' strategy as such reflections of staff were incorporated through a practical action plan by the headteacher. It was also dynamic and adaptable to meet rising needs of individual children through a collaborative evaluation by all the staff. This was more effective than any local or central government initiated training programme. The staff constantly talked to one another on and off task and evaluated children's progress in regular staff meetings. Children felt they were valued and respected. They were happy to talk about themselves to others and were happy to listen to others in return. We think that one of the reasons for this was because they were made to feel happy about who they are and what they offered as learners in the nursery environment.

In this book, we have taken a critical approach to successive government positions on multiculturalism and inclusive practice in schools. Our particular concern related to their contradictory positions on promotion of *language* and *inclusive approaches* to learning as two distinct and unrelated practices. We were disheartened to see OFSTED's criteria for school 'success' to be perceived merely as supporting bilingual children's acquisition of English and levels achieved in phonics, literacy and numeracy related tasks. Their refusal to back away from their position to view all learning in relation to English language has been the major stumbling block. We argued that both can be achieved through an inclusive and holistic view to language and learning where the learners' – whether monolingual or multilingual – social and cultural experiences are taken as starting points in all learning. We see learning as an accumulation of interrelated experiences of individuals' social and cultural activities. We challenged those that perceived the opposite, that somehow learning needs to be seen in different compartments somewhere 'out there' to be 'acquired' by inquisitive minds. We believe that most of such narrow views of language and learning are prevalent in some primary and secondary school settings. However, we believe that such negative practices are the fruits of limiting practices in early year's settings when young children set out fresh on their discovery learning. It is recognizing the crucial importance of early year's settings that guided our thinking in conducting our work in these settings.

In the book, we tried to explore the processes involved in transfer of children from early years to Reception classes. We found a sharp contrast in the way these settings were set up. We noticed that our focus children amid all the formal teaching of literacy and numeracy seemed rather lost at times. Understandably, the requirements of the National Curriculum and the standards have taken a priority over inclusive and multicultural practices. In this respect we sympathized with the challenging situations faced by the reception teachers we have observed. We had similar concerns about the lack of reference to the development of children's language, culture and identity in the EYFS guidelines. To us, it is inconceivable to think of young children's emotional development as separate from the nurturing of their language, culture and identity. If the government is really serious about promoting a truly multicultural and multilingual Britain in the future, it needs to stop playing lip-service to such important issues for our education system and for the cohesiveness of our society in the future.

In this respect we make the following recommendations:

- Closer attention to be paid to EYFS curriculum in Reception as well as better early years practice. There needs to be better links between EYC and Reception.
- More emphasis needs to be on the recognition of language, culture and identity in government documents and policy as well as in schools/nurseries/EYCs.

- The development of oral skills in English need to be explored in relation to young bilingual learners' home language which may be in more developed 'stage' due to the child's home experiences. For this reason, adults need to facilitate the use of children's home languages in order for them to meaningfully contextualize the use of English.
- Better training programmes for staff/providers in matters of cultural identity/language acquisition, equality to promote and develop the continuation of good early years practice in early years settings – already under threat from the formal curriculum.

This apparent indifference to inclusive practice has not only deprived some excellent schools of well-deserved credit for their good work, but has also prevented the dissemination of good practice to other schools. Our aim in this book has been partly to fulfil that task. We hope that we have made some contribution to early years practice in this field.

References

Abrami, P. C., Chambers, B., Poulson, C., De Simone, C., d'Apollonia, S. and Howden, J. (1995), *Classroom Connections: Understanding and Using Co-operative Learning*. Toronto: Harcourt Brace.

Aldrich, R. (1982), *An Introduction to the History of Education*. Sevenoaks: Hodder and Stoughton.

Alladina, S. and Edwards, V. (eds) (1991), *Multilingualism in the British Isles*. Longman: Africa, The Middle East and Asia.

Anwar, M. (1979), *The Myth of Return: Pakistanis in Britain*. London: Heinemann.

Baker, C. (1993), 'Bilingual Education in Wales', in Baetens Beardsmore (ed.), *European Typologies of Bilingual Education*. Clevedon: Multilingual Matters.

— (1996), *Foundation of Bilingual Education and Bilingualism*. Clevedon: Multilingual Matters.

— (2006), *Foundation of Bilingual Education and Bilingualism* (4th edn). Clevedon: Multilingual Matters.

Bakker, J. and Denessen, E. (2007), 'European Network about Parents in Education', *International Journal about Parents in Education*, 1, 188–99.

Bathurst, K. (1905), 'The Need for National Nurseries', in M. Woodhead and A. McGrath (eds) (1988), *Family, School and Society*. Milton Keynes: Open University Press.

Beardsmore, H. B. (ed.) (1993), *European Models of Bilingual Education*. Clevedon: Multilingual Matters.

Beardsmore, H. B. and Swain, M. (1985), 'Designing Bilingual Education: Aspects of Immersion and "European School" model', *Journal of Multilingual and Multicultural Development*, 6 (1), 1–15.

Berk, F. (1972), 'A Study of the Turkish Cypriot Community in Haringey with Particular Reference to Its Background, Its Structure and Changes Taking Place Within It', Unpublished M.Phil. Dissertation. University of York.

Bernstein, B. (1971), 'On the Classification and Framing of Educational Knowledge', in M. F. D. Young (ed.), *Knowledge and Control: New Directions for the Sociology of Education*. London: Collier-Macmillan.

— (1972), 'Education Cannot Compensate for Society', in A. Cashdan and E. Grugeon (eds), *Language in Education: A Source Book* (pp. 213–18). London and Boston: Routledge and Kegan Paul in association with the Open University.

Bettelheim, B. (1961), *The Informed Heart*. Great Britain: Thames and Hudson.

Bialystok, E. (1991), *Language Processing in Bilingual Children*. Cambridge: Cambridge University Press.

— (2001), *Bilingualism and Development: Language, Literacy and Cognition*. Cambridge: Cambridge University Press.

Bialystok, E., Craik, F. I. M. and Ryan, J. (2006), 'Executive Control in a Modified Anti-Saccade Task: Effects of Aging and Bilingualism', *Journal of Experimental Psychology: Learning, Memory, and Cognition*, 32, 1341–54.

Birdsong, D. and Molis, M. (2001), 'On the Evidence for Maturational Constraints in Second-Language Acquisition', *Journal of Memory and Language*, 44, 1–15.

Blair, M. and Bourne, J. (1998), *Making the Difference: Teaching and Learning Strategies in Successful Multi-Ethnic Schools* (Research Report No. 59). London: DfEE.

Blakeny, M. (1981), 'Survey of LEAs, National Association Multiracial Education (Report)', Derby.

Board of Education (1933), *Report of the Consultative Committee on Infant and Nursery Schools* (Hadow Report). London: HMSO.

— (1945 reprint), *Handbook of Suggestions for the Consideration of Teachers and Others Concerned in the Work of Public Elementary Schools*. London: HMSO.

Boos-Nünning, U. and Hohmann, M. (1986), *Towards Intercultural Education. A Comparative Study of the Education of Migrant Children in Belgium, England, France and the Netherlands*. London: CILT.

Bourdieu, P. (1990), *The Logic of Practice*. Stanford, CA: Stanford University Press.

Boys, R. (2008), 'Communication, Language and Literacy', in J. Basford and E. Hodson (eds), *Teaching Early Years Foundation Stage*. Exeter: Learning Matters.

Breiter, M. L. and Engelmann, S. (1966), *Teaching Disadvantaged Children in the Pre-School*. Englewood Cliffs, NJ: Prentice-Hall.

Briggs, A. (1992), *The Twentieth Century: The Pictorial History*. London: Reed International Publishing.

British Nationality Act (1981), London: HMSO.

British Nationality Law (1977), Discussion of Possible Changes, Cmnd. 6795. London: HMSO.

Brook, M. (1980), 'The Mother Tongue Issue in Britain: Cultural Diversity and Control?' *British Journal of Sociology of Education*, 1 (3), 237–55.

Bruce, T. (1987) *Early Childhood Education*. London: Hodder and Stoughton.

— (2005), *Early Childhood Education* (3rd edn). London: Hodder and Arnold.

Bruner, J. S. (1975), 'Language as an Instrument of Thought', in A. Davies (ed.), *Problems of Language and Learning*. London: Heinemann.

Bullock Report (1975), 'A Language for Life: Report of the Committee of Inquiry'. London: HMSO.

Byram, M. (1993), 'Bilingual or Bicultural Education and the Case of the German Minority in Denmark', in H. B. Beardsmore (ed.), *European Models of Bilingual Education*. Clevedon: Multilingual Matters.

CILT (2005), *Language Trends 2005: Community Language Learning in England, Wales and Scotland: CILT*. Clevedon: Multilingual Matters.

Coard, B. (1971), *How the West Indian Child Is Made Educationally Subnormal in the British School System: The Scandal of the Black Child in Schools in Britain*. London: New Beacon Books.

Coddington, D. (2003), *Let Parents Choose*. Auckland, NZ: Valentine Press.

Collier, V. P. and Thomas, W. P. (1997), 'Acquisition of Cognitive-Academic Second Language Proficiency: A Six Year study', Paper presented at the Intercultural Education Partnership European Seminar. London, 22–23 May.

Commission for Racial Equality (CRE) (1991), *Code of Practice for the Elimination of Racial Discrimination in Education.*. London: Commission for Racial Equality.

Commission of European Communities (CEC) (2008), Green Paper: 'Migration and Mobility: Challenges and Opportunities for EU Education Systems'. COM (3 July) 423 Final.

Commonwealth Immigrants Act (1962), Control of Immigration Statistics 1962/1963/1966, Cmnd. 2151, 2379,2658, 2979, 3258. London: HMSO.

— (1968), London: HMSO.

Commonwealth Immigrants Advisory Council (1964), Second Report, February 1964. London: HMSO.

Craft, M. (1981), *Teaching in a Multi-Cultural Society: The Task for Teacher Education*. Lewes, Sussex: Falmer Press.

Crook, C. (2000), 'Motivation and the Ecology of Collaborative Learning', in R. Joiner, D. Miell, K. Littleton and D. Faulkner (eds), *Rethinking Collaborative Learning*. London: Free Association Press.

Cummins, J. (1976), 'The Influence of Bilingualism on Cognitive Growth: A Synthesis of Research Findings and Explanatory Hypotheses', *Working Papers On Bilingualism*, 9, 1–43.

— (1977), 'Cognitive Factors Associated with the Attainment of Intermediate Levels of Bilingual Skills', *Modern Language Journal*, 61, 3–12.

— (1984), *Bilingualism and Special Education: Issues in Assessment and Pedagogy*. Clevedon: Multilingual Matters.

— (1989), *Empowering Minority Students*. Sacramento: California Association for Bilingual Education.

— (1996), *Negotiating Identities: Education for Empowerment in a Diverse Society*. California: Association for Bilingual Education; Cambridge: Cambridge University Press.

— (2000), *Language, Power and Pedagogy: Bilingual Children in the Crossfire*. Clevedon: Multilingual Matters.

— (2009), 'Multilingualism and Equity Beyond the Effectiveness Paradigm: Exploring Inspirational Pedagogy for Bilingual Students', Keynote presentation, Making Multilingualism Meaningful Conference, London Metropolitan University, 20 June 2009.

Dabydeen, D., Gilmore, J. and Jones, C. (eds) (2007), *Black British History*. Oxford: Oxford University Press.

Darcy, N. T. (1953), 'A Review of the Literature on the Effects of Bilingualism upon the Measurement of Intelligence', *Journal of Genetic Psychology*, 82, 21–57.

David, T. (1990), *Under Five-Under-Educated?* Milton Keynes: Open University Press.

David, T., Curtis, A. and Siraj-Blatchford, I. (1992), *Effective Teaching in the Early Years: Fostering Children's Learning in Nurseries and in Infant Classes*. Stoke on Trent: Trentham Books.

David, T., Powell, S. and Goouch, K. (2010), 'The World Picture', in G. Pugh and B. Duffy (eds), *Contemporary Issues in the Early Years* (5th edn). London: Sage.

De Boysson-Bardies, B. (2001), *How Language Comes to Children: From Birth to Two Years*. Cambridge: MIT Press.

De Houwer, A. (2005). 'Early Bilingual Acquisition: Focus on Morphosyntax and the Separate Development Hypothesis', in J. F. Kroll and A. M. B. De Groot (eds), *Handbook of Bilingualism: Psycholinguistic Approaches* (pp. 30–48). Oxford, New York: Oxford University Press.

Dearing, R. (1993), *The National Curriculum and Its Assessment Final Report*. London: SCAA.

Department for Business Innovation and Skills (BIS) (2009), *Impact Assessment: European Commission Proposal for a Directive to Implement Revised Framework Agreement on Parental Leave*. London: BIS.

Department for Children, Schools and Families (DCSF) (2008), *Parents as Partners in Early Learning Project* (PPEL). London: DCSF.

Department for Education (DfE) (2010), 'Annual School Census, Language Data Collection', DfE, Statistical Release for 2010 data.

— (2011), 'Review of the Statutory Framework for the Early Years Foundation Stage', The *Tickell Review*, July 2011. London: DfE.

Department for Education and Skills (DfES) (2006), *Excellent and Enjoyment: Learning and Teaching for Bilingual Pupils in the Primary Years*. London: OPSI.

— (2007a), *Practice Guidance for the Early Years Foundation Stage*. London: HMSO.

— (2007b), *Statutory Framework for the Early Years Foundation Stage*. London: DfES.

Department of Education and Science (DES) (1965), 'Circular 7/65: The Education of Immigrants'. London: HMSO.

— (1967), 'Children and Their Primary Schools: A Report of the Central Advisory Council for Education (England)'. *The Plowden Report*. London: HMSO.

— (1971), 'Education Survey 13: Education of Immigrants'. London: HMSO.

— (1980a), *A Framework for the School Curriculum: Proposals for Consultation by the Secretaries of State of Education and Science and for Wales*. London: HMSO.

— (1980b), *A View of the Curriculum* (HMI Series: Matters or discussion No. 11). London: HMSO.

— (1981), *Schools and Working Life*. London: HMSO.

— (1985), *The Curriculum from 5–16 Curriculum Matters 2*. (HMI Series). London: HMSO.

— (1988), Letter to the National Curriculum Council, London: HMSO.

Desforges, C. and Abouchaar, A. (2003), 'The Impact of Parental Involvement, Parental Support and Family Education on Pupil Achievement and Adjustment: A Literature Review'. *DfES Research Report* 433.

Deucher, M. and Quay, S. (2000), *Bilingual Acquisition: Theoretical Implications of a Case Study*. New York: Oxford University Press.

DeVillar, R. A. and Faltis, C. J. (1991), *Computers and Cultural Diversity*. Albany: State University of New York Press.

Diaz, R. M. (1985), 'Bilingual Cognitive Development: Addressing Three Gaps in the Current Research', *Child Development*, 56, 1376–88.

Dickinson, P. (1982), 'Facts and Figures: Some Myths', in J. Tierney (ed.), *Race Migration and Schooling*. Norfolk: Thetford Press.

Dickinson, K. D. and Tabors, P. O. (eds) (2001), *Beginning Literacy with Language: Young Children Learning at Home and School*. Baltimore, MD: Paul H Brookes Publishing.

Donaldson, M. (1978), *Children's Minds*. Great Britain: Fontana/Collins.

— (1992), *Human Minds*. London: Penguin.

Dowling, M. (2010), *Young Children's Personal, Social and Emotional Development* (3rd edn). London: Sage.

Drury, R. (2007), *Young Bilingual Learners at Home and School Researching Multilingual Voices*. Stoke on Trent: Trentham Books.

Dunn, J. (1996), 'The Emmanuel Miller Memorial Lecture 1995. Children's Relationships: Bridging the Divide between Cognitive and Social Development', *Journal of Child Psychology and Psychiatry*, 37 (5), 507–18.

Dweck, C. S. (2000), *Self-Theories: Their Role in Motivation, Personality and Development*. Hove, East Sussex: Psychology Press.

Early Years Foundation Stage (EYFS) (2008), 'Practice Guidance and Supporting Resources' – (CD pack – practice cards 1.2), Department for Children Schools and Families (DCSF).

Early Years Foundation Stage Review (2011), *The Tickell Report*, Department for Education (DfE).

Education Act (1980), London: HMSO.

'Education for All' (1985), The Report of the Committee of Inquiry into the Education of Children from Ethnic Minority Groups. London: HMSO.

Education Reform Act (1988), London: HMSO.

Eliot, L. (1999), *What's Going On in There?* London: Allen Lane.

Epstein, J. L., Sanders, M. G., Simon, B. S., Salinas, K. C., Jansorn, N. R. and Van Voorhis, F. L. (2002), *School, Family, and Community Partnerships: Your Handbook for Action* (2nd edn). Thousand Oaks, CA: Corwin.

Esser, H. (2006), 'Migration, Language and Integration', *AKI Research Review* 4.

European Commission (EC) (1993), Council Directive 93/34/EEC, *Employment Rights*.

European Community Commission (ECC) Directive (1977), 'Directive 77/486/EEC'. 'Education of the Children of Migrant Workers'. European Economic Commission.

Fabian, H. and Dunlop, A. W. (2006), *Outcomes of Good Practice in Transition Processes for Children Entering Primary School*. UNESCO.

Fletcher, S. S. F and Welton, J. (trans.) (1912), *Froebel's Chief Writings on Education*. London: Edward Arnold & Co.

Foot, P. (1969), *The Rise of Enoch Powell*. Harmondsworth: Penguin Books.

Galton, M., Simon, B. and Croll, P. (1980), *Inside the Primary Classroom*. London: Routledge and Kegan Paul.

Garcia, E. E. (1991), 'Effective Instruction for Language Minority Students: The Teacher', *Journal of Education*, 173 (2), 130–41.

Gee, J. P. (1996), *Social Linguistics and Literacies: Ideology in Discourses* (2nd edn). London: Taylor & Francis.

Genesee, F. (2004), 'What Do We Know about Bilingual Education for Majority Language Students?' in T. K. Bhatia and W. Ritchie (eds), *Handbook of Bilingualism and Multiculturalism* (pp. 547–76). Malden, MA: Blackwell.

— (2007), 'French Immersion and At-Risk Students: A Review of Research Evidence', *Canadian Modern Language Review/La Revue Canadienne des Langues Vivantes*, 63, 5 (August/aouˆ t), 655–88.

— (2008), 'Dual Language in the Global Village', in T. W. Fortune and D. J. Tedick (eds), *Pathways to Multilingualism: Evolving Perspectives on Immersion Education* (pp. 22–45). Clevedon, UK: Multilingual Matters.

Genesee, F., Boivin, I. and Nicoladis, E. (1996), 'Talking with Strangers: A Study of Bilingual Children's Communicative Competence', *Applied Psycholinguistics*, 17, 427–42.

Gertner, B. L., Rice, M. L. and Hadley, P. A. (1994), 'Influence of Communicative Competence on Peer Preferences in a Preschool Classroom', *Journal of Speech and Hearing Research*, 37, 913–23.

Gumperz, J. C. and Corsaro, W. A. (1977), 'Social-Ecological Constraints on Children's Communicative Strategies', *Sociology*, 11 (3), 411–34.

Harris, R. J. (1992), *Cognitive Processing in Bilinguals*. Amsterdam: North-Holland.

Hart, B. and Risley, T. R. (2005), 'The Early Catastrophe: The 30 Million Word Gap', *American Educator*, 27 (1), 4–9.

Hawkes, N. (1966), *Immigrant Children in British Schools*. London: Pall.

Heath, S. B. (1993), 'Inner City Life through Drama: Imagining the Language Classroom', *TESOL Quarterly*, 27 (2), 177–92.

Heath, S. B. and Mangiola, L. (1991), *Children of Promise: Literate Activity in Linguistically and Culturally Diverse Classrooms*. Washington, DC: National Education Association.

Heredia, R. and McLaughlin, B. (1992), 'Bilingual Memory Revisited', in R. J. Harris (ed.), *Cognitive Processing in Bilinguals*. Amsterdam: North-Holland.

Hester, H. (1984), 'Peer Interaction in Learning English as a Second Language: Theory into Practice', *Special Issue: Access to Meaning: Spoken and Written Language* 23 (3), 1984.

Holt, D. (ed.) (1993), *Co-operative Learning: A Response to Linguistic and Cultural Diversity*. Washington, DC: Center for Applied Linguistics.

Home Office (1986), Section 11 of the Local Government Act 1966, Circular 72/86.

Hummel, K. M. (1993), 'Bilingual Memory Research: From Storage to Processing Issues', *Applied Psycholinguistics*, 14, 267–84.

Immigration Act (1971), London: HMSO.

Inner London Education Authority (ILEA) (1987), Research and Statistics Report: Language Census RS 1157/87. London: ILEA.

International Symposium on Bilingualism, 9–12 April (1997), *Abstracts*. Department of Speech: University of Newcastle Upon-Tyne.

Isaacs, E. (1976), *Greek Children in Sydney, Canberra*. Australian National University Press.

Isaacs, S. (1932), *The Nursery Years*. London: Routledge and Kegan Paul.

Issa, T. (1987), 'Bilingual Education of Turkish Speaking Children in a Multicultural Environ-ment', Unpublished M.Sc. Dissertation. London: Polytechnic of the South Bank.

— (2005), *Talking Turkey: Language, culture and Identity of Turkish Speaking children in UK*. Stoke on Trent: Trentham Books.

Issa, T. and Öztürk, A. (2008), *Practical Bilingual Strategies for Multilingual Classrooms*. Leices-ter: UKLA Publications.

Johnson, J. S. and Newport, E. L. (1989), 'Critical Period Effects in Second Language Learning: The Influence of Maturational State on the Acquisition of English as a Second Language', *Cognitive Psychology*, 21, 60–99.

Jones, W. R. (1966), *Bilingualism in Welsh Education*. Cardiff: University of Wales.

Kardash, C. A., Amlund, J. T., Kulhavy, R. W. and Ellison, G. (1988), 'Bilingual Referents in Cognitive Processing', *Contemporary Educational Psychology*, 13, 45–57.

Keatley, C. W. (1992), 'History of Bilingualism Research in Cognitive Psychology', in R. J. Harris (ed.), *Cognitive Processing in Bilinguals*. Amsterdam: North-Holland.

Kenner, C. (2004), *Becoming Biliterate: Young Children Learning Different Writing Systems*. Stoke on Trent: Trentham Books.

Kessler, C. (ed.) (1992), *Co-operative Language Learning: A Teachers Resource Book*. Englewood Cliffs, NJ: Prentice-Hall Regents.

Khan, V. S. (1980), 'The Mother Tongue of Linguistic Minorities in England', *Journal of Multi-lingual and Multicultural Development*, 1 (1), 71–88.

King, R. L. (1979), 'Italians in Britain: An Idiosyncratic Immigration', *Association of Teachers of Italian Journal*, 29, 6–16.

Knight, C. (1990), *The Making of Tory Education Policy in Post War Britain, 1950–86*. Lewes: Falmer Press.

Kolers, P. (1963), 'Interlingual Word Association', *Journal of Verbal Learning and Verbal Behav-iour*, 2, 291–300.

Kuhn, A. (2000), 'A Journey through Memory', in S. Radstone (ed.), *Memory and Methodology* (pp. 179–96). Oxford and New York: Berg.

Labov, W. (1966), *The Social Stratification of English in New York City*. Washington, DC: Centre for Applied Linguistics.

Lambert, W. E. and Tucker, G. R. (1972), *Bilingual Education of Children: The St. Lambert Experiment*. Rowley, MA: Newbury House.

Lauren, U. (1991), 'A Creativity Index for Studying the Free Written Production for Bilinguals', *International Journal of Applied Linguistics*, 1 (2), 198–208.

Laurie, S. S. (1890), *Lectures on Language and Linguistic Method in School*. Cambridge: Cambridge University Press.

Lawton, D. (1989), *Education Culture and the National Curriculum*. Sevenoaks: Hodder and Stoughton.

Leman, J. (1993), 'The Bicultural Programmes in the Dutch-Language School System in Brussels', in H. A. Beardsmore (ed.), *European Models of Bilingual Education*. Clevedon: Multilingual Matters.

Lewis, R. (1988), *Anti-Racism: A Mania Exposed*. London: Quartet Books.

Macdonald, I., Bhavnani, R., Khan, L. and John, G. (1989), *Murder in the Playground: The Report of the Macdonald Inquiry into Racism and Racial Violence in Manchester Schools* (Burnage Report). London: Longsight Press.

MacKay, T. (2007), *Gee's Theory of D/discourse and ESL Research in Teaching English as a Second Language: Implications for the Mainstream*. Winnipeg, MB: University of Manitoba.

Maclure, J. S. (1986), *Educational Documents England and Wales 1816 to the Present Day* (5th edn). London: Methuen.

MacNaughton, G. (2003), *Shaping Early Childhood*. Maidenhead: Open University Press Mall Press for IRR.

McNeal, J. and Rogers, M. (1971), *The Multi-Racial School*. Penguin: Harmondsworth.

Maneva, B. and Genesee, F. (2002), 'Bilingual Babbling: Evidence for Language Differentiation in Dual Language Acquisition', in B. Skarbela, S. Fish and A. H.-J. Do (eds), *The Proceedings of the 26th Boston University Conference on Language Development* (pp. 383–92). Somerville, MA: Cascadilla Press.

Marian, V. and Kaushanskaya, M. (2009), 'The Bilingual Advantage in Novel Word Learning', *Psychonomic Bulletin & Review*, 16 (4) (August), 705–10.

Matthews, A. (1981), *Advisory Approaches to Multicultural Education*. London: Runnymede Trust.

Mehmet Ali, A. (1984), 'Why Are We Wasted', *Multi-Ethnic Education Review*, 4 (1), 7–12.

Meisel, J. M. (2001), 'The Simultaneous Acquisition of Two First Languages: Early Differentiation and Subsequent Development of Grammars', in J. Cenoz and F. Genesee (eds), *Trends in Bilingual Acquisition* (pp. 11–42). Amsterdam: John Benjamins.

Merriman, N. (ed.) (1993), *The Peopling of London: Fifteen Thousand Years of Settlement from Overseas*. London: Museum of London.

Ministry of Education (1963), *English for Immigrants*. London: HMSO.

Nanez, J. E., Padilla, R. V. and Maez, B. L. (1992), 'Bilinguality, Intelligence and Cognitive Information Processing', in R. V. Padilla and A. H. Benavides (eds), *Critical Perspectives on Bilingual Education Research*. Temple, AZ: Bilingual Press.

National Curriculum Council (NCC) (1990), 'Curriculum Guidance 3: The Whole Curriculum'. York: National Curriculum Council.

Ng Kwee Cho (1968), *The Chinese in London*. London: Oxford University Press.

Norwood Report (1943), Report of the Committee of the Secondary School Examinations Council. London: HMSO.

Nushe, D. (2008), 'Assessment of Learning Outcomes in Higher Education: A Comparative Review of Selected Practices', *OECD Education Working Paper*, No. 15. Paris: OECD.

Oswald, P. and Schulz-Benesch, G. (compilers) (1997), *Basic Ideas of Montessori's Educational Theory: Extracts from Maria Montessori's Writings and Teachings*. Oxford: Clio Press.

Paivio, A. (1986), *Mental Representations: A Dual Coding Approach*. Oxford: Oxford University Press.

— (1991), 'Mental Representations in Bilinguals', in A. G. Reynolds (ed.), *Bilingualism, Multiculturalism and Second Language Learning*. Hillsdale, NJ: Lawrence Erlbaum.

Parekh Report (2000), *The Future of Multi-Ethnic Britain: Report of the Commission on the Future of Multi-Ethnic Britain*. London: Profile Books.

Patterson, S. (1969), *Immigration and Race Relations in Britain, 1960–1967*. London: Oxford University Press for the Institute of Race Relations.

Pea, R. D. (1993), 'Practices of Distributed Intelligences and Design for Education', in G. Solomon (ed.), *Distributed Cognitions: Psychological and Educational Considerations* (pp. 47–87). Cambridge, UK: Cambridge University Press.

Peal, E. and Lambert, W. E. (1962), 'The Relationship of Bilingualism to Intelligence', *Psychological Monographs*, 76 (27), 1–23.

Phillips, M. and Phillips, T. (1998), *Windrush: The Irresistible Rise of Multi-Racial Britain*. London: Harper Collins.

Piller, I. (2001), 'Who, if Anyone, Is a Native Speaker?' *Anglistik. Mitteilungen des Verbandes Deutscher Anglisten*, 12 (2), 109–21.

Power, J. (1967), 'Immigrants in Schools', *Councils and Education Press* (pp. 179–96). Oxford, UK: Berg Imprint.

Proudfoot, M. J. (1956), European Refugees 1939–52: A Study in Forced Population Movement. London: Faber & Faber.

Race Relations Act (1968), London: HMSO.

— (1976), London: HMSO.

'Racial Discrimination' (1975), Cmnd. 6234. London: HMSO.

Ramsey, P. and Derman-Sparks, L. (1992), 'Multicultural Education Reaffirmed', *Young Children*, 47 (2), 10–11.

Robson, S. (2006), *Developing Thinking and Understanding in Young Children*. London: Routledge.

Rogers, P. I. (1997), 'From Butler to Baker: Education Since 1944', M.Ed. Dissertation, School of Education, University College of North Wales.

Rogoff, B. (2003), *Cultural Nature of Human Development*. Oxford: Oxford University Press.

Romaine, S. (1995), *Bilingualism* (2nd edn). Malden, MA: Blackwell.

Rose, E. J. B., Deakin, N., Abrams, M., et al. (1969), *Colour and Citizenship: A Report on British Race Relations*. London: Oxford University Press.

Rosen, H. (1973), *Language and Class: A Critical Look at the Theories of Basil Bernstein*. Bristol: Falling Wall Press.

Rose Review (2009), *Report into Early Reading and Phonics*. London: Department for Children, Schools and Families (DCSF).

Ross, A. (2000), *Curriculum: Construction and Critique*. London: Falmer Press.

Rousseau, J. J. (1760), *Emile*, trans. Barbara Foxley (1961 reprint). London: J. M. Dent.

Rumbold Report (1990), 'Starting with Quality'. The Report of the Committee of Inquiry into the Quality of the Educational Experience Offered to 3 and 4 Year Olds, chaired by Mrs Angela Rumbold CBE MP. London: HMSO.

Saer, D. J. (1923), 'The Effects of Bilingualism on Intelligence', *British Journal of Psychology*, 14, 25–38.

Saer, D., Smith, F. and Hughes, J. (1924), *The Bilingual Problem*. Wrexham: Hughes and Son.

Schieffelin, B. and Ochs, E. (1986), *Language Socialization across Cultures*. Cambridge: Cambridge University Press.

Schlesinger, A. Jr (1991), *The Disuniting of America*. New York: W. W. Norton.

'Section 11 of the Local Government Act' (1966), London: HMSO.

Shorrocks, D., Daniels, S., Frobisher, L., Nelson, N., Waterson, A. and Bell, J. (1992), 'The Evaluation of National Curriculum Assessment at Key Stage 1 (ENCA 1 project): Final Report'. London: SEAC.

Silber, K. (1960), *Pestalozzi: The Man and His Work*. London: Routledge and Kegan Paul.

Siraj-Blatchford, I. (2010), 'Diversity, Inclusion and Learning in the Early Years', in G. Pugh and B. Duffy, *Contemporary Issues in the Early Years* (5th edn) (pp. 151–64). London: Sage.

Skutnabb-Kangas, T. (1981), *Bilingualism or Not: The Education of Minorities*. Clevedon: Multilingual Matters.

Skutnabb-Kangas, T. and Cummins, J. (1988), *Minority Education: From Shame to Struggle*. Clevedon: Multilingual Matters.

Stanat, P. and Christensen, G. (2006), 'Where Immigrant Students Succeed – A Comparative Review of Performance and Engagement', in PISA 2003. Paris: OECD.

— (2007), 'Language Policies and Practices for Helping Immigrants and Second-Generation Students Succeed', The Transatlantic Task Force on Immigration and Integration, Migration Policy institute and Bertelsmann Stiftung.

Strachey (1977), *Denotational Semantics: The Scott-Strachey Approach to Programming Language Theory*. Cambridge: MIT Press.

Stubbs. M. (ed.) (1985), *The Other Languages of England: Linguistic Minorities Project*. London: Routledge and Kegan Paul.

Swain, M. and Lapkin, S. (1991), 'Additive Bilingualism and French Immersion Education: The Roles of Language Proficiency and Literacy', in A. G. Reynolds (ed.), *Bilingualism, Multiculturalism and Second Language Learning*. Hillsdale, NJ: Lawrence Erlbaum.

Swick, K. J. (1993), *Strengthening Parents and Families during the Early Childhood Years*. Champaign, IL: Stipes.

Taylor, M. J. and Hegarty, S. (1985), 'The Best of Both Worlds . . . ? A Review of Research into the Education of Pupils of South Asian Origin'. Windsor: NFER-Nelson.

Tizard, B. and Hughes, M. (1984), *Young Children Learning*. London: Fontana Press.

Tomlinson, S. (1983), *Ethnic Minorities in British Schools*. London: Heinemann.

— (1993), 'The Multicultural Task Group: The Group That Never Was', in A. King and J. Reiss (eds), *The Multicultural Dimension of the National Curriculum*. Falmer Press.

Tough, J. (1976), *Listening to Children Talking*. London: Ward Lock.

Townsend, H. E. R. (1971), *Immigrant Pupils in England: The LEA Response*. Slough: NFER.

Townsend, H. E. R. and Britten, E. M. (1973), 'Multiracial Education: Need and Innovation', *Schools Council Working Paper* 50. London: Evans/Methuen Education.

Trudgill, P. (1975), *Accent, Dialect and the School*. London: Edward Arnold.

Tunmer, W. E. and Herriman, M. L. (1984), 'The Development of Metalinguistic Awareness: A Conceptual Overview', in W. E. Tunmer, C. Pratt and M. L. Herriman (eds), *Metalinguistic Awareness in Children*. Berlin: Springer-Verlag.

Uccelli, P. and Paez, M. (2007), 'Narrative and Vocabulary Development of Bilingual Children from Kindergarten to First Grade: Developmental Changes and Associations among English and Spanish Skills', *Language, Speech, and Hearing Services in Schools*, 38 (3), 225–36.

Visram, R. (2002), *Asians in Britain: 400 Years of History*. London: Pluto Press.

Vygotsky, L. S. (1962), *Thought and Language*. Cambridge, MA: MIT Press.

— (1978), 'Interaction between Learning and Development', in M. Cole, V. John Steiner, S. Scribber and E. Souberman (eds), *Mind in Society: The Development of Higher Psychological Processes* (pp. 79–91). Cambridge: Harvard University Press.

Watson, J. L. (1975), *Emigration and the Chinese Lineage: The 'Mans' in Hong Kong and London*. Berkeley: University of California Press.

Wells, G. (1981), *Learning through Interaction: The Study of Language Development*. Cambridge: Cambridge University Press.

— (1986), *The Meaning Makers: Children Learning and Using Language to Learn*. London: Hodder and Stoughton.

— (1987), *The Meaning Makers*. Hodder & Stoughton.

'White Paper: Immigration from the Commonwealth' (1965), Cmnd. 2739. London: HMSO.

Wiles, S. (1985), 'Learning a Second Language', in G. Wells (ed.), *Perspectives on Language Learning*. London: Falmer Press.

Williams, C., Lewis, G. and Baker, C. (1996), *The Language Policy: Taking Stock, Interpreting and Appraising Gwynedd's Language Policy in Education*. North Wales: Gwynedd Education Authority.

Winder, R. (2004), *Bloody Foreigners*. London: Abacus.

Wittek, F. (1992), 'The Historical and International Context for Current Action on Intercultural Education', in E. Reid and H. Reich (eds), *Breaking the Boundaries*. Clevedon: Multilingual Matters.

Woodhead, M. and McGrath, A. (eds) (1988), *Family, School and Society*. Milton Keynes: Open University Press.

Wright, J. (1982), 'Bilingualism in Education', *Issues in Race and Education*. London: Issues in Race and Education.

Wyse, D., Jones, R. and Bradford, H. (2008), *Teaching English, Language and Literacy*. New York: Taylor & Francis.

Young, K. (1983), 'Ethnic Pluralism and the Policy Agenda in Britain in Ethnic Pluralism and Public Policy', *International Journal of Psychology*, 28 (2), 185–201.

Useful websites

Declaration of the Rights of the Child
www.un.org/cyberschoolbus/humanrights/resources/child.asp

Hadow Report
www.educationengland.org.uk/documents/hadow1933/3312.html

Pugh, G. (2006), Putting Children First
www.nurseryworld.co.uk/news/716362/Putting-children-first/?DCMP=ILC-SE

The Refugee Council
www.refugeecouncil.org.uk

Rumbold Report (1990), *Starting with Quality* DES
www.educationengland.org.uk/documents/rumbold/rumbold01.html

Index

Page numbers in **bold** denote tables.